GAME CHANGER$

HOW NAME, IMAGE, AND LIKENESS LAW CREATES COLLEGE MILLIONAIRES

Mitchell F. Crusto

AMERICANBARASSOCIATION
ABA Publishing

Cover design by Sara Wadford/ABA Design

Printed in the United States of America.

29 28 27 26 25   5 4 3 2 1

Library of Congress Cataloging-in-Publication Data

Names: Crusto, Mitchell F., author.
Title: Game Changers: How Name, Image, and Likeness Law Creates College Millionaires Mitchell F. Crusto.
Description: Chicago : American Bar Association, 2025. | Includes bibliographical references and index. | Summary: "College athletes are benefiting from a revolution in college sports. Due to a change in the law, they are permitted to be paid for their notoriety, that is, the use of their name, image, and likeness, commonly referred to as "NIL.""– Provided by publisher.
Identifiers: LCCN 2025029316 (print) | LCCN 2025029317 (ebook) | ISBN 9781639056415 (paperback) | ISBN 9781639056422 (epub)
Subjects: LCSH: College sports–Law and legislation–United States. | College sports–Economic aspects–United States. | Commercialism in sports–United States. | College athletes–Legal status, laws, etc.–United States.
Classification: LCC KF3989 .C78 2025 (print) | LCC KF3989 (ebook) | DDC 344.73/099–dc23/eng/20250621
LC record available at https://lccn.loc.gov/2025029316
LC ebook record available at https://lccn.loc.gov/2025029317

ISBN 978-1-63905-641-5

Discounts are available for books ordered in bulk. Special consideration is given to state bars, CLE programs, and other bar-related organizations. Inquire at Book Publishing, ABA Publishing, American Bar Association, 321 N. Clark Street, Chicago, Illinois 60654–7598.

www.shopABA.org

I dedicate this book to my uncle, Rolland J. "Speedy" Curtis, an African American civil rights leader who, after integrating the U.S. Marines during World War II, integrated the football team at the University of Southern California in 1951.

Contents

Preface vii
Acknowledgments ix

Introduction 1

Chapter 1:
Chase Young and Reggie Bush: Tarnished Sterling Careers and a Call for Justice 9

Chapter 2:
Edward O'Bannon, Shawne Alston, and Grant House: Millions for Past NIL Abuse 27

Chapter 3:
Livvy Dunne: The Crowned Princess of Social Media Influence 51

Chapter 4:
Bronny James: Eyes on the Prize 69

Chapter 5:
Bryce Underwood: "Pay to Play?": Big Money and Cooperatives 89

Chapter 6:
Arch Manning: Playing the Long Game to Brand Dynasty 117

Chapter 7:
Shedeur Sanders: Maximizing One's Value 139

Chapter 8:
Angel Reese: Persistence in Achieving One's Goals 167

Chapter 9:
Dr. Myron Rolle: Pursuit of One's Education 187

Chapter 10:
Caitlin Clark: Wealth Creator for Women Athletes 203

Conclusion:
How Law Can Create Wealth Opportunities and NIL Power Secrets 239

Further Reading 247
Index 249
About the Author 253

Preface

This book describes the legal, financial, and cultural victory that college athletes have won in establishing the right to own and control their name, image, and likeness ("NIL"). Its thesis or centralizing idea is that the law can create substantial wealth opportunities for young people, including those from socially or economically disadvantaged backgrounds. This is evidenced by the change in the NIL law, which facilitates wealth opportunities for college athletes. Consequently, NIL deals are an important opportunity for college athletes to be paid for their fame, but those deals should be explored in an informed, sophisticated manner. The case studies found in this book are presented to guide players, their parents, colleges, boosters, collectives, lawyers, sports agents, promoters, and endorsers in making informed, beneficial decisions relative to NIL deals. Further, I hope to inform the public about college NIL deals and promote their support for these deals, despite critics who believe that they are detrimental to college sports.

The stories of and the lessons from these college NIL superstars show us that dreams can, in fact, become reality. Not just for college athletes but for everyone. Hence, this book guides both college athletes and non-athletes in critical strategies, skills, and techniques to help everyone achieve incredible dreams. Consequently, *Game Changers* is valuable to many audiences, including everyone who participates in or follows college or high school sports and sports in general; everyone who is particularly interested in understanding NIL deals, including present and former players, parents of athletes, school administrators, lawyers, business persons, sports agents, and educators; everyone interested in media, advertising, law, equality, and culture; and everyone who wishes to capitalize on the use of their name, image, and likeness.

Acknowledgments

Thanks to the Henry F. Bonura Jr. Family; the Rosario Sarah LaNasa Memorial Fund; colleagues at various academic programs, including the American Association of Law Schools, the John Mercer Langston Writers Workshops, Loyola University New Orleans College of Law, the Southeastern Association of Law Schools; and to research assistants Cody Bernheisel and LaTreshia Hamilton. Additionally, thanks to the editorial staff of the law reviews who have published my scholarship on NIL law, including at Harvard University, Stanford University, the University of Miami, Washington and Lee University, and the *Journal of Legal Aspects of Sport.* Further, I am eternally grateful to Lorraine Murray, Executive Editor, ABA Publishing, for her belief in this project as well as for the editorial support of Apex CoVantage. Special thanks to the National College Players Association for their impactful work in achieving legal rights for college athletes.

Introduction

Maybe that first Nike deal wouldn't have been as low as it was. . . . It would have changed the game. [Michael Jordan] would have potentially approached his contracts with Nike differently. Looking at his Funko Pop collectibles or the fact that people still wear his UNC jersey, to reap the benefits from it today, we're talking making trillions at this point.

—Jasmine Jordan, daughter of Michael Jordan[1]

Caitlin Clark, Olivia Dunne, Bronny James, Arch Manning, Angel Reese, Shedeur Sanders, and Bryce Underwood are current or recent college sports icons who are among the country's youngest millionaires.[2] They are on the pathway to join the ranks of sports and entertainment billionaire megastars. These megastars include Leonardo DiCaprio, Robert Downey Jr., LeBron James, Jay-Z, Magic Johnson, Michael Jordan, Kim Kardashian, Lionel Messi, Neymar, Tyler Perry, Rihanna, Cristiano Ronaldo, Taylor Swift, Oprah Winfrey, and Tiger Woods.[3]

Today, college and even high school athletes are earning millions of dollars and are benefitting from a revolution in college sports. Due to a change in the law, they are now permitted to be paid for their notoriety, that is, the use of their name, image, and likeness, commonly referred to as "NIL."[4] As a result of these changes, NIL is the most important and the least understood development in college sports. It is transformative as it allows college athletes to be paid for their notoriety as well as be compensated for their athletic performances. However, NIL is also controversial, raising questions as to whether it will result in the death of college sports[5] and whether the "professionalization" of college sports will compromise the educational mission of colleges and decimate the financial integrity of many colleges.[6] Please note that the NCAA refers to college athletes as student-athletes.

Game Changers: How Name, Image, and Likeness Law Creates College Millionaires celebrates some of the most successful college superstars when it comes to NIL deals. This book will demystify the nature of NIL, what it means, and how it operates. The Prime Video documentary, *The Money Game*,[7] produced by Shaquille O'Neal, showcased the lives of some of these superstars. While each athlete's narrative featured in this book could comprise an entire book, this book extracts from each one an invaluable secret on how to become a college NIL millionaire. Each chapter presents a case study of how the most successful college athletes are becoming the country's youngest millionaires thanks to NIL deals.

OVERVIEW: WHAT IS NIL?

NIL refers to the name, image, and likeness law that currently grants college athletes the right to make money in certain ways, which do not violate the National Collegiate Athletic Association's ("NCAA")[8] eligibility rules that determine whether a person can play sports for NCAA colleges. There are three types of NIL deals that benefit college athletes. In an endorsement deal, a college athlete is often paid by a business to endorse or promote a product or service. Some of these deals have made college athletes millionaires. One such example is where Nike paid Caitlin Clark to promote the sale of Nike shoes during her college years. Another type of lucrative NIL deal is where supporters of a college or boosters arrange to compensate an athlete when that athlete plays for the boosters' college. These deals are often for millions of dollars and are paid to the most sought-after high school athletes by way of booster organizations known as collectives. One such NIL deal involved a collective in support of the University of Michigan's decision to recruit and enroll its star quarterback Bryce Underwood. The third type of NIL deal is new, following a 2025 court-approved settlement in *House v. NCAA*[9] which, among other things, allows colleges to directly pay players to play for a particular college. This type of NIL deal comes with court-approved requirements and restrictions, such as a limitation or a cap on the annual total payments. Chapter 1 elaborates on the types of NIL deals and illustrates examples of different NIL deals. In addition to these types of NIL deals, former college athletes are being compensated in lawsuits in which they have sued and are suing the NCAA and others for the wrongful use of the athletes' NIL.

College athlete NIL deals greatly vary.[10] Many college athletes do not have an NIL deal because they have no notoriety of value in the marketplace or have little value to the teams for which they play.[11] On the other end of the spectrum are the high-profile players who are commanding megabucks in NIL money in the millions of dollars.[12] A selective few have national brand endorsement deals, such as Bronny James, who inked a lucrative contract with Nike while he was a high school student.[13] The highest-paid NIL players are high-profile young men who play football or basketball and some young women who play basketball.[14] A few are negotiating equity deals where they share in the ownership of businesses. For example, on June 2, 2025, Michigan's running back Justice Haynes secured an ownership stake in Loom Juice in a new NIL deal.[15] Notwithstanding, one major exception is Louisiana State University gymnast Livvy Dunne, who proves that having a significant social media following can garner substantial NIL deals, with reportedly over 13.4 million social media followers in 2024.[16]

NCAA Prohibited NIL

NIL is relatively new and is the most important development in college sports. Historically, college athletes were prohibited from receiving compensation of any kind from any source, whether from inside or outside of their colleges. This restriction was called the "amateurism" or "eligibility" rule,[17] which required that for college athletes to maintain their amateur status, they were strictly forbidden from receiving funds or support from sources outside of NCAA member schools.[18] Consequently, under the NCAA rules, its players are restricted to school-granted benefits, such as scholarships.[19] These school benefits and restrictions meant that athletes, particularly those from economically disadvantaged backgrounds, lacked financial resources to meet their basic needs,[20] such as facing food insecurity after the school cafeterias were closed.[21] In fact, tuition shortfalls amount to thousands of dollars per year, with 86% of NCAA college athletes living below the poverty line while usually required to live on campus, attend offseason workouts, and travel to games all over the country.[22] These financial pressures, in addition to having to meet both academic and rigorous sports challenges, placed a tremendous emotional and psychological strain on college athletes, particularly on African American young men with disadvantaged backgrounds.[23] One aspect of the NCAA rules was to forbid players from benefiting from the use of their name, image, or likeness.[24] As a result, college athletes missed out on millions of dollars that they might have earned but for the amateurism rule. By limiting student compensation and restricting their rights to their NIL, the NCAA and its member schools received substantial financial benefits from prohibiting their players from being compensated.[25] Most important, the NCAA rules were strictly enforced, often resulting in players or schools being severely punished for alleged violations.

Legal Basis for Change

State laws and a Supreme Court decision provide two legal bases or justifications for NIL law. State NIL laws note that it would be unfair to deny college students who are athletes the opportunity to financially benefit from their NIL when college students who were not athletes enjoyed such opportunities.[26] These laws relied on the right of publicity[27] and equal protection principles.[28] The second legal basis of NIL law resulted from the Supreme Court's 2021 decision in *NCAA v. Alston*.[29] In a nutshell, the Court held that the NCAA was subject to the federal antitrust laws, which means that the NCAA's rules should not monopolize or restrain trade.[30] Consequently, the NCAA should not unduly restrict the labor and property rights of its athletes. In combination, these two legal bases facilitated the current NIL laws that provide college athletes the power to contract NIL deals and not lose their eligibility to play college sports. In addition to these two legal bases for the creation of NIL law for college athletes, both the Supreme Court and state governments recognized the inherent inequity in how the NCAA and its member colleges were exploiting the labor and fame of their college athletes under its rules.[31]

ROADMAP

Chapters 1 and 2 of this book provide a picture of college sports before the creation of NIL law and how the law changed to permit NIL deals. In addition to providing a history of NIL law, these beginning chapters provide two of the ten power secrets to achieving NIL millionaire status.

Following those background chapters, Chapters 3 through 10 present additional power secrets of some well-known past and present NIL college millionaires. The narrative of each of these NIL superstars gives us invaluable insights into how NIL deals work. These college sport superstars include Olivia Dunne, Bronny James, Bryce Underwood, Arch Manning, Shedeur Sanders, Angel Reese, Dr. Myron Rolle, and Caitlin Clark.

Overall, *Game Changers* provides invaluable information on how NIL works and educates on how college NIL athletes have negotiated and are negotiating their paths to becoming some of the youngest American millionaires.

Endnotes

1. *Michael Jordan's Daughter Jasmine Jordan Says NIL Deals Could've Made Her Father "Trillions,"* AfroTech (Mar. 13, 2023), https://afrotech.com/jasmine-jordan-michael-jordan-nil-deals ("Michael Jordan signed a five-year, $2.5 million deal with Nike back in 1984").
2. *See generally*, Paul Rudder, *Who Is the Highest Paid College Athlete? NIL Endorsement Deal Money in NCAA Sports*, AS (updated Jan. 1, 2025), https://en.as.com/ncaa/who-is-the-highest-paid-college-athlete-nil-endorsement-deal-money-in-ncaa-sports-n/.
3. Devin Sean Martin, *The World's Celebrity Billionaires 2024*, Forbes (updated Apr. 3, 2024), https://www.forbes.com/sites/devinseanmartin/2024/04/02/the-worlds-celebrity-billionaires-2024-taylor-swift-kim-kardashian-oprah/; Mohammad Jazib, *[Updated] Top 10 Richest Celebrities in the World 2024*, Jagran Josh (Nov. 18, 2024), https://www.jagranjosh.com/general-knowledge/list-of-richest-celebrities-in-the-world-1721194031-1; *50 Highest-Paid Athletes of All-Time*, Sportico (Mar. 7, 2024), https://www.sportico.com/feature/highest-paid-athletes-all-time-1234711562/; *Influential Sports Stars*, TicketSource, https://www.ticketsource.us/influential-sports-stars (accessed on Mar. 11, 2025). (In terms of influence, Ronaldo is a social media superstar with over 100 million Twitter followers and 444 million Instagram followers.)
4. "Name, image, and likeness" or "NIL" herein is defined as laws and regulations relating to college athletes' right to benefit financially from the use of their name. *See generally*, Greg Daugherty, *What Is NIL? Understanding Name, Image, and Likeness Rules*, Investopedia (updated May 29, 2024), https://www.investopedia.com/name-image-likeness-8558991. Cole Claybourn, *Name, Image, Likeness: What College Athletes Should Know About NCAA Rules*, U.S. World & News (Feb. 8, 2024), https://www.usnews.com/education/best-colleges/articles/name-image-likeness-what-college-athletes-should-know-about-ncaa-rules.
5. Manu Raju, Clare Foran, & Morgan Rimmer, NCAA Leaders Warn College Sports at Risk of "Permanent Damage" without Action from Congress, CNN.

com (Dec. 3, 2023), https://www.cnn.com/2023/12/03/politics/ncaa-college-sports-at-risk-nil/index.html.

6. E. Gordon Gee & Kent Syverud, The Demise of College Sports as We Know Them (Oct. 4, 2024), https://www.chronicle.com/article/the-demise-of-college-sports-as-we-know-them.
7. The Money Game (2024), https://www.imdb.com/title/tt31048383/ (a documentary series following LSU student athletes as they navigate the NIL era in college sports); Olivia Deffes, *New Prime Video Docuseries 'The Money Game' Sheds Light on LSU Athletics and its NIL Earners,* INREGISTER (Sept. 10, 2024), https://www.inregister.com/features/new-prime-video-docuseries-the-money-game-sheds-light-on-lsu-athletics-and-its-nil-earner.
8. *See* NCAA, "What Is the NCAA?," ncaa.org (accessed Mar. 1, 2021) (reporting that, as of March 2021, the NCAA was composed of "[n]early half a million college athletes [who] make up the 19,886 teams that send more than 57,661 participants to compete each year in the NCAA's 90 championships in 24 sports across 3 divisions").
9. 545 F. Supp. 3d 804 (2021) (aka In re College Athlete NIL Litigation). The Plaintiffs alleged that the NCAA and conferences engaged in an "overarching conspiracy" to (a) "fix the amount that student-athletes may be paid for licensing, use, and sale of their names, images, and likeness—at zero; and (b) foreclose student-athletes from the market for licensing, use, and sale of their names, images, and likenesses entirely"). Case 4:20-cv-03919-DMR Document 1 Filed 06/15/20 Page 7, available at https://www.courtlistener.com/docket/17248915/1/in-re-college-athlete-nil-litigation/.545 F. Supp. 3d 804 (2021). *See* Michelle Brutlag Hosick, *Settlement Documents Filed in College Athletics Class-Action Lawsuits,* NCAA (July 26, 2024), https://www.ncaa.org/news/2024/7/26/media-center-settlement-documents-filed-in-college-athletics-class-action-lawsuits.aspx.
10. *See generally,* Albert Samaha, Emily Giambalvo, Jesse Dougherty, & Artur Galocha, *College Sports' Money Machine: The Hidden NIL Economy of College Sports,* WASH POST (Oct. 21, 2024), https://www.washingtonpost.com/sports/interactive/2024/nil-money-deals-college-sports-athlete-pay/.
11. *See generally,* Data Dashboard, NCAA.org, https://nilassist.ncaa.org/data-dashboard/, accessed June 25, 2025 (reporting that the "average total athlete earnings" that was disclosed to the NCAA for January 1, 2024 to the end of October 31, 2024 was $21,916, while the "median total athlete earnings" was only $512).
12. Paul Rudder, *Who Is the Highest Paid College Athlete?* AS (update Mar. 25, 2024), https://en.as.com/ncaa/who-is-the-highest-paid-college-athlete-nil-endorsement-deal-money-in-ncaa-sports-n/.
13. *See infra* Chapter 4.
14. *See generally,* The On3 NIL Deal Tracker, https://www.on3.com/nil/deals/, last accessed June 25, 2025. (It provides updated NIL Deals across the NCAA for college and high school athletes that has been reported by players, collectives, agents and media. On3 does not disclose deal financial terms as financial data is undisclosed and private to the athlete.)

15. Nick Schultz, *Michigan RB Justice Haynes Secures Ownership Stake in Loom Juice in New NIL Deal,* On3 (June 2, 2025), https://www.on3.com/nil/news/michigan-rb-justice-haynes-secures-ownership-stake-in-loom-juice-in-new-nil-deal/.
16. Josh Sanchez. *Livvy Dunne NIL Net Worth 2024: How Much Is Olivia Dunne Worth?* SPORTS ILLUSTRATED (Sept. 10, 2024), https://www.si.com/onsi/athlete-lifestyle/news/livvy-dunne-nil-net-worth. *See also infra* Chapter 3.
17. "Amateurism rules" refers to the body of NCAA rules, under which college teams are only allowed to compensate their athletes with scholarships that cover the costs of attending school. *See Amateurism, National Collegiate Athletic Association (2023), https://www.ncaa.org/sports/2014/10/6/amateurism.aspx. See also* NCAA DIVISION I MANUAL 64–77 (NCAA, 1998) (setting forth the amateurism and athletics eligibility requirements including: (1) Athletes will lose their amateur status and become ineligible for NCAA play if he or she is compensated for his or her athletic skills in that sport; (2) an NCAA member institution or affiliate is permitted to use the physical appearance, name, and pictures of a student-athlete for both charitable and educational purposes; (3) *a student-athlete will lose his or her ability to participate in NCAA sporting events if he or she either accepts or receives payment through commercial advertisement, promotion, or endorsement*). (Emphasis added.)).
18. *Id.*
19. Armstrong Williams, *Time to Pay College Athletes,* NEWSMAX (Apr. 9, 2014, 7:47 AM), https://www.newsmax.com/ArmstrongWilliams/NCAA-college-athletes-nlrb/2014/04/09/id/564508/.
20. *Id.*
21. *See Paying College Athletes—Top 3 Pros and Cons,* PROCON.ORG (Jan. 21, 2022), https://www.procon.org/headlines/paying-college-athletes-top-3-pros-and-cons/ ("Erin McGeoy, a former water polo athlete at George Washington University, explained, 'a common occurrence was that we would run out of meal money halfway through the semester and that's when I started to run into troubles of food insecurity'").
22. *Id.*
23. Some commentators have likened the NCAA's exploitation of its players to the enslavement of Black people or of Black labor during the era of Jim Crow. *See, e.g.,* Brandi Collins-Dexter, *NCAA's Amateurism Rule Exploits Black Athletes as Slave Labor,* ANDSCAPE (Mar. 27, 2018), https://andscape.com/features/ncaas-amateurism-rule-exploits-black-athletes-as-slave-labor/; Brando Simeo Starkey, *College Sports Aren't like Slavery. They're like Jim Crow,* THE NEW REPUBLIC (Oct. 31, 2014), https://newrepublic.com/article/120071/ncaa-college-sports-arent-slavery-theyre-jim-crow.
24. *See supra* note 17. NCAA Division I Manual (Overland Park, KS: NCAA 1998); Bylaw 12 ((1) ([A]fter student-athletes enroll at an NCAA school, they may no longer promote or endorse a product or allow their name, image, or likeness to be used for commercial or promotional purposes"),
25. *See* Eliott C. McLaughlin, *California Wants its College Athletes to Get Paid, but the NCAA Is Likely to Put Up Hurdles,* CNN (Oct. 2, 2019, 9:00 AM), https://edition

.cnn.com/2019/10/01/us/california-sb206-ncaa-fair-pay-to-play-act/index.html ("With the signing of California's Fair Pay to Play Act, Gov. Gavin Newsom . . . says the law is about rebalancing a power structure in which NCAA universities receive more than $14 billion annually and the nonprofit NCAA receives more than $1 billion, 'while the actual product, the folks that are putting their lives on the line, putting everyone on the line, are getting nothing'").

26. *See, e.g.*, California's Fair Pay to Play Act, originally known as California Senate Bill 206, allows collegiate athletes to acquire endorsements and sponsorships while still maintaining athletic eligibility, https://leginfo.legislature.ca.gov/faces/billTextClient.xhtml?bill_id=201920200SB206. *See also* Greg Daugherty, *What Is NIL? Understanding Name, Image, and Likeness Rules,* INVESTOPEDIA (updated May 29, 2024), https://www.investopedia.com/name-image-likeness-8558991 (reporting that "as of October 2023, at least 30 states and the District of Columbia had such laws on the books" citing Business of College Sports, Tracker: High School NIL, https://businessofcollegesports.com/high-school-nil/).
27. The right of publicity, aka publicity rights or personality rights, is defined as the right of all individuals to control commercial use of their NIL or other identifying aspects of their identities. Federal appeals court Judge Jerome N. Frank coined the term "the right of publicity" in the case of *Haelan Laboratories, Inc. v. Topps Chewing Gum, Inc.*, 202 F.2d 866 (2d Cir. 1953), which recognized a baseball player's interest in his photograph on a baseball card. *Id.* at 868–69. To date, the right of publicity has been recognized either in state common (judge-made) law or in state statutes, with more than half the states recognizing the right in one form or another.
28. The Equal Protection Clause of the Fourteenth Amendment mandates that individuals in similar situations be treated equally by the law. *See* U.S. CONST. amend. XIV, § 1, the Equal Protection Clause of the Fourteenth Amendment which provides, "nor shall any State . . . deny to any person within its jurisdiction the equal protection of the laws."
29. 594 U.S. 69 (2021) (holding that while the NCAA could regulate its players' compensation, restrictions on that compensation would be subjected to antitrust scrutiny under a "rule of reason" analysis and the ordinary rule of reason's fact-specific assessment of their effect on competition).
30. The Sherman Antitrust Act of 1890 (26 Stat. 209, 15 U.S.C. §§ 1–7) is a United States antitrust law that prescribes the rule of free competition among those engaged in commerce. *See generally*, ANTITRUST ENFORCEMENT AND INTELLECTUAL PROPERTY RIGHTS: PROMOTING INNOVATION AND COMPETITION (REPORT), U.S. DEPARTMENT OF JUSTICE AND FEDERAL TRADE COMMISSION (April 2007), https://www.justice.gov/sites/default/files/atr/legacy/2007/07/11/222655.pdf.
31. Antitrust laws "should not be a cover for exploitation of the student athletes." Justice Brett Kavanaugh, concurring opinion in *NCAA v. Alston. See* Eliott C. McLaughlin, *California Wants its College Athletes to Get Paid, but the NCAA Is Likely to Put Up Hurdles,* CNN (Oct. 2, 2019, 9:00 AM), https://edition.cnn.com/2019/10/01/us/california-sb206-ncaa-fair-pay-to-play-act/index.html.

1

Chase Young and Reggie Bush: Tarnished Sterling Careers and a Call for Justice

Show me the money![1]

—Rod Tidwell (football player) to Jerry Maguire (sports agent)[2]

OVERVIEW

Chase Young and Reggie Bush are two of the many college athletes whose sterling college careers and financial fortunes were tarnished because of the NCAA's prohibition on college athletes' benefitting financially from their notoriety and athletic performance. The only benefit allowed was athletic scholarships, which were insufficient to provide for the students' basic needs and were not guaranteed. The NCAA took the position that college athletes were amateurs and should be free of potential conflicts that might include bribery that might affect their play. Notwithstanding, the NCAA, college coaches, athletic directors, and university administrations enjoyed the largesse of the billions of dollars in media revenue, contributions from donors, and other revenue sources such as ticket sales. To enforce its hold on its athletes, the NCAA strictly enforced its amateurism/eligibility rules, punishing players and their colleges for even minor infractions, which often resulted in suspension and forfeiture of awards. Both Chase Young and Reggie Bush were severely sanctioned for minor rule violations. Today, these and many other college athletes who were subject to the NCAA rules would be college NIL millionaires, rather than tainted sources of embarrassment. Their NIL power secret is flying past injustice and adversity to achieve successful, lucrative professional sports careers.

TARNISHED STERLING CAREERS AND A CALL FOR JUSTICE

In 2019, Chase Young was the star football player for The Ohio State University Buckeyes. The Buckeyes were then and are now a member of the NCAA. During his junior season, Young broke the school's single-season sack record, earned a unanimous First-Team All-American nomination, and received yet another Defensive Player of the Year award. However, in November 2019, Young was suspended from play "due to a possible NCAA issue that the Department of Athletics [was] looking into."[3] It was later reported that in 2018, Young had borrowed money from a family friend to purchase an airline ticket for his girlfriend to attend the prestigious Rose Bowl in Pasadena, California.[4] By the time Young was suspended in November 2019, he had already repaid the loan. Despite this fact, the NCAA claimed that by taking the loan, Young had violated the NCAA amateurism rules (hereinafter "rules"). Under the NCAA's "amateurism" or "eligibility" rules, its college athletes were prohibited from receiving funds of *any* kind related to their play, other than scholarships that cover the costs of attending school. The NCAA ultimately suspended Young for two games, which likely contributed to his lost bid for the highly coveted Heisman Trophy.[5] Young's misfortune illustrates how many college athletes were negatively impacted by the NCAA's extreme enforcement of its amateurism rules. Despite these early setbacks, Chase Young continued to excel in professional football. On July 23, 2020, he signed a four-year rookie contract with the Washington Redskins (now Commanders) for $34.56 million.[6] He is currently a defensive end for the NFL's New Orleans Saints. As to NIL deals, he has appeared in advertisements for Chipotle, Under Armour, and eBay. Notwithstanding his successful career in the NFL, had the current changes in NIL law been available years prior to 2021, Chase Young would not have needed to borrow funds to buy a plane ticket for his girlfriend. Under the current NIL law, he would have undoubtedly been a NIL college millionaire.

As tragic a story, Chase Young's narrative is not an isolated story of how the NCAA's rules harmed college players' reputations and peace of mind. Another notable example of the severity of the NCAA's enforcement of its rules involved the University of Southern California ("USC") Trojans' star running back Reggie Bush, who, in 2010, was stripped of his 2005 Heisman Trophy, following allegations that his family had accepted cash and living arrangements from a sports agent. In addition to penalizing players for rule violations, the NCAA has severely punished its member schools for non-compliance, including financial penalties and sanctions. Related to the Reggie Bush matter, on June 10, 2010, the NCAA put USC on probation for four years and vacated its last two wins of the 2004 season, including the 2005 Orange Bowl, as well as all its wins in the 2005 season. They also banned the Trojans from bowl games in 2010 and 2011 and denied them thirty scholarships over three years.[7] Once again, like Chase Young, had the current NIL law been in effect in 2005, Reggie Bush would have been an NIL college millionaire. Recognizing the inequity of the NCAA rules at that time, on August 23, 2023, Reggie Bush filed a lawsuit against the NCAA, USC, and Pac-12 conference, seeking compensation for their use of his NIL.[8] Further, on April 24, 2024, following changes in the NIL laws and years of legal actions by Bush to clear his name, the Heisman Trust announced that it would be reinstating Reggie Bush's 2005 Heisman Trophy, which they did.[9]

Young's and Bush's narratives of alleged violations of the NCAA rules are not isolated stories of how the NCAA's rules harmed players' reputations. Unfortunately, over the years, there were many such NCAA allegations against college players. For example, Terrelle Pryor, Ohio State's starting quarterback from 2008 to 2010, confessed to selling his conference championship rings on eBay, as well as accepting improper discounts from a local tattoo parlor over a period of at least two years, and consequently was suspended for the first five games of the 2011 season.[10] In 2010, USC basketball superstar O.J. Mayo was held ineligible for the 2007–2008 season, for allegedly receiving improper gifts before and during his time at USC.[11] Further, in 2010, The University of Alabama's ("Alabama") defensive tackle Marcell Dareus was ruled ineligible for two games after an NCAA investigation determined that he received improper benefits during two trips to Miami for agent-hosted parties and was ordered to pay $1,787 to a charity of his choice before returning to play for the Alabama Crimson Tide.[12]

Parenthetically, Reggie Bush is not the only ex-college athlete who has sued the NCAA for compensation for their prior athletic careers following a change in the NIL laws that favor college athletes. For example, in June 2024, a group of ten players on North Carolina State University's 1983 NCAA championship-winning basketball team sued the NCAA and the Collegiate Licensing Company to seek compensation for the use of their names, images, and likenesses.[13] Further, in September 2024, Denard Robinson, Braylon Edwards, and several former Michigan stars sued the NCAA and the Big Ten Network, claiming reimbursement of more than $50 million during their college careers because of the NCAA's ban on athletes being compensated for name, image, and likeness.[14] These lawsuits are likely to be followed by other former players who are seeking retroactive payment for their NIL rights.

NIL LAW AND DEALS

Narratives of Chase Young and other college athletes who were severely punished for even minor infractions illustrate how strictly the NCAA enforced its rules and how the NCAA's enforcement tarnished the otherwise sterling careers of many young athletes. However, in 2021, that situation changed after the law permitted college athletes to benefit from their NIL. Since then, many college athletes have contracted with third parties such as Nike, for shoe endorsement deals. Several players have become millionaires due to NIL deals while still in college. These opportunities are directly the result of a change in the NIL law.

So, what is NIL and how are college athletes becoming millionaires due to a change in the NIL law? As previously noted, "NIL" is shorthand for "name, image, and likeness" and is how college athletes can make millions from their notoriety.[15] NIL law permits college athletes "the right to publicity" that ordinary citizens already have. Today, college athletes can be paid for the use of their NIL in several ways. That includes appearing in advertising campaigns, selling ads on their social accounts, selling merchandise, starting their own sports camps, starting their own businesses, selling signed memorabilia, making paid appearances, delivering speeches for money, and arranging autograph signings.[16] As a result, college superstars have signed lucrative deals with top athletic brand names like Nike, Adidas, and Under Armour, as well as with non-athletic brands such as T-Mobile, Sam's Club, and Amazon.[17] For example, Angel Reese is paid for endorsing Reese's Peanut Butter Cups;[18] Colorado lineman Tommy Brown stripped down to model Shinesty underwear;[19] and Arkansas wide receiver Trey Knox included his dog, Blue, in a deal with him to endorse PetSmart products.[20] What's more, the athletes are legally permitted to use and often employ agents, lawyers, and other professionals to facilitate these NIL deals.

What is meant by the individual words "name," "image," and "likeness"?[21] The use of a player's name is somewhat obvious, such as Nike putting Michael Jordan's name on a shoe. Equally easy to discern is the use of the "Air Jordan" image on Nike advertisements. That would also include using a photograph of Livvy Dunne on the packaging for athletic gear.[22] However, what is meant by likeness? To help differentiate it from "image"—as in a photograph or recognizable drawing of a particular athlete—USA Volleyball, that sport's governing body, describes "likeness" as "your 'semblance.'"[23] It elaborates: "Think the outline of Michael Jordan on the Jordan brand. Arnold Palmer's signature on Arizona Iced Tea. Think EA Sports' popular and profitable video games that depicted former NCAA athletes by using their height, body type, number, and playing style—but never their name or exact image."[24] Incidentally, the On3 NIL Deal Tracker lists all NIL deals across the NCAA for college and high school athletes being reported by players, collectives, agents, and media.[25]

NIL has a controversial impact on the trajectory of college sports. That is because it is the only means by which college athletes can be legally compensated for their role or status as athletes. As such, it is a great boon for the athletes, while being a perceived threat to the NCAA's control of college sports. NIL deals have two related developments that make for greater financial opportunities for college athletes. The first development is the NCAA "Transfer Portal,"[26] which was created in the fall of 2018 and facilitates an athlete who wishes to transfer to another college.[27] The second development is the realignment of college football conferences,[28] which is resulting in greater competition for top talent. NIL, combined with the Transfer Portal and the realignment of college football conferences, has been transformative in college sports. Some critics have deemed NIL to be the death of college sports.[29]

A NIL deal is essentially a legal contract or agreement, between a player and a third party, such as Nike. Under these deals, a player licenses the use of their name, image, or likeness to endorse a product or service by appearing in commercials, ads, and digital content. Players are paid in cash or in kind for promoting products or services, such as cars, groceries, and athletic apparel. Further, they are paid to create social media content on platforms like YouTube, TikTok, Instagram, podcasts, or other outlets, getting paid by advertisers through subscriptions or other means: autograph signings, public appearances, and speaking engagements; licensing their name or image to be used in advertisements, video games, memorabilia, apparel, or other media; hosting sports camps and training clinics for aspiring athletes, charging participation fees; and partnering with local businesses for promotions, appearances, endorsements, or joint marketing initiatives.[30] It has been reported that although national brands are continuing to expand how they engage student-athletes as promoters in marketing campaigns, social media remains the main tactic in many endorsement deals.[31] The increasing market value of NIL is due in great part to the proliferation of social media.[32] For example, LSU gymnast Livvy Dunne, who has millions of social media followers, has signed million-dollar NIL deals.[33]

College athlete NIL deals greatly vary in the amount of compensation from thousands to millions of dollars per year. Many college athletes do not have an NIL deal because they have no notoriety or value in the marketplace. After the first year of NIL deals, it was reported that nearly half a million college athletes signed NIL deals.[34] It was reported that, in 2024, the "median total athlete earnings" on NIL deals was only $512.[35] On the other end of the spectrum are the high-profile players who are commanding megabucks in NIL money in the millions of dollars.[36] The amount of money involved in a NIL deal depends on the value a player can bring to influence markets, such as a decision to purchase a certain brand of athletic equipment.[37] A select few have national brand endorsement deals, such as Bronny James who inked a lucrative contract with Nike while he was a high school student.[38] The highest-paid NIL players are high-profile, star football or basketball young men.[39] Notwithstanding, one major exception is LSU gymnast Livvy Dunne, who has millions of social media followers.[40] A high-profile player is typically represented by a seasoned sports agent and accompanied by a team of lawyers, accountants, tax professionals, and social media experts.[41]

Those third parties who contract with players are generally not the player's college, although a few states are allowing players to contract NIL deals with their college.[42] This is a growth market compared to international, professional sports. One example of the potential value of NIL for college athletes is that of the world-famous soccer great, Cristiano Ronaldo. He reportedly has 545 million Instagram followers and commands nearly $4 million per post![43] That does not include other revenue he receives from the sale of T-shirts, trading cards, and other NIL revenue.[44] Further, consider the financial value of an avatar in a fantasy football league.[45] Overall, these "corporate" sponsor NIL deals for brand endorsements reportedly account for 20% of NIL money. Notwithstanding, there are NIL deals that involve players' decisions as to which colleges they enroll in and play for.

That second type of NIL deal involves players contracting with third parties called "collectives" that are composed of college donors or boosters who traditionally donate money to a college's athletic department. Currently, 80% of NIL money is raised by "NIL collectives," nonprofit entities indirectly affiliated with a school that receives donations from boosters, alumni, and fans of a particular school, then pay the funds to college athletes.[46] Again, the players would receive money for endorsing services such as promoting a car dealership or a product like a brand of pizza. However, these "collective" NIL contracts are used as a device to recruit a player to attend a particular college.[47] However, this practice has been frowned upon by the NCAA and criticized by lesser-funded colleges. The NCAA rules prohibit the use of a NIL deal to recruit an athlete to play for a particular college. This rule remains controversial and is the subject of litigation. In 2014, a federal judge in Tennessee granted a preliminary injunction that prohibits the NCAA from enforcing its own rules against pay-to-play in recruiting. Notwithstanding, the University of Oregon ("Oregon") reportedly engaged in a large sum of money collective arrangements to fill its football roster.[48] Further, many of the top schools have active internal programs to facilitate their athletes signing NIL deals.[49] Hence, NIL collectives can negotiate deals with recruits without the apparent fear of NCAA sanctions.[50]

In the past, NIL collectives have applied for and received tax-exempt status from the Internal Revenue Service ("IRS").[51] However, in June 2023, the IRS Office of Chief Counsel explained that many organizations that develop paid NIL opportunities for student-athletes are *not* eligible for tax-exempt status under IRC § 501(c)(3) "because the private benefits they provide to student-athletes are not incidental both qualitatively and quantitatively to any exempt purpose furthered by that activity."[52] This will likely change how NIL agreements are structured and the status or type of institutions they contract with going forward.[53] That means that some of the revenue that would have gone to the NCAA and its school members—all of whom are tax-exempt, nonprofit entities—would now become taxable. Hence, whereas boosters and/or collectives who contributed directly to a college or university's athletic program would have received a tax deduction as a charitable donation, those same boosters who form cooperatives to help recruit players via NIL deals have been instructed by the IRS that those NIL funds are not tax deductible.[54]

Hence, this chapter provides the nature of NIL, its background, and how college athletes won their NIL rights. It shows how the law creates winners and losers, levels unlevel playing fields, and controls the flow of wealth to those denied opportunities to achieve it. Granting college athletes their NIL rights is righteous; however, it remains controversial. The NIL world for college athletes was not always green. Prior to 2021, the NCAA prohibited its athletes from receiving any compensation of any type, under severe penalty for even minor violations.[55] That included forbidding college athletes from being paid for the use of their NIL. Notwithstanding, following years of lawsuits by former college athletes, the law changed to protect college athletes' right to profit from their NIL, which includes their personal brands, endorsements, social media influence, and their playing for a given team. Consequently, in 2021, the NCAA amended its rule to permit its players to contract NIL deals, with restrictions.

A review of revenue sharing that college athletes receive shows both the importance of NIL deals to player compensation and how players are still under-compensated. In 2023, its second year of existence, NIL revenues were estimated to total $1.2 billion.[56] College sports is a multi-billion-dollar enterprise. According to a November 2021 report, NCAA college athletic programs receive sports-related revenue from many and varied sources, including distributions from the NCAA and conferences; broadcast rights; royalties/advertising/sponsorship; contributions from alumni and others; endowment/investment income; ticket sales and concessions; guarantees and options; sports camps; direct governmental support; direct and indirect university institutional support; and student fees.[57] A surprising leading source of revenue for all NCAA colleges comes from institution and government supports (37%) and for Division I colleges (29%).[58] The second-most significant revenue source comes from colleges' share of media revenue (all colleges, 18%; Division I, 21%),[59] including from March Madness in basketball[60] and their share of conference/bowl game media revenue in football.[61] In 2024, the leading college conferences reported near multi-millions in revenue, including the Big Ten ($879.9 million); the SEC ($852.6 million); the ACC ($707 million); the Pac-12 ($603.9 million); and the Big 12 ($510.7 million).[62] College sports revenue, as well as that of the NCAA, including media revenue, is generally tax-exempt because of their tax-exempt status under section 501(c)(3) of the Internal Revenue Code, while revenue from professional sports is taxable.[63] Further, college sports contribute to many multi-billion-dollar industries, including legal and illegal sports-betting;[64] fantasy sports;[65] and gaming.[66]

Before the change in NIL law, the student-athletes only received scholarships/financial aid. Today, NIL is making some college athletes instant millionaires. Since NIL payments go directly to athletes, the new financial opportunities can begin to bridge the vast gap between the student athletes that generate revenue at an estimated 7% and revenues to professional athlete compensation at approximately 50% of revenues.[67] Hence, even with NIL deals, which are generally not distributed equally among players, college athletes are not being equitably compensated for their contribution to college sports.

NIL POWER SECRET #1: FOLLOW CHASE YOUNG AND REGGIE BUSH'S POWER PLAY TO FLY PAST ADVERSITY

Chase Young and Reggie Bush are two of the many college athletes who were demonized by the NCAA's use of its amateurism rule to tarnish the otherwise sterling reputations of college athletes, particularly those who were African American superstars.[68] Today, college athletes can benefit from the use of their NIL, and some are becoming multi-millionaires in the process. Unfortunately, many former athletes did not have the law on their side for many years and suffered personal humiliation and had to recover from their tarnished, previously sterling reputations. Fortunately, Reggie Bush ultimately had the Heisman Trophy returned to him. Chase Young was not given to the chance to obtain one, following what was clearly a minor infraction of the NCAA rules.

Chase Young and Reggie Bush have both gone on to have successful professional football careers with the NFL. Notwithstanding, one can imagine the emotional burden put on the shoulders of these players when they were mere teens in college, as well as the lingering sense of being victims caught on the wrong side of unjust laws. Their power secret is the ability to continue to excel despite setbacks that negatively impacted their careers and their status in society. Recovering from injustice and a stain on one's reputation is not an easy task. Seeking redress and overdue apologies are vital to recovering from victimization. Seeking compensation for the emotional and financial damage done to these and other former and present college athletes is both right and just.

Next, we will see how the law has awarded millions of dollars to past athletes who have successfully sued the NCAA and its member schools for retroactive compensation for the use of the players' NIL.

Further Reading

Associated Press, *Auburn Releases Cam Newton Docs,* ESPN (Nov. 4, 2011), https://www.espn.com/college-football/story/_/id/7190987/auburn-tigers-records-reveal-details-cam-newton-scandal.

Bailey Brautigan, *Cam Newton and 10 College Athletes in Scandal: Is it Their Fault or the System?,* Bleacher Report (June 2, 2018), https://bleacherreport.com/articles/514177-10-college-athletes-involved-in-scandals-is-it-their-fault-or-the-system.

Bryce Young Says he Was a Doordash Driver While at Alabama to Earn Extra Money, FOX Sports (Aug. 3, 2023), https://www.foxsports.com/stories/nfl/bryce-young-says-he-was-a-doordash-driver-while-at-alabama-to-earn-extra-money.

Chuck Shilken, *Reggie Bush Lawsuit Accuses USC, Pac-12, NCAA of Profiting from his NIL "Without Compensating Bush One Penny,"* LA Times (Sep. 24, 2024), https://www.latimes.com/sports/usc/story/2024-09-24/reggie-bush-lawsuit-usc-pac-12-ncaa-nil.

Don Yaeger, *Tarnished Heisman: Did Reggie Bush Turn his Final College Season into a Six-Figure Job?* (2008).

Jeff Zimbalist & Michael Zimbalist, *Youngstown Boys* (2013), https://www.imdb.com/title/tt3377022/.

Margaret J. Goldstein, Meet Bryce Young: Carolina Panthers Superstar (2024).

Pete Thamel, *Auburn is Cleared in Investigation into Newton,* N.Y. Times (Oct. 12, 2011), https://www.nytimes.com/2011/10/13/sports/ncaafootball/auburn-is-cleared-in-investigation-into-cam-newtons-recruitment.html.

Endnotes

1. "Show Me the Money" means that if you really appreciate what I bring to the table, then pay me accordingly. The phase was first used in a demand made by an underpaid, unappreciated Black, outstanding athlete to his white, desperate for business, sports' agent, that the agent can prove his ability to deliver on substantial compensation and appreciation.
2. Jerry Mcguire (1996), https://www.imdb.com/title/tt0116695/?%20ref_=fn_al_tt_1.
3. Diamaris Martino, *Ohio State's Star Football Player Suspended for Accepting Loan,* CNBC (Nov. 8, 2019), https://www.cnbc.com/2019/11/08/ohiostates-star-football-player-suspended-for-accepting-loan.html (reporting on a statement made by Ohio State's Associate Athletics Director).
4. Jordan Heck, *"Free Chase Young": Criticism of the NCAA Trends on Social Media after Ohio State Star's Suspension,* Sporting News (Nov. 9, 2019), https://www.sportingnews.com/us/ncaa-football/news/chase-young-suspensionohio-state-ncaa/arx41omz2l47191iwyw5ju398.
5. *See* Bruce Hooley, *Ohio State's Justin Fields, Chase Young 3–4 in Heisman Voting,* Sports Illustrated (Dec. 14, 2019), https://www.si.com/college/ohiostate/football/ohio-states-chase-young-justin-fields-watch-burrow-win-heisman (reporting that Young lost the Heisman bid to Joe Burrow).
6. Matt Johnson, *Chase Young Signs Rookie Contract with Washington,* Sportsnaut (updated July 23, 2020), https://sportsnaut.com/chase-young-signs-rookie-contract-with-washington/.
7. *See* Shehan Jeyarajah, *How Did Reggie Bush Lose His Heisman Trophy? Answering Key Questions with Ex-USC Star Back Among Award Winners,* CBS Sports (Apr. 24, 2024), https://www.cbssports.com/college-football/news/how-did-reggie-bush-lose-his-heisman-trophy-answering-key-questions-with-ex-usc-star-back-among-award-winners/.
8. *See* J. Brady McCollough, *Former USC Star Reggie Bush Sues the NCAA for Defamation and Seeks His Heisman Trophy,* LA Times (updated Aug. 23, 2023), https://www.latimes.com/sports/usc/story/2023-08-22/reggie-bush-ncaa-lawsuit-defamation. (Attached to the report is a copy of the lawsuit, https://ca-times.brightspotcdn.com/12/f6/1c3eb7c643debff1c369b24c3801/bush-ncaa-complaint.pdf.)

9. *See* David Cobb, *Reggie Bush's 2005 Heisman Trophy Reinstated as Former USC Trojans Star Wins Long Battle*, CBS SPORTS (Apr. 24, 2024), https://www.cbssports.com/college-football/news/reggie-bushs-2005-heisman-trophy-reinstated-as-former-usc-trojans-star-wins-long-battle/.
10. *See generally*, Bailey Brautigan, *Cam Newton and 10 College Athletes in Scandal: Is It their Fault or the System?*, BLEACHER REPORT (Nov. 10, 2010), https://bleacherreport.com/articles/514177-10-college-athletes-involved-in-scandals-is-it-their-fault-or-the-system (interesting that all 10 athletes discussed in these "scandals" are African American men).
11. *Id.*
12. *Id.*
13. Doric Sam, *10 Players from 1983 NC State MCBB Championship Team Sue NCAA over NIL*, BLEACHER REPORT (June 10, 2024), https://bleacherreport.com/articles/10124294-10-players-from-1983-nc-state-mcbb-championship-team-sue-ncaa-over-nil.
14. Ralph D. Russo, *Denard Robinson and Braylon Edwards Are among Former Michigan Players Suing NCAA and Big Ten Network*, AP (Sept. 10, 2024), https://apnews.com/article/michigan-lawsuit-ncaa-d82d7420d16afa06a91c2253cd20f21f.
15. *See generally*, Greg Daugherty, *What Is NIL? Understanding Name, Image, and Likeness Rules*, INVESTOPEDIA (updated May 29, 2024), https://www.investopedia.com/name-image-likeness-8558991.
16. James Parks, *NIL in College Football: Here's What You Need to Know, and What's Next*, SPORTS ILLUSTRATED (Jan. 17, 2024), https://www.si.com/fannation/college/cfb-hq/ncaa-football/college-football-nil-rule-changes-what-you-need-to-know.
17. Sara Coello, *What Is NIL in College Sports? How Do Athlete Deals Work?*, ESPN (Sept. 26, 2024), https://www.espn.com/college-sports/story/_/id/41040485/what-nil-college-sports-how-do-athlete-deals-work.
18. *Id.*
19. *Shinesty Signs Groundbreaking NIL Deal, Mints College Football's First Professional Underwear Supermodel*, SHINESTY (Oct. 28, 2022), https://www.shinesty.com/press-releases/tommy-brown.
20. Chance Linton, *Arkansas WR Trey Knox Lands Promotional Deal with PetSmart*, 247SPORTS (July 1, 2021), https://247sports.com/article/arkansas-football-trey-knox-lands-promotional-deal-with-petsmart-under-new-nil-rules-name-image-likeness-167296461/.
21. Greg Daugherty, *What Is NIL? Understanding Name, Image, and Likeness Rules*, INVESTOPEDIA (updated May 29, 2024), https://www.investopedia.com/nil-and-the-ncaa-8599762.
22. *Id.*
23. *Id.*
24. *Id.* quoting USA Volleyball. "An Overview of Name, Image, and Likeness in College Sports," https://usavolleyball.org/resource/an-overview-of-name-image-and-likeness-in-college-sports/.
25. *NIL Deal Tracker*, ON3, https://www.on3.com/nil/deals/ (last accessed Mar. 11, 2025).

26. Greg Johnson, *What the NCAA Transfer Portal Is... and What It Isn't*, NCAA (Oct. 8, 2019), https://www.ncaa.org/news/2023/2/8/media-center-what-the-ncaa-transfer-portal-is-and-what-it-isn-t.
27. Tom VanHaaren, *College Football's New Transfer Portal Windows, Explained*, ESPN (Nov. 9, 2022), https://www.espn.com/college-football/story/_/id/34967085/college-football-new-transfer-portal-windows-explained.
28. Lawrence Price, *"College Football Conference Realignment Breakdown for 2024–25: Teams in New Conferences,"* NCAA (Sept. 8, 2024), https://www.ncaa.com/news/ncaa/article/2024-08-22/college-football-conference-realignment-breakdown-2024-25-teams-new-conferences.
29. Manu Raju, Clare Foran, & Morgan Rimmer, *NCAA Leaders Warn College Sports at Risk of 'Permanent Damage' Without Action from Congress*, CNN (Dec. 3, 2023), https://www.cnn.com/2023/12/03/politics/ncaa-college-sports-at-risk-nil/index.html.
30. Richard Pianoforte, *Insights: For Student Athletes, NIL Means Visibility, Income—and Taxes*, FIDUCIARY TRUST INT'L (Aug. 23, 2023), https://www.fiduciarytrust.com/insights/article-detail/for-student-athletes-nil-means-visibility-income-and-taxes.
31. *See* Nelson Granados, *The Sports Agent of the NIL Era: A Social Media Savvy Life Coach*, FORBES (May 23, 2023), https://www.forbes.com/sites/nelsongranados/2023/05/23/the-sports-agent-of-the-nil-era-a-social-media-savvy-life-coach/amp/; *NIL x Social Media*, STUDENT-ATHLETE INSIGHTS (Oct. 9, 2022), https://studentathleteinsights.com/blog/name-image-likeness-nil-insider-14.
32. *See* Dan Whateley & Ashley Rodriquez, *How NIL Deals and Brand Sponsorships Are Helping College Athletes Make Money*, INSIDER (Sept. 19, 2023), https://www.businessinsider.com/how-college-athletes-are-getting-paid-from-nil-endorsement-deals.
33. *See infra* Chapter 3.
34. *Understanding NIL Compensation for College Athletes: 5 Things to Know*, FOOTBASKET.COM (Nov. 10, 2022), https://www.footbasket.com/2022/11/understanding-nil-compensation-for.html. "Still, the fastest and possibly easiest way college athletes can make money from NIL is through social media affiliate marketing. Even micro-influencers with fewer than 10,000 followers on social media, can profit from their followers. The micro-influencer trend has gained popularity because when you get people with smaller followings to promote a service or produce, the things they suggest appear more genuine. Posting sponsored content can earn you hundreds or even thousands of dollars per month, depending on the size of your following." *Id.*
35. *See generally*, Data Dashboard, NCAA.org, https://nilassist.ncaa.org/data-dashboard/, accessed June 25, 2025 (reporting that the "average total athlete earnings" that was disclosed to the NCAA for January 1, 2024 to the end of October 31, 2024 was $21,916, while the "median total athlete earnings" was only $512).
36. *See On3 NIL Valuations*, ON3.COM (updated on June 26, 2025), https://www.on3.com/nil/rankings/player/nil-valuations/.

37. *Id.*
38. *See infra* Chapter 4.
39. *See On3 NIL Valuations*, ON3.COM (updated on June 26, 2025), https://www.on3.com/nil/rankings/player/nil-valuations/.
40. *See infra* Chapter 3.
41. *See generally*, NCAA NIL Assist, NCAA.org (2025), https://nilassist.ncaa.org/ (last assessed June 26. 2025).
42. Email from National College Players Association to author (Dec. 7, 2024, at 2:00:06 PM EST). "[A]t least four states (CA, GA, IL, and VA) have NIL laws that already allow their universities to pay NIL compensation directly to their athletes and prohibit universities from complying with conference or NCAA rules that would restrict such pay."
43. *See* Chris De Silva, *Sport's Highest Earners Per Instagram Post*, NINE'S WIDE WORLD OF SPORTS (Dec. 25, 2022), https://wwos.nine.com.au/news/highest-earning-sports-stars-on-instagram-lionel-messi-cristiano-ronaldo-virat-kohli/ab1bcaaf-0c00-4779-8c67-227a4079aa7f#22.
44. Riccardo Zazzini, *Cashing in on the Beautiful Game: Ronaldo's Net Worth Breaks the Bank*, HIGHSNOBIETY (last accessed Oct. 8, 2023), https://www.highsnobiety.com/p/cristiano-ronaldo-net-worth/ ("As of 2023, Forbes estimates his net worth at a cool $500 million, making him one of the wealthiest athletes in the world").
45. Dora Mekouar, *Why Millions of Americans Spend Billions on this Fantasy*, VOICE OF AMER. NEWS (Sept. 3, 2019), https://www.voanews.com/a/usa_all-about-america_why-millions-americans-spend-billions-fantasy/6175070.html (reporting that, in 2019, the fantasy sports industry was worth over $7 billion).
46. Serena Morones & Paul Heidt, *Following the Money in College Sports*, MORONES ANALYTICS (lastaccessedMar.11,2025),https://moronesanalytics.com/following-the-money-in-college-sports/#_ftnref6.citing.
47. *See* Morgan Moriarty, *Bryce Underwood NIL Money, Explained: What to Know about Michigan's "Champions Circle" Behind $10.5m Recruiting Flip*, SPORTING NEWS (Nov. 26, 2024), https://www.sportingnews.com/us/ncaa-football/news/bryce-underwood-nil-money-explained-michigan-champions-circle/243a41ba76189ecd313ad693. (Bryce Underwood NIL with a collective affiliated with the University of Michigan, which is reportedly worth $10 million, as discussed in Chapter 7.).
48. Arden Cravalho, *How Much Money Built Oregon Ducks Current Roster*, MSN (Aug. 27, 2024), https://www.msn.com/en-us/sports/other/how-much-nil-money-built-oregon-ducks-current-football-roster/ar-AA1pwwF7?ocid=socialshare&pc=DCTS&cvid=b12c0ae7ca014b06906a30d70a11d971&ei=15.
49. *Ranked: Which American College Has the Most NIL Athletes?*, ESSENTIALLYSPORTS (Sept. 20, 2024), https://www.msn.com/en-us/sports/other/ranked-which-american-college-has-the-most-nil-athletes/vi-AA1qUjPC?ocid=socialshare&pc=DCTS&cvid=b14eb3a93a29407db7e0c3fc7e837377&ei=31.

50. *See* Stewart Mandel, *NCAA Recruiting Pay-for-Play Is Here, and the Only Surprise Is How Fast it Happened*, THE ATHLETIC, NY TIMES (Feb. 23, 2024), https://www.nytimes.com/athletic/5296175/2024/02/23/ncaa-nil-paying-recruits-tennessee-injunction/.
51. *Name, Image, and Likeness (NIL) Collectives*, TAXPAYER ADVOC. SERV. (updated Nov. 19, 2024), https://www.taxpayeradvocate.irs.gov/get-help/general/nil/nil-collectives/.
52. Office of Chief Counsel, Internal Revenue Service, Memorandum, Number: AM 2023–004 (June 9, 2023).
53. *See* Tax Policy Center Briefing Book, *State and Local Tax Policies*, https://www.taxpolicycenter.org/briefing-book/how-do-state-and-local-individual-income-taxes-work (last accessed July 14, 2024).
54. *Id.*
55. Cole Claybourn, *Name, Image, Likeness: What College Athletes Should Know about NCAA Rules*, U.S. WORLD & NEWS (Feb. 8, 2024), https://www.usnews.com/education/best-colleges/articles/name-image-likeness-what-college-athletes-should-know-about-ncaa-rules.
56. Serena Morones & Paul Heidt, *Following the Money in College Sports*, MORONES ANALYTICS, https://moronesanalytics.com/following-the-money-in-college-sports/#_ftnref6 (last accessed Mar. 11, 2025) (citing *At Two: Two Years of Name, Image and Likeness in College Sports*, OPENDORSE, https://biz.opendorse.com/wp-content/uploads/2023/06/NILatTwo.pdf#gf_46) (last accessed Mar. 11, 2025).
57. *Trends in Division I Athletics Finances*, NCAA RESEARCH, https://ncaaorg.s3.amazonaws.com/research/Finances/2021RES_D1-RevExpReport.pdf (last accessed Mar. 11, 2025).
58. *Id.*
59. *Id.*
60. "The NCAA ended the 2023 fiscal year with $1.3 billion in revenue and $870 million in net assets, according to a copy of the association's audited financial statement. . . . On the expense side of its ledger, the NCAA reported distributing $670 million to its Division I members (up from $657 in FY22) and spending $192 million on its D-I championships programs and NIT tournament ($170 million in FY22)." Daniel Libit & Eben Novy-Williams, *NCAA Took in Record Revenue in 2023 on Investment Jump*, SPORTICO (Feb. 1, 2024), https://www.sportico.com/leagues/college-sports/2024/ncaa-revenue-2023-financials-1234765147/. *See also NCAA Generates Nearly $1.3 Billion in Revenue for 2022–23*, ESPN (Feb. 1, 2024), https://www.espn.com/college-sports/story/_/id/39439274/ncaa-generates-nearly-13-billion-revenue-2022-23.
61. "In June 1984, a tectonic shift in college sports occurred when the Supreme Court ruled in *NCAA v. Board of Regents* (of the University of Oklahoma) that the NCAA's control of television deals represented a restraint of trade. This landmark decision ushered in a free market system for revenue generation, in lieu of an

NCAA-regulated system. Subsequently, the Bowl Championship Series and the College Football Playoff ('CFP') led to large television deals for post season competition. The Big-10 Conference formed its own television network in 2007 and most major conferences followed their lead over the next decade" (citing Brandon Marcello, *Why the NCAA Doesn't Control College Football and Never Will*, 247SPORTS (July 23, 2020), https://247sports.com/article/-why-1984-supreme-court-ruling-explains-why-ncaa-does-not-control-college-football-amid-coronavirus-covid-19-pandemic-149461659/).

"After the 1984 Supreme Court decision, conferences stepped into the position of negotiating television rights on behalf of their member schools. Collegiate athletic conferences, non-profit organizations comprised of 8–16 member schools, are governed by boards made up of university presidents responsible for budgeting, hiring conference commissioners, enforcing rules, and admitting new schools.[8] Conference commissioners manage the day-to-day operations and hold significant sway over shaping revenue for the conferences, given that university presidents often lack experience in sports business matters" (footnotes omitted). Serena Morones & Paul Heidt, *Following the Money in College Sports*, MORONES ANALYTICS, https://moronesanalytics.com/following-the-money-in-college-sports/#_ftnref6 (last accessed Mar. 11, 2025).

62. *Bulked-up Big Ten and SEC Set to Dominate College Football on and off the Field*, ALA. DAILY NEWS (Aug. 25, 2024), https://aldailynews.com/bulked-up-big-ten-and-sec-set-to-dominate-college-football-on-and-off-the-field/#:~:text=According%20to%20tax%20filings%20released,%24707%20million%20in%202022%2D23.
63. *See* Scott Hodge, *The Big Business of Tax-Free College Sports*, TAX FOUND. (Aug. 21, 2023), https://taxfoundation.org/blog/college-sports-tax-free-revenue/ (reporting "Furthermore, since broadcasting companies can deduct the cost of making payments to college athletic conferences on their income tax return, it means that TV income to athletic conferences is never subject to federal income taxes and is effectively subsidized by other taxpayers").
64. *See generally, Sports Betting in the United States—Statistics & Facts*, STATISTICA, https://www.statista.com/topics/8581/sports-betting-us/#topicOverview (last accessed Mar. 15, 2025) ("In May 2018, when the U.S. Supreme Court overturned the Professional and Amateur Sports Protection Act, giving states the power to legalize sports betting. As of September 2024, there were 38 states in the U.S. where sports betting was legal to different degrees. Since then, the industry has gone from strength to strength, with revenue generated from sports betting in the U.S. increasing from around 400 million U.S. dollars in 2018 to over 11 billion U.S. dollars in 2023"). "U.S. bettors are expected to wager more than $2.72 billion on this year's men's and women's national tournaments using legalized sportsbooks, according to the American Gaming Association (AGA)." *See* Kristopher J. Brooks, *How Much Money Is Bet on March Madness? The 2024 NCAA Tournament Is Expected to Generate Billions*, CBS NEWS (Mar. 21, 2024), https://www.cbsnews.com/news/march-madness-ncaa-tournament-2024

-bet-money-online-sports-gambling/. Further, the NCAA reported that "[s]ports wagering activity is widespread on college campuses—67% of students living on campus are bettors and tend to bet at a higher frequency. 41% of college students who bet on sports have placed a bet on their school's teams and 35% have used a student bookmaker." *See* Saquandra Heath, *NCAA Releases Sports Wagering Survey Data,* NCAA (May 24, 2023), https://www.ncaa.org/news/2023/5/24/media-center-ncaa-releases-sports-wagering-survey-data.aspx.

65. Ayrton Ostly, *What Is Fantasy Football? A Beginner's Guide for the American Pastime,* USA Today (Sept. 29, 2024), https://www.usatoday.com/story/sports/nfl/fantasy/2024/09/29/fantasy-football-explained-format-scoring-drafts/75434713007/.
66. *See, e.g.*, EA Sports, https://www.ea.com/sports (last accessed Mar. 11, 2025).
67. Serena Morones & Paul Heidt, *Following the Money in College Sports,* Morones Analytics, https://moronesanalytics.com/following-the-money-in-college-sports/#_ftnref6. (last accessed Mar. 11, 2025) (according to the 2022 Annual Report of the Green Bay Packers, players receive approx. 49% of revenues).
68. *See* Demand that the U.S. Congress Guarantee Fair Pay for College Athletes in Every State, Color of Change, https://act.colorofchange.org/sign/congress_fairpay?source=coc_main_website (last visited Feb. 24, 2022) (reporting several awful stories of the National Collegiate Athletic Association's ("NCAA") mistreatment of Black athletes, including Chase Young).

2

Edward O'Bannon, Shawne Alston, and Grant House: Millions for Past NIL Abuse

"[T]raditions alone cannot justify the NCAA's decision to build a massive money-raising enterprise on the backs of student-athletes who are not fairly compensated."

—Brett Kavanaugh, Associate Justice of the U.S. Supreme Court[1]

OVERVIEW

Edward O'Bannon, Shawne Alston, and Grant House are former college athletes who successfully sued and consequently helped deliver millions of dollars to other former college athletes for the illegal use of their NIL by the NCAA and its member colleges. These lawsuits sought billions of dollars for former or current college athletes. Their NIL power secret is seeking changes in the law and the NCAA rules to ensure that players retain their NIL rights even after graduating from college.

SUCCESSFULLY SUING FOR A SHARE OF THE WEALTH

As previously mentioned, many former college athletes have filed lawsuits against the NCAA for a share of the use of the players' NIL. Most noteworthy are lawsuits that have changed the NIL law to provide college athletes the present opportunity to benefit from their NIL. In addition to changing the NIL law to favor college athletes, these groundbreaking cases sought and have awarded former players millions and potentially billions in retroactive compensation for the NCAA's monopolization of the players' NIL. What follows next are the stories of three former colleges athletes who were the lead plaintiffs in these lawsuits.

Edward O'Bannon is a former NBA basketball player who was a power forward for the University of California, Los Angeles ("UCLA") Bruins on their 1995 NCAA championship team. In July 2009, he was the lead plaintiff in *O'Bannon v. NCAA*,[2] an antitrust class-action lawsuit against the NCAA over the organization's use for commercial purposes of the images of its former student athletes, which resulted in the discontinuation of NCAA video games. On August 8, 2014, a federal district court judge ruled that upon graduation, a former college athlete should become entitled to financial compensation for the NCAA's commercial uses of the player's image, particularly in video games, as the defendants had violated the Sherman Act and other federal antitrust law.[3] In September 2015, the Ninth Circuit Court of Appeals affirmed, in part, and reversed, in part, the district court's ruling.[4] Consequently, the NCAA was ordered to pay the plaintiffs $42.2 million in fees and costs.[5] Moreover, because of the *O'Bannon* decision, many other class-action lawsuits were filed by student-athletes against the NCAA and colleges, challenging other restrictions on educational funds as being anti-competitive.[6] While the college athletes received some benefits from the *O'Bannon* decision, the courts still failed to recognize the students' property rights in their NIL or their labor rights.

In 2019, following the *O'Bannon* decision, Shawne Alston, a former West Virginia University Mountaineers running back, and former University of California, Berkeley center Justine Hartman, as representatives of several former NCAA players, filed several lawsuits in federal court, which were consolidated under *NCAA v. Alston*,[7] challenging the NCAA restrictions on educational compensation for athletes.[8] In March 2019, a federal judge ruled that the NCAA restrictions on "non-cash education-related benefits" violated antitrust law under the Sherman Act.[9] The court required the NCAA to allow for certain types of academic benefits beyond the previously established full scholarships from the *O'Bannon* decision, such as for "computers, science equipment, musical instruments, and other tangible items not included in the cost of attendance calculation but nonetheless related to the pursuit of academic studies."[10] Moreover, the district court in *Alston* barred the NCAA from preventing athletes from receiving "post-eligibility scholarships to complete undergraduate or graduate degrees at any school; scholarships to attend vocational school; tutoring; expenses related to studying abroad that are not included in the cost of attendance calculation; and paid post-eligibility internships."[11] However, the court held that the conferences within the NCAA may still limit cash or cash-equivalent awards for academic purposes.[12] The court based the decision on the large compensation discrepancy between the NCAA and the students.[13] The NCAA appealed to the U.S. Ninth Circuit.

In May 2020, the Ninth Circuit upheld the district court's decision.[14] It noted that the NCAA had a necessary interest in "preserving amateurism and thus improving consumer choice by maintaining a distinction between college and professional sports."[15] Notwithstanding, the Ninth Circuit agreed with the district court's finding that the NCAA practices relative to some specific restrictions violated antitrust law.[16] Judge Smith penned a concurrence and noted that the NCAA's treatment of its players is "not the result of free market competition . . . [t]o the contrary, it is the result of a cartel of buyers acting in concert to artificially depress the price that sellers could otherwise receive for their services. Our antitrust laws were originally meant to prohibit exactly this sort of distortion."[17] Subsequently, the NCAA started a review of its policies related to players' compensation for NIL, while it appealed the case to the U.S. Supreme Court.

On March 31, 2021, the U.S. Supreme Court heard arguments in *NCAA v. Alston*.[18] In June 2021, the Supreme Court affirmed the lower court decisions in a unanimous decision. The centerpiece of this case was the antitrust protection under *NCAA v. Board of Regents*,[19] as it relates to the NCAA's eligibility standards and compensation.[20] The plaintiffs had claimed the NCAA's rules violate the Sherman Act, which prohibits contracts, combinations, or conspiracies "in restraint of trade or commerce."[21] The Court noted that courts have interpreted the Sherman Act's prohibition on restraints of trade to prohibit only restraints that are "undue."[22] Further, the Court observed that courts assess whether a restraint is undue using the "rule of reason" standard,[23] which requires a fact-finding of market power and structure to decide what a restraint's actual effect is on competition.[24] In response to the plaintiff's antitrust allegations, the NCAA argued that its business should enjoy a special exception that excludes it from antitrust law or at least be given special leeway under antitrust law.[25] On this issue, the Court sided with the college athlete plaintiffs, stating that college sports is a trade and, therefore, cannot unduly restrain athletes from the marketplace.[26]

However, the Court relented in its attack on the NCAA. On the one hand, it affirmed the district court's findings of undue restraints in certain NCAA rules limiting the education-related benefits schools otherwise could make available to student-athletes, including paid internships, post-graduate scholarships, tutoring, or education abroad.[27] But, on the other hand, the Court failed to rule on the NCAA's rules limiting players' education-related benefits.[28] Moreover, the Court expressly stated that it is *not* an undue restraint for the NCAA, or conferences within it, to define what those educational benefits are,[29] leaving the restrictions on amateur status partially undisturbed. Hence, Justice Neil Gorsuch, writing for a unanimous Court, affirmed the lower court's injunction against the NCAA's restrictions on players' compensation.[30] However, the Court explicitly stated that since the student-athletes did not renew their "across-the-board challenge" to the NCAA's compensation restrictions,"[31] the Court's review was limited to "those restrictions now enjoined."[32]

The most significant takeaway from the *Alston* case is that the Court advised the NCAA that it could *not* use the federal antitrust laws as a justification for its rules regulating players' compensation.[33] In a concurring opinion, Justice Kavanaugh was more direct in attacking the NCAA's undue control over its players' rights, emphasizing that "the NCAA's current compensation regime raises serious questions under the antitrust laws."[34] While the *Alston* decision is regarded as a landmark decision that supports the right for student-athletes to profit from their NIL, the Court's *Alston* decision did *not* expressly answer the question of whether college athletes are legally entitled to their NIL and, if so, its legal basis. Rather, the Court appeared to guide the NCAA's behavior, letting them know that their prohibition of players' NIL would be difficult to defend against in the courts.

For newcomers to the issue of NIL and college sports, one might ask what is their relationship to antitrust law? Oddly enough, the answer is huge. We must digress to provide some context before moving forward. The Sherman Act, *inter alia,* prohibits activities that restrict interstate commerce and competition in the marketplace.[35] The NCAA had taken the position that they were broadly exempted from the antitrust law. The NCAA argued that as they are a nonprofit entity engaged in the charitable activity of education, they are exempt from the antitrust laws. However, in *O'Bannon* and *Alston,* the courts stripped the NCAA's broad antitrust protection relative to its amateurism rule that denied players the right to benefit from their NIL. Most importantly, the penalty for federal antitrust violations is *triple* damages, which means NIL was facing substantial financial exposure in future lawsuits. This leads to a discussion of the third of the pivotal NIL cases.

In 2020, Arizona State University swimmer Grant House and Texas Christian University basketball player (Oregon in 2020) Sedona Prince filed a lawsuit against the NCAA, to share in broadcasting revenue.[36] *In House v. NCAA,*[37] the plaintiffs sought in federal court $1.4 billion in damages representative of the NIL revenue they could have earned if it had been allowed during their enrollment.[38] This lawsuit tested the boundaries of the NCAA's restrictions on its players' NIL rights. In 2023, U.S. District Judge Claudia Wilken ruled that potentially thousands of NCAA athletes could be grouped into a class that may have been harmed.[39] Under antitrust law, damages would be tripled if the NCAA loses, resulting in a $4.2 billion exposure. In 2024, the judge reviewed a nearly $2.8 billion proposed, controversial settlement, in which the NCAA and its members colleges have agreed to pay past and current athletes.[40] On June 6, 2025, Judge Wilken approved a settlement of a class action lawsuit for nearly $2.8 billion.[41] Under the terms of the settlement, the NCAA agreed to a revenue-sharing model that allows member colleges to distribute funds up to $20 million to Division I athletes who have played since 2016 and a removal of caps on athletic scholarships.[42] For the first time in the history of college sports, the NCAA and its member college will be legally permitted to pay their athletes to play their sports. In summary, these three groundbreaking decisions have resurrected somewhat dormant antitrust law to take down a major economic and political force in American life, the NCAA.[43]

Equally important to the judicial development of NIL law is the passage of NIL legislation by several states. Following the *O'Bannon* decision, in 2019, in response to the then-pending litigation and public opinion in favor of players having control over their NIL,[44] the State of California passed S.B. 206, the Fair Pay to Play Act. This law permits student-athletes to capitalize on their NIL for sponsorships and endorsements, free from the NCAA rules.[45] The new law also prohibits universities from implementing rules that prohibit student-athletes from earning compensation or denying scholarships to athletes who choose to market their NIL.[46] S.B. 206 does not require universities to pay student-athletes themselves; as a result, the net cost to the NCAA and its collegiate members would be zero, as all compensation is paid for by third-party endorsers.[47] The law is based on an equal protection argument that, relative to benefiting from their NIL, NCAA schools cannot treat athletes differently from other college students.[48] For example, a film major who doesn't play a varsity sport is permitted to generate income by making YouTube videos, but a film major who is also an intercollegiate athlete may not.[49] The California law along with the Supreme Court's *Alston* decision facilitated the movement that has resulted in a majority of states that have enacted pro-NIL, player-protection laws. These laws are not universal, and some states have not passed or have reversed their NIL laws.[50] Further, the NCAA has resisted NIL deals but has slowly permitted them, with restrictions and regulations.

As a result of the lawsuits and the state laws that sought to preempt the NCAA when it comes to college players' NIL, on June 30, 2021, the NCAA suspended its previous NIL rules and announced an "interim" policy that allowed college athletes across the nation to be paid for their fame.[51] The NCAA said that athletes in states with applicable laws "can engage in NIL activities that are consistent with the law of the state where the school is located" and instructed schools in other states to set their own guidelines with minimal restrictions. The NCAA stressed that rules that prohibited pay-to-play and recruiting inducements still were in force and effect. In announcing its new policy, the NCAA offered "guidance to college athletes, recruits, their families, and member schools" in the form of four bullet points, reprinted here as they appeared in the association's press release at the time: "(1) Individuals can engage in NIL activities that are consistent with the law of the state where the school is located. Colleges and universities may be a resource for state law questions. (2) College athletes who attend a school in a state without an NIL law can engage in this type of activity without violating NCAA rules related to name, image, and likeness. (3) Individuals can use a professional services provider for NIL activities. And (4) Student-athletes should report NIL activities consistent with state law or school and conference requirements to their school."[52] Notwithstanding, the NCAA pointed to the inconsistency in NIL law, which varies state by state, and called for the federalization of NIL laws and regulations.[53] To date, that federalization has not happened, despite many bills that have been proposed in Congress.[54] In summary, prior to a change in the NIL laws, college athletes were denied the right to benefit from their NIL. That all changed after a series of successful lawsuits that were filed by past and present college athletes to seek compensation for their play and for the use of their NIL. In their lawsuits, they claimed that the NCAA had violated federal antitrust laws. Federal protection of college athletes' rights to access national markets takes us to the next discussion. That discussion shows that college sports have become a major industry, and it is only fair that the athletes who are responsible for the revenue should receive a fair share.

NCAA'S AMATEURISM RULE AND WEALTH INEQUITY

To understand how college athletes can become millionaires, we need to introduce who the NCAA is[55] and describe how its rules had prohibited its athletes from receiving any compensation related to their athlete status, particularly from NIL deals. The NCAA is an organization formed in 1906 that regulates the college athletics of its member colleges and the athletes who play for those colleges. According to the NCAA, there are over 500,000 college athletes across all three divisions who "compete for about 1,100 member schools in all 50 states, the District of Columbia, Puerto Rico, and even Canada. . . . Student-athletes strive to end each season at one of the NCAA's 90 championships in 24 sports."[56]

Prior to a change in the NIL law, the NCAA could terminate a player's eligibility to play if a player received any compensation for their athletic skills or "if he or she either accepts or received payment through commercial advertisement, promotion, or endorsement."[57] By denying a student compensation and restricting their rights to their NIL, the NCAA and its member schools received billions of dollars from their sports programs, mainly in the form of advertising and television media.[58] Notwithstanding the NCAA's prohibition against NIL deals, many NCAA players, particularly those who were award-winning players, would have likely earned millions of dollars per year in advertising and promotional deals, more than enough to take care of them, their families, and their friends' financial needs.

In fact, one study shows that NCAA college football stars could earn as much as $2.4 million per year if they were paid equitably for the financial benefits that they bring to the NCAA and its member colleges.[59] One analysis concluded that when applied to Instagram followers for college athletes from the 2019–2020 school year, annual NIL endorsement revenue estimates would be $700,000 for LSU's Joe Burrow, $440,000 for Alabama's Tua Tagovailoa, $390,000 for the University of Oklahoma's Jalen Hurts, and in the $5,000–$30,000 range for less popular athletes.[60] Hence, current and past players have sued the NCAA and its member colleges for failing to compensate them *both* for their play and for the unauthorized use of their NIL to benefit the NCAA. Their legal claims include that athletes should be treated as employers of their colleges, that they should be allowed to unionize, and that they have an equitable right to share in the revenue that their colleges and the NCAA received because of the athletes' play.

In the leading cases against the NCAA, the courts noted that the NCAA and its members have received substantial financial benefits from prohibiting their players from being compensated.[61] The Supreme Court in *Alston* has documented the obvious inequity in the distribution of wealth, in which the coaches, administrators, and school greatly benefit primarily from media contracts for college football and basketball. That inequity is clear evidence that the players are not being justly compensated for the expropriation of their labor and/or for their NIL, as is provided in the dicta of the majority decision in *Alston* and in the concurring opinion of Justice Brett Kavanaugh, as described next.[62] In Justice Gorsuch's majority opinion, he pointed out that the historical rationale for the NCAA amateurism rules has become questionable in today's economic environment.[63] While recognizing the benefits that the NCAA and its members bestow on its athletes, Justice Gorsuch noted that the NCAA has become a "sprawling enterprise" and "a massive business."[64] The Court documented the obvious inequities in compensation between what the leadership of the NCAA receives, what some member colleges receive, and what some coaches receive, as compared to what the athletes receive:[65]

> The president of the NCAA earns nearly $4 million per year. Commissioners of the top conferences take home between $2 to $5 million. College athletic directors average more than $1 million annually. And annual salaries for top Division I college football coaches approach $11 million, with some of their assistants making more than $2.5 million.[66]

On the other end of the spectrum, college athletes of NCAA member colleges are severely limited in what they are compensated, usually to the cost of tuition, room, board, and fees.[67] In the *Alston* case, these former college athletes argued that their compensation was grossly unfair and that the NCAA is a monopoly with an unfair competitive advantage.[68] Less subdued than Justice Gorsuch's majority opinion,[69] Justice Kavanaugh stated, "Today . . . the Court holds that the NCAA has violated the antitrust laws."[70] He "adds [his] concurring opinion to underscore that the NCAA's remaining compensation rules also raise serious questions under the antitrust laws."[71] What follows, in his opinion, is Justice Kavanaugh's scathing attack on the inequities in the NCAA's compensation of the players. He points out the following: (1) The NCAA has a monopoly on the college sports market, which suppresses players' compensation;[72] (2) "The NCAA's business model would be flatly illegal in almost any other industry in America";[73] and (3) "Price-fixing labor is price-fixing labor."[74]

In reference to the inequity in what the NCAA top executives, coaches, and university administrators are paid compared to what the players receive, Justice Kavanaugh stated: "It is highly questionable whether the NCAA and its member colleges can justify not paying students athletes student-athletes a fair share of the revenues on the circular theory that the defining characteristic of college sports is that the colleges do not pay student athletes student-athletes."[75] This observation was very explicit when he observed:

> The bottom line is that the NCAA and its member colleges are suppressing the pay of student-athletes who collectively generate billions of dollars in revenues for colleges every year. Those enormous sums of money flow to seemingly everyone except the student-athletes. College presidents, athletic directors, coaches, conference commissioners, and NCAA executives take in six- and seven-figure salaries. Colleges build lavish new facilities. But the student-athletes who generate the revenues, many of whom are African American and from lower-income backgrounds, end up with little or nothing.[76]

Justice Kavanaugh's critique of the gross wealth inequities in college athletics is evidence of unjust compensation in a takings analysis or unjust enrichment under equitable principles.

His concurring opinion ends with a warning message to the NCAA and its members:

> [T]raditions alone cannot justify the NCAA's decision to build a massive money-raising enterprise on the backs of student-athletes who are not fairly compensated. Nowhere else in America can businesses get away with agreeing not to pay their workers a fair market rate on the theory that their product is defined by not paying their workers a fair market rate. And under ordinary principles of antitrust law, it is not evident why college sports should be any different. The NCAA is not above the law.[77]

What follows is an elaboration of the *Alston* Court's view of the unjust compensation that the NCAA players receive, compared to that of the NCAA executive, coaches, and the school leadership. In its fiscal year that ended August 31, 2019, the NCAA, a private, nonprofit enterprise, reported revenues of over $1.1 billion, with a positive increase in net assets of $70 million and net assets of just under a half of a billion dollars.[78] It receives most of its annual revenue from two sources: television and marketing rights for the Division I Men's Basketball Championship and ticket sales for all championships.[79] It proudly reported that about 60% of its annual revenue—around $600 million—is annually distributed directly to Division I member schools and conferences, while more than $150 million funds Division I championships.[80] At the same time, close to $170 million, or about 15% of its annual revenue, went to student-athlete services and championship support, including costs for insurance, drug testing, and additional support (nearly $65 million); general and administrative expenses (nearly $45 million); and association-wide expenses, including legal services (nearly $60 million).[81] NCAA President Mark Emmert's base salary for the calendar year 2019 was $2.5 million and his total compensation was $2.9 million, according to the association's 2019 federal tax return.[82]

Similarly, states and their college-level educational institutions reap substantial financial benefits from their membership with the NCAA. For example, a state like California receives millions every year from the NCAA through its state-owned member colleges.[83] California's Governor Gavin Newsom, in supporting college athletes' rights, noted that the Fair Pay to Play Act would rebalance a power structure in which NCAA universities receive more than $14 billion annually, and the nonprofit NCAA receives more than $1 billion, "while the actual product, the folks that are putting their lives on the line . . . are getting nothing."[84]

Then there are the incredible salaries[85] paid to some NCAA coaches of state-owned schools,[86] which rival the highest-paid salaries of professional coaches.[87] For example, in 2020, the top ten highest-paid football coaches for state-owned NCAA institutions ranged from $6 million to $9.3 million.[88] Moreover, the 2020 NCAA men's basketball coach salaries for state schools in the top ten are equally shocking, ranging from $4 million to $8 million.[89] With these salaries, it is hard to argue that college sports have not become highly commercialized and extremely profitable for some.

In the *Alston* case,[90] some former college athletes argued that their compensation was grossly unfair and that the NCAA is a monopoly with an unfair competitive advantage.[91] As previously noted, Justice Kavanaugh agreed with their contention. One scholarly analysis found that while players are valued or worth millions to these universities and the NCAA, 86% of college athletes live below the poverty line, with many qualifying for and receiving government Pell Grants.[92] In addition to devaluing their labor, the players claimed they were negatively impacted by the NCAA's former prohibition on their receiving funds from their NIL.[93] These claims were advanced in litigation in which the players sought to enhance their compensation for their play, through a demand that they are permitted to benefit financially from their NIL.[94]

In their book, *The End of College Football,* Nathan Kalman-Lamb and Derek Silva document some startling numbers of gross inequity in compensation in college football.[95] The institutions that comprise the NCAA produce $18.9 billion in annual revenue. This value is driven primarily by football, principally in the athletic departments of what have until recently been called the Power Five Institutions. In 2022, 49 athletic departments each earned more than $100 million of revenue, with 22 pulling in more than $150 million, and six more than $199 million. Coaches are the primary beneficiaries of this largesse. As of 2023, 36 college football coaches earn $5 million or more annually: 18 of those earn more than $7 million per year and 10 earn more than $9 million. Additionally, 66 *assistant* football coaches earn $1 million per year or more and 21 strength coaches make $500,000 or more. Athletic department administrators also directly benefit. In 2021, 51 athletic directors earned $700,000 or more in annual salaries, with 25 of those earning $1 million or more. For example, one source reported the salaries of some of the top college athletic directors as The University of Texas's Chris Del Conte, $2.85 million; Alabama's Greg Byrne, $2.31 million; Ohio State's Ross Bjork, $2 million; University of Tennessee, Knoxville's Danny White, $2.2 million; Texas A&M University's Trev Alberts, $2 million; LSU's Scott Woodward, $1.85 million; The University of Florida's Scott Stricklin, $1.725 million; Michigan's Warde Manuel, $1.227 million; University of Georgia's Josh Brooks, $1.275 million salary; Texas Tech University's Kirby Hocutt, $1.64 million; University of Arkansas's Hunter Yurachek, $1.5 million; and University of Illinois's Josh Whittman, $1.5 million.[96]

Shockingly, the salaries of the head coaches for men's football and basketball and the colleges' athletic directors are notably higher than the salaries of their college presidents. Further evidence of the inequity in college coaches' salaries and players' compensation is the 2024 announcement that the University of North Carolina, Chapel Hill, Tar Heels hired the legendary New England Patriots head coach Bill Belichick to be the college football's head coach in a five-year $50 million contract.[97] Further, UNC reportedly committed to increasing its NIL package for football from $4 million to $20 million, as part of its effort to land Belichick.[98]

To understand the NCAA's amateurism rules, one needs to appreciate the related issue of player compensation. In addition to denying players their NIL rights, the NCAA prohibited its member schools from compensating their athletes for their play, restricting benefits to athletic scholarships,[99] usually limited to the cost of tuition, room, board, and fees.[100] These restrictions meant that athletes, particularly those from economically disadvantaged backgrounds, lacked the financial resources to meet their basic needs and would face food insecurity after the school cafeterias were closed.[101] In fact, tuition shortfalls amount to thousands of dollars per year, with 86% of NCAA college athletes living below the poverty line, while usually required to live on campus, attend offseason workouts, and travel to games all over the country.[102] These financial pressures, in addition to having to meet both academic and rigorous sports' challenges, place a tremendous emotional and psychological strain on college athletes.

Hence, in the *Alston* case, the Court documented and criticized the inequitable way that the NCAA and its member colleges fail to compensate its players, under the assertion that college sports is an enterprise of amateurism. As the Court pointed out, college sports is big business and compensates its football and basketball coaches and athletic directors on a scale of professional sports. Notwithstanding, the Court failed to dictate a remedial solution to this problem. That is, the Court failed to order a revenue-sharing protocol as well as failing to rule on the players' right to the benefit of their NILs. As a result, the law relating to the fair compensation of college athletes, whether through NIL or as employees of their colleges, was and is still being hammered out in the legislatures, in the courts of law, and in the court of public opinion.

YOUTH SHARING IN THE WEALTH

Notwithstanding the developing nature of NIL law, NIL can address some of the wealth inequity between the young and the old in this country.[103] Relative to such inequity, NIL is especially valuable to younger Americans, both college athletes and non-college athletes. This inequity results from a conscious and unconscious transfer of wealth from young people,[104] of both their nonvirtual and virtual selves,[105] to upper-class, white adult men. I refer to this wealth transferal phenomenon as "intergenerational wealth displacement."[106]

"Intergenerational wealth displacement" (a term I coined) is the legal and illegal, conscious and unconscious, transfer of wealth from younger Americans, particularly those from disadvantaged communities, to adults, particularly wealthy, senior, white males, as one dynamic that resulted in an age-related wealth gap. Households headed by people aged 65 or older are 47 times wealthier than households where the median age is 35 years or younger. One example of a nonvirtual, inequitable transfer of wealth is the high debt load that many students pay for college, graduate, and professional schools and its subsequent negative impact on their quality of life.[107] As such, rights to one's NIL are of particular interest to millennials, Generation Z, and Generation A who are currently living off the fruits of their persona due to the proliferation of social media. For example, a 19-year-old influencer, Josh Richards, made nearly a thousand dollars a minute as a TikTok star.[108] As social media influencers and brand ambassadors, NIL as property provides college athletes and other young people the opportunity to earn well-needed wealth. Consequently, the NCAA athletes' controversy should be a public concern because it further highlights the need to address wealth inequity, particularly at the intersection of age, race, gender, and class.[109] One thing is certain: sports will never be the same as NIL evolves further.

Consequently, most states now protect college athletes' right to capitalize on the use of their NIL, and the NCAA has changed its rules to permit limited benefits from NIL. However, NIL deals are still regulated by state law, NCAA regulations, and school policies. For example, most college policies require athletes to report the details of any potential deals with their schools, and some require school approval before a player can sign an NIL deal. Further, many schools reserve the right to keep their athletes from advertising certain products, like drugs and alcohol.[110]

Hence, for many years, the NCAA denied its athletes the opportunity to share in the enormous wealth that derived from media coverage and the licensing of players' NIL, particularly men's football and basketball. The NCAA strictly enforced its rules, which tarnished the sterling reputation of alleged violators. In response, some past and present college athletes sued the NCAA and its members, seeking compensation for the NCAA's use of the players' NIL. Following a series of successful lawsuits, most states have enacted laws that grant college athletes the right to benefit from their NIL.[111] Consequently, the NCAA amended its rules to allow its athletes to make money from their NIL, with restrictions. Further, the Supreme Court ruled that the NCAA is not entitled to a broad exemption from federal antitrust laws. This decision means that other player lawsuits against the NCAA could move forward, with the possible remedy of treble damages under federal antitrust laws. As a result of these lawsuits, O'Bannon, Alston, and House, as representatives of past and present college athletes, received remediation from the NCAA for their taking of the players' NILs.

The law often creates winners and losers. In the instance of college athletes, the change in the law creates a major financial opportunity for college athletes. It now permits college athletes to contract to be paid for the use of their NIL, primarily to endorse products or to play for a particular college. As we shall see in the following chapters, that change means some college athletes are making millions of dollars through NIL deals.

NIL POWER SECRET #2: ADOPT O'BANNON, ALSTON, AND HOUSE'S PASSION FOR JUSTICE

Edward O'Bannon, Shawne Alston, and Grant House are former college athletes who delivered millions and potentially billions of dollars to past, present, and future college athletes from the NCAA, the college conferences, and vendors for the illegal use of players' NIL. Their names will be forever legends as college athletes who struggled for justice and obtained a share of the revenue from college sports. Their power secret is harnessing the legal system to achieve just compensation for the unauthorized use of players' NIL and for the monopolization of the labor and property rights of student athletes. Understanding the legal system and having the resources and staying power to bring about change is one of the most powerful secrets that every college athlete should emulate to ensure their NIL rights. Doing so can result in millions of dollars and can provide a lifetime of revenue, even after a player has graduated from college.

Further Reading

Ben Strauss, *Ex-Athlete's Battle for Scholarship Upgrades: "I Feel Like I Helped My Brothers,"* N.Y. TIMES (Feb. 12, 2017), https://www.nytimes.com/2017/02/12/sports/a-football-scholarship-is-a-full-ride-but-it-doesnt-mean-a-free-one.html.

Ed O'Bannon, COURT JUSTICE: THE INSIDE STORY OF MY BATTLE AGAINST THE NCAA (2018).

John Wright, *A New Era: Understanding the Historic NCAA v. House Settlement*, AVE MARIA SCHOOL OF L. (Jan. 28, 2025), https://www.avemarialaw.edu/house-settlement/.

Mark Schlabach, *Basketball Players Sue NCAA over NIL Use in March Madness Promos*, ESPN (July 2, 2024), https://www.espn.com/mens-college-basketball/story/_/id/40480858/basketball-players-sue-ncaa-nil-use-march-madness-promos.

N.Y. State Attorney Gen., *Attorney General James Sues NCAA for Imposing Unfair Restrictions on Student Athletes' Careers*, AG.NY.GOV (May 1, 2024), https://ag.ny.gov/press-release/2024/attorney-general-james-sues-ncaa-imposing-unfair-restrictions-student-athletes. VA Off. of the Attorney Gen., *Attorney General Miyares Sues NCAA over NIL Restrictions*, OAG.STATE.VA.US (Jan. 31, 2024), https://www.oag.state.va.us/media-center/news-releases/2680-january-31-2024-attorney-general-miyares-sues-ncaa-over-nil-restrictions.

Endnotes

1. *See NCAA v. Alston*, 141 S. Ct. 2141, 2169 (2021), at 2168 (Kavanaugh, J., concurring).
2. *O'Bannon v. NCAA*, 7 F. Supp. 3d 955, 1009 (N.D. Cal. 2014) ("[T]he Court finds that this restraint does violate antitrust law").
3. *Id.* at 1009.
4. *O'Bannon v. NCAA*, 802 F.3d 1049 (9th Cir. 2015). The NCAA appealed to the Supreme Court which did not grant certiorari.
5. *O'Bannon v. NCAA*, 739 F. App'x 890 (9th Cir. 2018).
6. *See* Michael McCann, *Why the NCAA Lost Its Latest Landmark Case in the Battle over What Schools Can Offer Athletes*, SPORTS ILLUSTRATED (Mar. 8, 2019), https://www.si.com/college/2019/03/09/ncaa-antitrust-lawsuit-claudia-wilken-alston-jenkins.
7. *See* In re NCAA Athletic Grant-In-Aid Cap Antitrust Litig., 375 F. Supp. 3d 1058, 1065 (N.D. Cal. 2019).
8. *Id.* at 1062.
9. *Id.* at 1110.
10. *Id.* at 1088.
11. *Id.*
12. *Id.*
13. *Id.* at 1089.
14. In re NCAA Athletic Grant-In-Aid Cap Antitrust Litig., 958 F.3d 1239, 1244 (9th Cir. 2020).
15. Wolters Kluwer trade report (Trade Reg. Rep. P 81227 (C.C.H.), 2020 WL 3549287).
16. *Id.*
17. *Id.* at 1267 (Smith, J., concurring).
18. *NCAA v. Alston*, 594 U.S. 69, 141 S. Ct. 2141 (2021).

19. *NCAA v. Bd. of Regents*, 468 U.S. 85, 101, 119–20 (1984) (invalidating NCAA's restrictive television licensing scheme under rule of reason standard but noting that college sports is "an industry in which horizontal restraints on competition are essential if the product is to be available at all").
20. *See generally*, Robert Barnes & Rick Maese, *Supreme Court Will Hear NCAA Dispute Over Compensation for Student-Athletes*, WASH. POST (Dec. 16, 2020), https://www.washingtonpost.com/politics/courts_law/supreme-court-ncaa/2020/12/16/90f20dbc-3fa9-11eb-8db8-395dedaaa036_story.html (reporting the NCAA oversees rules related to student athletes that play in their athletics programs, which, inter alia, limit the type of compensation that the school could give to student athletes as to distinguish college athletics from professional sports, disallowing "non-cash education-related benefits" such as scholarships and internships so that there is no apparent "pay to play" aspects).
21. *NCAA v. Alston*, 141 S. Ct. 2141, 2169 (2021), at 2151 (quoting 15 U.S.C. § 1).
22. *Id.* (quoting *Ohio v. Am. Express Co.*, 138 S. Ct. 2274, 2283 (2018)).
23. *Id.* (quoting *Texaco Inc. v. Dagher*, 547 U.S. 1, 5 (2006)).
24. *Id.* at 2151 (quoting *Ohio v. Am. Express Co.*, 138 S. Ct. 2274, 2284 (2018)).
25. *Id.* at 2159.
26. *Id.*
27. *Id.* at 2164.
28. *Id.* at 2147.
29. *Id.* at 2165.
30. *NCAA v. Alston*, 594 U.S. 69, 141 S. Ct. 2141(2021) 141 S. Ct. 2141, 2169 (2021).
31. *Id.* at 2151.
32. *Id.* at 2162–63 (holding that the district court's injunction did not invite future courts to "micromanage" the NCAA but rather constituted a permissible antitrust remedy).
33. *NCAA v. Alston*, 594 U.S. 69, 141 S. Ct. 2141, 2165 (2021).
34. *Alston*, 141 S. Ct. at 2169 (2021) (Kavanaugh, J., concurring).
35. The Sherman Antitrust Act, 15 U.S.C. §§ 1–7, is a United States antitrust law that prescribes the rules of free competition for those engaged in interstate commerce. *See* LEGAL INFO. INST., Sherman Antitrust Act, CORNELL L. SCH., https://www.law.cornell.edu/wex/sherman_antitrust_act (last accessed Apr. 1, 2022).
36. *House v. NCAA*, *Hubbard v. NCAA*, and *Carter v. NCAA* have been consolidated into one case. *See* Michelle Brutlag Hosick, *Settlement Documents Filed in College Athletics Class-Action Lawsuits*, NCAA (July 26, 2024), https://www.ncaa.org/news/2024/7/26/media-center-settlement-documents-filed-in-college-athletics-class-action-lawsuits.aspx.
37. 545 F. Supp. 3d 804 (2021) (aka In re College Athlete NIL Litigation). The Plaintiffs alleged that the NCAA and conferences engaged in an "overarching conspiracy" to (a) "fix the amount that student-athletes may be paid for licensing, use, and sale of their names, images, and likeness—at zero; and (b) foreclose student-athletes from the market for licensing, use, and sale

of their names, images, and likenesses entirely"). Case 4:20-cv-03919-DMR Document 1 Filed 06/15/20 Page 7, available at https://www.courtlistener.com/docket/17248915/1/in-re-college-athlete-nil-litigation/.545 F. Supp. 3d 804 (2021).

38. *Id.*
39. *Id.*
40. *Id.*
41. Case No. 20-cv-03919 CW IN RE: COLLEGE ATHLETE NIL LITIGATION OPINION REGARDING ORDER GRANTING MOTION FOR FINAL APPROVAL OF SETTLEMENT AGREEMENT (Re: Dkt. No. 717), https://swimswam.com/wp-content/uploads/2025/06/Grant-House-vs-NCAA-Order-Granting-Final-Approval-to-Settlement.pdf.
42. Eddie Pells, *A $2.8 Billion Settlement Will Change College Sports Forever. Here's How,* AP NEWS.COM (updated 9:55 AM CDT, June 7, 2025), https://apnews.com/article/ncaa-house-settlement-aa3169056e8194aeebf34495641bce0b.
43. Related to this legal issue but separate and still in litigation is whether the NCAA and is members violated the labor rights of its players.
44. Michael T. Nietzel, *Americans Now Overwhelmingly Support College Athletes Earning Endorsement and Sponsorship Money,* FORBES (Feb. 11, 2020), https://www.forbes.com/sites/michaeltnietzel/2020/02/11/americans-now-overwhelmingly-support-college-athletes-earning-endorsement-and-sponsorship-money/.
45. S.B. 206, 2019 Leg., Reg. Sess. (Cal. 2019) ("[Under S.B. 206] an athletic association, conference, or other group or organization with authority over intercollegiate athletics, including, but not limited to, the National Collegiate Athletic Association, shall not prevent a student of a postsecondary educational institution participating in intercollegiate athletics from earning compensation as a result of the use of the student's name, image, or likeness."); *See also Governor Newsom Signs SB 206, Taking on Long-Standing Power Imbalance in College Sports,* CAL. STATE PORTAL: OFF. OF GOVERNOR GAVIN NEWSOM (Sept. 30, 2019), https://www.gov.ca.gov/2019/09/30/governor-newsom-signs-sb-206-taking-onlong-standing-power-imbalance-in-college-sports/; Gregg E. Clifton & Nicholas A. Plinio, *New Jersey Grants Name, Image, Likeness Rights to Collegiate Student Athletes,* JACKSON LEWIS: COLLEGIATE & PRO. SPORTS BLOG (Sept. 15, 2020), https://www.collegeandprosportslaw.com/uncategorized/new-jersey-grants-nam e-image-likeness-rights-to-collegiate-student-athletes/.
46. *Id.*
47. *Id.*
48. *See* Billy Witz, *A State Skirmish over N.C.A.A. Amateurism Rules Has Quickly Become a National Battle,* N.Y. TIMES (June 21, 2021), https://www.nytimes.com/2020/12/28/sports/ncaa-amateurism-rules.html.
49. *Id.*
50. *NIL College Rules,* ON3, https://www.on3.com/nil/laws/college/ (last accessed Dec. 10, 2024); Braly Keller, *High School NIL: State-By-State Regulations for Name, Image and Likeness Rights,* OPENDORSE (Sept. 16, 2024), https://biz.opendorse.com/blog/nil-high-school/.

51. Michelle Brutlag Hosick, *"NCAA Adopts Interim Name, Image and Likeness Policy,"* NCAA (June 30, 2021), https://www.ncaa.org/news/2021/6/30/ncaa-adopts-interim-name-image-and-likeness-policy.aspx.
52. *Id.*
53. *See infra* Conclusion.
54. *Id.*
55. *See* National Collegiate Athletic Association, ENCYC. BRITANNICA (June 17, 2024), https://www.britannica.com/topic/National-Collegiate-Athletic-Association. S*ee also Overview,* NCAA, https://www.ncaa.org/sports/2021/2/16/overview.aspx (last accessed June 20, 2024).
56. *Id.*
57. Tim Tucker, *NIL Timeline: How We Got Here and What's Next,* ATLANTA J. & CONST. (Mar. 18, 2022), https://www.ajc.com/sports/georgia-bulldogs/nil-timeline-how-we-got-here-and-whats-next/EOL7R3CSSNHK5DKMAF6STQ6KZ4/.
58. *See NCAA v. Alston,* 141 S. Ct. 2141 (2021) (the majority opinion noting how college sports has become a huge economic enterprise).
59. *See* Tom Huddleston Jr., *College Football Stars Could Be Earning as Much as $2.4 Million per Year, Based on NCAA Revenues: Study,* CNBC (Sept. 2, 2020), https://www.cnbc.com/2020/09/02/howmuch-college-athletes-could-be-earning-study.html; s*ee also* Tommy Beer, *NCAA Athletes Could Make $2 Million a Year if Paid Equitably, Study Suggests,* FORBES (Sept. 1, 2020), https://www.forbes.com/sites/tommybeer/2020/09/01/ncaa-athletes-could-make-2-million-a-year-if-paid-equitably-study-suggests/.
60. *See also* AJ Maestas & Jason Belzer, *How Much is NIL Worth to Student Athletes?,* ATHLETIC DIR. U, https://athleticdirectoru.com/articles/how-muchis-nil-really-worth-to-student-athletes/ (last accessed Feb. 26, 2022).
61. *See* Eliott C. McLaughlin, *California Wants its College Athletes to Get Paid, but the NCAA is Likely to Put Up Hurdles,* CNN (Oct. 2, 2019), https://edition.cnn.com/2019/10/01/us/california-sb206-ncaa-fair-pay-to-play-act/index.html ("With the signing of California's Fair Pay to Play Act, Gov. Gavin Newsom. . . . says the law is about rebalancing a power structure in which NCAA universities receive more than $14 billion annually and the nonprofit NCAA receives more than $1 billion, 'while the actual product, the folks that are putting their lives on the line, putting everyone on the line, are getting nothing'").
62. *See NCAA v. Alston,* 141 S. Ct. 2141, 2154 (2021), at 2168 (Kavanaugh, J., concurring).
63. *Id.* at 2150.
64. *Id.*
65. *Id.* at 2151.
66. *Id.*
67. *See generally,* David J. Berri, *Paying NCAA Athletes,* 26 MARQ. SPORTS L. REV. 479, 479 (2016); Comment, *Ending the Amateurism Façade—Pay College Athletes,* 9 HOUS. L. REV. 158, 167 (2019).
68. Joel Mitnick & Ngoc Pham Hulbig, *Supreme Court to Weigh in College Sports: The Intersection of Antitrust and "Amateurism,"* 12 NAT'L L. REV., No. 99, 2020, https://www.natlawreview.com/article/supreme-court-to-weigh-college-sports-intersection

-antitrust-and-amateurism (explaining that plaintiffs in Alston argued "that the top athletic teams are operating a system that acts as a classic restraint of trade in violation of Section 1 of the Sherman Act" and that, absent those restraints "student-athletes would be compensated at a level more commensurate with their value to their universities, conferences, and the NCAA").

69. *See Id.* at 2147–66.
70. *Id.* at 2166 (Kavanaugh, J., concurring).
71. *Id.* at 2166–67 ("[T]here are serious questions whether the NCAA's remaining compensation rules can withstand ordinary 'rule of reason' scrutiny").
72. *Id.* at 2168 ("The NCAA acknowledges that it controls the market . . . set the price for student athlete labor . . . that the student athletes currently have no meaningful ability to negotiate with the NCAA over the compensation rules").
73. *Id.* at 2167 ("Law firms cannot conspire to cabin lawyers' salaries in the name of providing legal services out of a 'love of the law'").
74. *Id.* at 2168 ("Or to put it in more doctrinal terms, a monopoly cannot launder its price-fixing of labor by calling it product definition").
75. *Id.* at 2168.
76. *See Id.*
77. *Id.* at 2169.
78. Nat'l Collegiate Athletic Ass'n, NCAA Consolidated Financial Statements: Aug. 31, 2020 & 2019 (2020), https://ncaaorg.s3.amazon aws.com/ncaa/finance/2019–20NCAAFIN_FinancialStatement.pdf.
79. *Finances*, NCAA, https://www.ncaa.org/finances (last accessed Feb. 14, 2022).
80. *Id.*
81. *Id.*
82. *See* Steve Berkowitz, *NCAA President Mark Emmert Credited with $2.9 Million in Total Pay for 2019 Calendar Year*, USA Today (July 19, 2021), https://www.usatoday.com/story/sports/college/2021/07/19/ncaa-mark-emmert-total-pay-2019/8015855002/.
83. *See* Dan Murphy, *California Defies NCAA as Gov. Gavin Newsom Signs into Law Fair Pay to Play Act*, ESPN (Sept. 30, 2019), https://www.espn.com/college-sports/story/_/id/27735933/california-defies-ncaa-gov-gavin-newsom-signs-law-fair-pay-play-act.
84. *See* Eliott C. McLaughlin, *California Wants its College Athletes to Get Paid, But the NCAA Is Likely to Put Up Hurdles*, CNN (Updated 9:00 AM EDT, Oct. 2, 2019), https://www.cnn.com/2019/10/01/us/california-sb206-ncaa-fair-pay-to-play-act/index.html/.
85. Salaries are only one form of financial benefit that these coaches receive. For instance, they have major endorsement contracts, consulting contracts, shoe contracts, as well as directors on corporate boards, which come close to or exceed their contracts with their schools. As a result, many of the top coaches have tremendous net worth. *See, e.g.*, *Nick Saban Net Worth*, Celebrity Net Worth, https://www.celebritynetworth.com/richest-athletes/richest-coaches/nick-saban-net-worth/ (last accessed Mar. 11, 2024). *See also* Anthony Riccobono, *Nick Saban Net Worth: Salary, Contract Extension Put Alabama HC Among Highest-Paid Coaches*, Int'l Bus. Times

(June 7, 2021), https://www.ibtimes.com/nick-saban-net-worth-salary-contract-extension-put-alabama-hc-among-highest-paid-3219602 (reporting that Saban signed an eight-year deal worth at least $74.4 million in the summer of 2018 and that, with his $9.1 million salary and $950,000 in bonuses, Saban became the first college football coach to make over $10 million in a season last year).

86. These salaries highlight state-owned schools to emphasize the governmental takings of players' persona. Nevertheless, the coaches private school members of the NCAA make comparably, incredibly high salaries. For example, Duke University's basketball coach Mike Krzyzewski received total annual pay of $7,044,221. *See Men's Basketball Head Coach Salary*, USA TODAY (updated Mar. 13, 2024), https://sports.usatoday.com/ncaa/salaries/mens-basketball/coach. Texas Christian University's football coach Gary Patterson received total annual pay of $6.1 million. *See College Football Head Coach Salaries*, USA TODAY (updated Oct. 16, 2024), https://sports.usatoday.com/ncaa/salaries.
87. *Id.*
88. *Id.* (reporting salaries for Nick Saban of Alabama ($9.3 million), Ed Orgeron of LSU ($8.9 million), Dabo Swinney of Clemson ($8.3 million), Jim Harbaugh of Michigan ($8 million), Jimbo Fisher of Texas A&M ($7.5 million), Kirby Smart of Georgia ($6.9 million), Lincoln Riley of Oklahoma ($6.5 million), and Dan Mullen of Florida ($6 million)).
89. *2021 NCAA Basketball Coach Pay – Updated as of Mar. 9, 2021*, USA TODAY, https://sports.usatoday.com/ncaa/salaries/mens-basketball/coach (last visited Aug. 5, 2021) (reporting salaries for John Calipari of Kentucky State ($8 million), Chris Beard of Texas Tech ($5 million), Rick Barnes of Tennessee ($4.9 million), Roy Williams of North Carolina ($2.5 million), Tom Izzo of Michigan State ($4 million), and Fred Hoiberg of Nebraska ($4 million)).
90. *See NCAA v. Alston*, 141 S. Ct. 2141, 2155 (2021).
91. *See* Joel Mitnick & Ngoc Pham Hulbig, *Supreme Court to Weigh in College Sports: The Intersection of Antitrust and "Amateurism,"* 12 NAT'L L. REV., No. 99, 2020, https://www.natlawreview.com/article/supreme-court-to-weigh-college-sports-intersection-antitrust-and-amateurism.
92. *See* Armstrong Williams, *Time to Pay College Athletes*, NEWSMAX (Apr. 9, 2014), https://www.newsmax.com/ArmstrongWilliams/NCAA-college-athletes-nlrb/2014/04/09/id/564508/.
93. *See* Joel Mitnick & Ngoc Pham Hulbig, *Supreme Court to Weigh in College Sports: The Intersection of Antitrust and "Amateurism,"* 12 NAT'L L. REV., No. 99, 2020, https://www.natlawreview.com/article/supreme-court-to-weigh-college-sports-intersection-antitrust-and-amateurism. The NCAA total control over players' NIL depressed the value of their NIL, where the NCAA is a monopsonist, the sole procurer of players' NIL. *Id.*
94. *See, e.g.*, *NCAA v. Alston*, 141 S. Ct. 2141, 2155 (2021).
95. Nathan Kalman-Lamb & Derek Silva, THE END OF COLLEGE FOOTBALL: ON THE HUMAN COST OF AN ALL-AMERICAN GAME (2024).

96. Matt Johnson, *Highest Paid Athletic Directors 2024: Texas, Ohio State, Tennessee Ads Among Top Salaries*, SPORTSNAUT (May 17, 2024), https://sportsnaut.com/college-football/lists/highest-paid-athletic-directors/.
97. Craig Meyer & John Leuzzi, *Bill Belichick Contract Details: Contract Length, Salary for New North Carolina Football Coach*, USA TODAY (Dec. 11, 2024), https://www.usatoday.com/story/sports/college/football/2024/12/11/bill-belichick-contract-details-length-salary-north-carolina-unc-football/76931669007/.
98. *Id.*
99. *See* NCAA DIVISION I MANUAL 64–77 (NCAA, 1998) (setting forth the amateurism and athletics eligibility requirements).
100. Sarah Lytal, *Ending the Amateurism Façade: Pay College Athletes*, HOUSTON L.R. (Apr. 18, 2019), https://houstonlawreview.org/article/7835-ending-the-amateurism-facade-pay-college-athletes.
101. Armstrong Williams, *Time to Pay College Athletes*, NEWSMAX (Apr. 9, 2014), https://www.newsmax.com/ArmstrongWilliams/NCAA-college-athletes-nlrb/2014/04/09/id/564508/.
102. *See Paying College Athletes—Top 3 Pros and Cons*, PROCON.ORG (Jan. 21, 2022), https://www.procon.org/headlines/pay ing-college-athletes-top-3-pros-and-cons/.
103. *See* Matthew Yglesias, *New Federal Reserve Data Shows How the Rich Have Gotten Richer*, VOX (June 13, 2019), https://www.vox.com/policy-and-politics/2019/6/13/18661837/inequality-wealth-federal-reserve-distributional-financial-accounts ("[T]he rich have gotten richer and inequality has grown[.]" In fact, the Federal Reserve data indicates that from 1989 to 2019, wealth became increasingly concentrated in the top 1% and top 10% and that the gap between the wealth of the top 10% and that of the middle class is over 1,000%; and increases another 1,000% as compared to the top 1%, hence the term "wealth gap").
104. *See* Christopher Ingraham, *The Staggering Millennial Wealth Deficit, in One Chart*, WASH. POST (Dec. 3, 2019), https://www.washingtonpost.com/business/2019/12/03/precariousness-modern-young-adulthood-one-chart/ ("[Millennials'] financial situation is relatively dire. They own just 3.2 percent of the nation's wealth. To catch up to Gen Xers, they'd need to triple their wealth in just four years. To reach boomers, their net worth would need a sevenfold jump").
105. This "exploitation" includes the lawful and unlawful commercial use of virtual or digital images, data, and information, referred to as "personally identifiable information," usually by big business or government. See Christos Giakoumopoulos *et al.*, *Handbook on European Data Protection Law*, E.U. AGENCY FUNDAMENTAL RTS., 29–31 (2018), https://fra.europa.eu/sites/default/files/frauploads/fra-coe-edps-2018-handbook-data-protection_en.pdf (protecting data rights among EU Member States for individuals, strengthening mandated data protection requirements, and imposing significant legal responsibilities on entities handling personal data). No similar protections exist in U.S. law, except for the State of California's California Consumer Privacy Act (CCPA). *See* Office of the Attorney General, California Consumer Privacy Act (CCPA) Fact Sheet, CAL. DEP'T OF JUST. (2019),

https://www.oag.ca.gov/system/files/attachments/press_releases/CCPA%20Fact%20Sheet%20%2800000002%29.pdf).

106. *See* Annalyn Censky, *Older Americans Are 47 Times Richer Than Young*, CNN (Nov. 28, 2011), https://money.cnn.com/2011/11/07/news/economy/wealth_gap_age/index.htm.

107. *Id.* ("Some of those trends come hand in hand with more young people attending college, which can be a double-edged sword. While those college credentials could lead to income gains for many young people down the road, surging tuition costs are also leaving them burdened by more student loans than prior generations.")

108. *See* Jade Scipioni, *Here's How Many Social Media Followers You Need to Make $100,000*, CNBC (May 20, 2021), https://www.cnbc.com/2021/04/30/how-much-money-you-can-make-off-social-media-following-calculator.html; Raktim Sharma, *How Do Influencers Make Money on Instagram?*, YAHOO! FIN. (Mar. 31, 2021), https://ca.sports.yahoo.com/news/how-do-influencers-make-money-through-instagram-083707019.html (discussing how influencers use their NIL as branding to influence marketing, promotional, and affiliate deals).

109. *See, e.g.*, Vanessa Williamson, *Closing the Racial Wealth Gap Requires Heavy, Progressive Taxation of Wealth*, BROOKINGS INST. (Dec. 9, 2020), https://www.brookings.edu/research/closing-the-racial-wealth-gap-requires-heavy-progressive-taxation-of-wealth/ ("The median white household has a net worth 10 times that of the median Black household. . . . The total racial wealth gap, therefore, is $10.14 trillion").

110. Sara Coello, *What Is NIL in College Sports? How Do Athlete Deals Work?*, ESPN (Sept. 24, 2024), https://www.espn.com/college-sports/story/_/id/41040485/what-nil-college-sports-how-do-athlete-deals-work.

111. *See* Braly Keller, *NIL Incoming: Comparing State Laws and Proposed Legislation*, OPENDORSE (May 23, 2023), https://biz.opendorse.com/blog/comparing-state-nil-laws-proposed-legislation/.

3

Livvy Dunne: The Crowned Princess of Social Media Influence

"There are so many professional leagues for men's sports after college, but there's such a small time frame for women to capitalize."[1] "[But on] July 21, 2021, the NIL rule changed, and that's the day my life changed."[2]

—Olivia "Livvy" Dunne[3]

Olivia "Livvy" Dunne did not invent the Internet; she did something far more ingenious! What do you get when you combine artistic athleticism, beauty, grace, and business-savvy marketing genius with NIL? Her name is Livvy Dunne and she has a powerful NIL secret.

OVERVIEW

In July 2021, the NCAA announced that they would allow college athletes to earn money from deals marketing their NIL. Livvy Dunne is ranked the top woman among college athletes with social media followers in the multi-millions, with over 10 million and counting on TikTok, Instagram, and Twitter alone.[4] In 2022, she reported in a *New York Times* piece that she was earning "seven figures" annually in endorsements.[5]

In 2023, she admitted to being paid over $500,000 for a sponsored social media post.[6] Dunne is a top NIL superstar, who defies all NIL norms. Almost all of the leading college NIL superstars are men, who are phenomenal football or basketball athletes, many with brand-name surnames, whereas Dunne is exceptional. She is a woman who competes in gymnastics and was not born with a famous last name.

Dunne's NIL power secret is how to merge college athletics, NIL, and social media. She has been criticized for marketing her sexuality, but is dedicated to equal opportunities for women in sports and NIL deals. Dunne is one of six athletes featured in Amazon Prime Video's six-part docuseries, *The Money Game*,[7] which provides a deep dive into the seismic impact that NIL has had on some of LSU's most famous sports stars.[8] She is clearly on her way to joining the top social influencers, such as Cristiano Ronaldo, with 632 million followers @cristiano, earning $3,234,000 per post; Lionel Messi, with 500 million followers @leomessi, earning $2,597,000 per post; and Selena Gomez, with 429 million followers @ selenagomez, earning $2,558,000 per post.[9] As of December 29, 2024, On3 listed Dunne as the college athlete with the fourth highest position, with an On3 valuation of $4.2 million, behind Shedeur Sanders ($6.5 million), Travis Hunter ($5.7 million), and Arch Manning ($5.5 million).[10] Parenthetically, an On3 valuations of a college athlete is not the same as their net worth or the value of their actual NIL deals. Many news reporters have mistakenly represented the On3 valuations as the players' actual NIL income. However, as NIL deals are private, we do not actually know how much a player is being paid from them.[11] Notwithstanding, in 2024, Dunn's estimated net worth was reportedly $2.3 million.[12]

OUTSTANDING GYMNAST

Dunne is one of the most accomplished artistic gymnasts in recent history and comes from a family that values hard work and athletics.[13] She was born on October 1, 2002, in Westwood, New Jersey, and grew up in Hillsdale, also in New Jersey.[14] While she was not born into a famous sports family, she was blessed with athletic genes: Her mother was a gymnast and cheerleader, and her father played football at Rutgers University.[15] Dunne was homeschooled by her mother.[16] Following in the path of her mother, Livvy started gymnastics at the age of three.[17]

Dunne began her competitive career at the age of five.[18] At the age of six, she was a New Jersey state champion in Level 4 and set scoring records in the bars, beam, floor exercise, and all-around.[19] Although already an accomplished gymnast in her childhood, Dunne continued to excel into her adolescence. During the 2017 elite season, she competed successfully at the U.S. Classic in Chicago, returning home with three medals for beam and floor, and 5th place all-around.[20] She also competed at P&G championships in California where she won medals on floor and beam.[21] In 2018, she made her senior debut in Jesolo, Italy, and competed at the 2018 U.S. Classic and 2020 USA National Championships in Boston.[22] She also began competing in Level 10, winning first place in the all-around at the Atlanta Centennial Classic in Georgia, the Classic Rock Invitational in Arizona, and Elevate the Stage in Ohio. She qualified with a top score in the Elevate the State meet for the 2020 Nastia Cup held in Milwaukee, Wisconsin, on March 6, 2020.[23]

In 2020, Dunne joined the LSU Tigers gymnastics team at their main campus in Baton Rouge, Louisiana, on a full athletic scholarship.[24] However, in 2021, she experienced a setback as she underwent surgery for a leg injury.[25] Despite this and other injuries, Dunne went on to earn more awards.[26] She continues to be an extremely successful gymnast to this day.[27] In addition to her athletic achievements, Dunne, an interdisciplinary studies major, has excelled academically, being named on the SEC Academic Honor Roll, which celebrates college athletes who excel in the classroom.[28]

Clearly, Livvy Dunne's name will go down in college sports records as an outstanding gymnast. However, despite her outstanding success as a gymnast, Dunne knew that she needed to be more than just a great athlete. She was and is acutely aware that she is a woman who does not have a famous surname and who does not play a sport that has a professional league to go to after college. Fortunately, she had the foresight and was media savvy in preparing for the opportunity that the change in NIL law would deliver to her.

LEADING NIL SUPERSTAR, SOCIAL MEDIA INFLUENCER

While Livvy Dunne has a record of athletic achievement, her notoriety is setting a different kind of record. She is the leader of college athletes who are social media influencers. Before describing Dunn's success as a social media influencer, it is essential to provide some context for that success, including the technology that made it possible, and how she harnessed that technology to become the Princess of NIL Social Media Influencers.

Technology Creates Opportunity

What makes America great is that it is the land of opportunity. Throughout our nation's history, those opportunities often derived from new technologies.[29] Benjamin Franklin's "discovery" of electricity, Thomas Edison's invention of the lightbulb, and Henry Ford's assembly line manufacturing system are a few examples of how harnessing technological developments leads to great notoriety and wealth. Today, we are experiencing another transformational scientific revolution, the Information Age, or the Digital Revolution.[30] The hallmark of the Information Age is social evolution that is driven by a combination of computer microminiaturization advances, modernized information systems, and Internet communications.[31] To understand how the Information Age has impacted social evolution, it is important to understand human needs and how those needs are influenced.

How is social behavior influenced by the dissemination of information or opinion? The answer is in the social sciences. In 1955, Dr. Morton Deutsch and Dr. Harold Gerard, at the Research Center for Human Relations, New York University, described two psychological needs that lead humans to conform to the expectations of others.[32] One of these needs is our craving to be liked, or normative social influence, an influence to conform to the positive expectations of others.[33] Furthermore, in 1958, Harvard psychologist Herbert Kelman identified three broad varieties of social influence. One is "identification," which is when people are influenced by someone who is liked and respected, such as the opinion or behavior of a celebrity.[34] Additionally, by the early 2000s, communication technology included personal computers, cell phones, gaming devices, and Internet access. This became a worldwide phenomenon with digital technology and the arrival of the World Wide Web.[35] Consequently, the human need to be liked, influenced by someone who is liked, combined with the modern digital communication technology of the Internet, has revolutionized marketing. Today, in addition to mass media broadcasting via television, radio, and streaming services, social media platforms, such as Facebook, Instagram, TikTok, and YouTube, are a vital part of social media influence.

The Nature and Success of Social Media Influencers

Now that we better understand the technology underlying the existence of social media, let's spend some time understanding what is meant by social media. In 2004, the term "social media" was first used to describe social networking services. A social networking service is a type of online social media platform that social media influencers use to build social networks or social relationships with other people. They usually share similar personal or career content, interests, activities, backgrounds, or real-life connections.

That leads one to wonder, "How do social media influencers make money?" Social media influencers have several ways to get paid.[36] They are compensated for (1) sponsored posts and brand collaborations to promote products or services; (2) affiliate marketing where they earn a commission for every sale made through their unique affiliate links; and (3) selling products and merchandise of their own creations, such as clothing lines, beauty products, or digital goods.[37] The amount of money they are paid for their services varies, including (1) engagement rate, where they have genuine interactions with their followers, which makes promotional content more effective; (2) niche market, where they have passionate communities, which often attract higher-paying brand deals due to targeted marketing opportunities, such as tech reviews, health and wellness, and personal finance; and (3) consistency and content quality, where they post often, which keeps followers engaged and helps grow the audience over time.[38]

The technology and the market opportunity exist for anyone to become a social influencer. However, becoming a social media influencer is not a reliable way for a young adult to get rich quickly. While some social media influencers do earn substantial incomes, achieving this level of success requires creating consistent, high-quality content that resonates with an audience, as well as engaging regularly with followers.[39] For a college athlete who is already committing substantial time practicing and playing a sport, in addition to their academic obligations, becoming a social media influencer is another drain on a person's time and energy. It also requires technical expertise and a big personality.

Dunne's Leadership as a Social Media Influencer

While it might appear that Dunne was an instant social media and NIL success, her rise to the top of college athletes with NIL deals was developed over many years. She started early in developing followers for her social media influencer platform; as of April 4, 2017, she had 8,602 followers on her Instagram account.[40] In 2020, she joined the social media platform TikTok.[41] In those days, Dunne could not make money as a social media influencer due to prohibitive NCAA rules which did not allow high school or college athletes to be paid for their NIL.

In 2021, her hard work began to pay off big after the NCAA changed their rules to permit their athletes restricted rights to benefit from their NIL. In an *N.Y. Post* article, Jenna Lemoncelli reported that since 2021, when NIL guidelines changed, Dunne has made an estimated $9.5 million from NIL deals.[42] Her NIL deals reportedly include contracts with American Eagle, Nautica, Snapchat, Microsoft, Raising Cane's, Ulta Beauty, Purina, and Accelerator energy drink, where she charged an average of $125,000 to companies for a social media post promoting their products.[43] As of February 2023, Dunne was the most-followed NCAA athlete on social media, with more than 8 million followers on TikTok and 5 million on Instagram.[44] As of December 2024, Dunne was the highest-valued women's college athlete with an estimated NIL valuation of $4.2 million, and a reported 13.7 million followers.[45] Sports Illustrated reported that "[a]ccording to the TikTok calculator, Dunne makes approximately $12,866 per video, and according to the Instagram Money Calculator, with her 5.37 million, 8.56% engagement rate and an average of 458,000 likes per post, Dunne can charge anywhere from $49,600 to $67,100 for a post, $24,800 to $33,600 for a story and $64,000 to $87,000 for a sponsored Instagram reel."[46]

Dunne's popularity and outstanding Internet following will likely lead to other, non-sports-related financial opportunities. For example, she was on the cover of Sports Illustrated for NIL 25 and was one of two college athletes featured in the 2023 Sports Illustrated Swimsuit Issue.[47] She was also featured on a billboard in New York City's famous Times Square for Nautica.[48] She will likely continue to get endorsement deals, particularly for products and services oriented to women, that have provided women influencers a niche market, which includes cosmetics, perfume, clothing, and feminine products. Based upon the current trajectory of her notoriety, Dunne will likely join the upper ranks of women who are social media "personalities," with media appearances as music stars, television dancers such as in *Dancing with the Stars,* and movie stars. She has reportedly already dabbled in rapping.[49] Further, to add to her public profile, she is dating professional baseball pitcher Paul Skenes, a former player for the LSU baseball team.[50] Without a doubt, Livvy Dunne has successfully integrated NIL, college athletics, and social media influence to earn the title of Princess of NIL Social Media Influencers.

THE VALUE OF BEING A COLLEGE ATHLETE

On July 8, 2024, Dunne announced via her social media channels that she would return for a fifth and final season with the LSU Tigers in 2025, stating that she was "not Dunne yet."[51] One might wonder why a newly minted NIL millionaire might choose to stay in college for a fifth year?

Most of the highly-valued NIL college athletes are men in football, basketball, and baseball, where players vie for even bigger money playing for professional sports teams after they graduate from college. However, with the rise of the Women's National Basketball Association ("WNBA"), college women who play basketball are developing a market for post-graduated careers. Unfortunately, such high-income opportunities do not typically exist for other college sports, with some exceptions, such as golf and tennis. Additionally, women's gymnastics, particularly due to Simone Biles and other members of the U.S. Olympic women's gymnastics team, has grown in popularity. For example, during the 2024 Paris Olympics, Simone Biles and Team USA Gymnastics drew record viewership numbers for NBC.[52] Hence, someone who is well-known and a social media influencer as a college athlete, but do not participate in a sport that does not have a post-graduate professional team, may choose to extend their days on a college campus.

For Dunne, her decision to play for LSU for a fifth year is a smart business choice. She likely recognizes the value of associating with LSU's highly acclaimed athletic program, which was recently the subject of a nationally televised docuseries about NIL and college sports at LSU titled *The Money Game.*[53] Further, she knows that college sports often receive greater media coverage than many professional sports, particularly women's gymnastics. In addition, LSU offers her a popular platform, supportive infrastructure, media coverage, and teamwork.

So, what is Dunne's reason for staying on at LSU? Her answer is that she loves her sport and wants to capitalize on being a college athlete for a little longer.[54] Since she is getting NIL deals relating to her gymnastic capability and her following on social media, it makes sense for her to continue to stay in college for another year.[55] Further, she gets the media coverage that comes with being a college athlete, being in the limelight and networking of LSU.[56] Moreover, unfortunately, she does not have anywhere to go for gymnastics after she graduates college, except for the Olympics.[57]

Notwithstanding the reasons for staying at LSU for another year, that decision comes with risks. Dunne must be aware that the rigors of gymnastics come with the risk of injury, as she had previously been sidelined through sports-related injuries. Many promising athletic careers have abruptly ended due to a sports injury.[58] Sports injuries have implications for NIL deals, as reflected in former Philadelphia Eagle Chris Maragos's jury award of $43.5 million for medical negligence charged to the healthcare team and the surgeon who performed his knee surgery in 2017, which caused the end of his football career.[59]

Perhaps Dunne should take a lesson from the 2024 romantic sports drama film, *Challengers*, where a highly awarded tennis star with substantial NIL prospects, played by the renowned actress and singer Zendaya, suffers from a career-ending injury incurred in a college tennis tournament.[60] In addition, one may question whether Dunne should stay in college rather than focus on continuing to develop her brand as a social media influencer. With a massive social media following of more than 8 million followers on TikTok and 5 million on Instagram, it is reasonable to say that she does not need to stay in college to be popular.[61] Clearly, her brand is not limited to or reliant upon her being a college athlete, as she already has non-sports-related deals, such as modeling for magazines and being a brand ambassador for products such as clothing.[62] Additionally, there are many non-sports-related deals that she can invest her time and attention in, including opening businesses and more endorsements,[63] such as Mr. Beast's Feastables line[64] or Logan Paul and KSI's Prime line of beverages.[65] The sky is truly the limit once you obtain a level of fame similar to that of social media personalities like Dunne.

Perhaps, Dunne would be better off investing her time breaking into niche markets of products designed for women that her male counterparts would have a harder time exploiting.[66] These products include cosmetics, women's clothing, perfumes, and other similar female products. For example, the Kardashians[67] have all sorts of products that are female-designated,[68] including SKIMS (underwear and shapewear),[69] Lemme (vitamin supplements), Dash (Clothing Boutique),[70] Arthur George (Socks),[71] Kylie Cosmetics,[72] and SKKN BY KIM.[73] In addition, women are also breaking into markets that have been male-dominated, such as food and beverage as well as lines of athletic wear and shoes, including Nike.[74]

Whether it is a wise move or not, Dunne's decision to remain at LSU for another year will likely bear fruit in another way. That is, it is the perfect platform for her dedication toward promoting gender equality.

CHAMPION OF GENDER EQUALITY

Promoting Gender Equality

Perhaps an additional reason Dunne has decided to stay another year at LSU is her role as a champion of gender equality in sports. During her time at LSU, she has used her social media platform as an advocate for gender equality and empowerment, particularly relative to NIL deals. She has spoken out on various issues related to women's rights, to advocate for equal opportunities for women in sports, to promote positive body image, and to encourage open conversations about mental health issues.[75] Consequently, in July 2023, she announced her partnership with Bayou Traditions to launch *The Livvy Fund*, a program to connect female student athletes at LSU with top brands to secure NIL endorsement deals.[76] Through her social media presence and public speaking engagements, Dunne has shared her own experiences and insights to raise awareness about the challenges women face in society.[77] Additionally, she has supported initiatives and organizations that work toward advancing women's rights and empowering women and girls.[78] Her advocacy for women's equal rights in college sports comes at a time when historical federal protections of women's rights, that is, Title IX, are under attack.[79]

Title IX[80]

Women in college sports have come a long way and still have a long way to go before reaching equality with their male counterparts.[81] The movement toward gender equality was greatly facilitated by the enactment of Title IX of the Civil Rights Act of 1964.[82] Title IX of the Education Amendments of 1972 is a federal civil rights law that prohibits discrimination on the basis of sex, including in college athletic programs, or activities that receive federal funding regardless of real or perceived sex, gender identity, and/or gender expression.[83] Since Title IX required colleges to have opportunities for women athletes to compete similar to those available to athletes who are men, it has given many women the opportunity to compete and a path to college.[84]

Historically, women in college athletics have a disproportionate opportunity in sports when it comes to their male counterparts. Title IX is extremely important for women because of the inequalities of opportunity that persist in college sports to this day. For example, the gap in the 2021–2022 academic year between men's and women's sports opportunities showed that in that last year alone, colleges provided women with 67,591 fewer sporting opportunities than they provided for men.[85] Title IX was and is necessary because, due to the high viewership in athletic events for men's athletics and the lack of viewership in women's athletics, there generally would be a deficit in income when it came to women's sports.[86] Therefore, most colleges would rather favor high media generating men's sports because it would be more profitable for those colleges, compared to low or no media revenue sports.[87] Most importantly, in addition to equal opportunity not hindered by a student's gender, Title IX has led to creating a pathway toward the development of professional sports leagues for women athletes.[88] Further, it has provided invaluable employment opportunities for women as coaches and athletic administrators.[89]

Inequality in NIL Deals

Notwithstanding Title IX legal requirements and the success of women in college sports, women athletes have not achieved equality of status or pay for NIL deals. Generally, women in NIL deals have been limited to basketball and gymnastics.[90] Further, there are inequities in the revenue that college women receive in NIL deals compared to what men can command.[91] While surprisingly female college athletes are, on average, striking more deals than males, men still make more money. For example, between February 2023 and February 2024, female athletes landed more deals on average (3.5) compared to men (2.5), but male athletes made up 57% of NIL deals overall, per SponsorUnited.[92] Some of the most successful female college athletes relative to NIL deals include Livvy Dunn (13.6 million followers), the University of Miami's Haley and Hanna Cavinder (each with 5.3 million followers), the University of Connecticut's ("UConn") Paige Bueckers (5.1 million followers), and LSU's Flau'jae Johnson (with 3.7 followers).[93]

However, the rise in popularity of women's athletics does not end with Livvy Dunne; many more notable names, such as Caitlyn Clark, Angel Reese, and Simone Biles, have been making headway for their respective sports and increasing viewership. During the regular season, games featuring Clark and the Indiana Fever nearly tripled other WNBA games in TV viewership, averaging 1.178 million viewers compared to 394,000, according to FOX Sports executive Michael Mulvihill.[94] The WNBA All-Stars game featuring Angel Reese and Caitlyn Clark was viewed by a record 3.44 million people on July 23, 2024.[95] The WNBA is not the only sport that has gained attention due to rising stars. Gymnastics has seen increased popularity, particularly due to Simone Biles and her expertise.[96] An Olympic competition that featured Simone Biles showed that 12.7 million people tuned in across NBC and Peacock for the daytime competition, which ranks among NBC's most-watched Olympic weekday daytime events ever.[97] Relative to gender equality in NIL college deals, positive change is coming but not fast enough.

NIL POWER SECRET #3: MIMIC OLIVIA DUNNE'S MASTERY OF SOCIAL MEDIA INFLUENCE

Livvy Dunne is so many things: an outstanding athlete, a savvy social media entrepreneur, and the "Joan of Arc" for leveling the playing field for women athletes. Dunne's NIL power secret is the ability to merge college athletics, NIL, and social media as a clear path to becoming a multi-millionaire in college. Becoming a social media influencer is one of the most powerful secrets that every college athlete should emulate. Doing so can result in millions of dollars and can provide a lifetime of revenue, even after a player has graduated from college.

Further Reading

Adobe Express, *How to Become a Social Media Influencer in 6 Easy Steps*, Adobe (May 5, 2023), https://www.adobe.com/express/learn/blog/how-to-become-an-influencer.

Joe Anderson, *13 Steps to Draft Your Influencer Contract In 2025 (+ Template)*, Mighty Scout, https://mightyscout.com/blog/13-steps-to-draft-your-influencer-contract-template (last accessed Mar. 17, 2025).

Ryan Gaydos, *LSU Star Olivia Dunne Gives Athletes Great Advice about NIL: 'Put all that Money Away,'* Fox Business (May 24, 2023), https://www.foxbusiness.com/sports/lsu-star-olivia-dunne-gives-athletes-great-advice-nil-put-all-money-away. Dunne recommends finding an agent as the first step for NIL success.

Steve Dudash, *College Athletes & the NIL: A New Marketing Frontier*, Forbes (Aug. 30, 2024), https://www.forbes.com/sites/greatspeculations/2024/08/30/college-athletes-the-nil-a-new-marketing-frontier/.

Endnotes

1. *From an Emmy-Winning AIDS Activist to Librarians Fighting Book Bans: People's 2023 Women Changing the World*, People (Mar. 1, 2023), https://people.com/human-interest/women-changing-the-world-2023/.
2. Joshua Rogers, *Livvy Dunne Is a Gymnastics Star Worth $9.5m but Couldn't Capitalize on Social Media Popularity until Major Rule Change*, talkSPORT (Sept. 11, 2024), https://talksport.com/sport/2044132/livvy-dunne-nil-lsu-money-game-amazon-net-worth/; Maleehah Shakeel, *My Life Changed": Olivia Dunne Breaks Silence on $4 Million Net Worth Ahead of Gymnastics Documentary on Amazon Prime*, Essentially Sports (Aug. 15, 2024), https://www.msn.com/en-us/sports/other/my-life-changed-olivia-dunne-breaks-silence-on-4-million-net-worth-ahead-of-gymnastics-documentary-on-amazon-prime/ar-AA1oSQyc.
3. *Id.*
4. Julie Mazziotta, *Olivia Dunne Is the Highest-Paid NCAA Female Athlete—and Wants "Equal Opportunities for Men and Women,"* People (Mar. 6, 2023), https://people.com/sports/olivia-dunne-highest-paid-ncaa-female-athlete-equal-opportunities-men-and-women/; Jason Fray, *The 25 Highest-Paid Collegiate Athletes in 2024*, New Arena (Aug. 6, 2024), https://newarena.com/sports/the-25-highest-paid-collegiate-athletes-in-2024/.
5. Kurt Streeter, *New Endorsements for College Athletes Resurface an Old Concern: Sex Sells*, N.Y. Times (Nov. 11, 2022), https://www.nytimes.com/2022/11/08/sports/ncaabasketball/olivia-dunne-haley-jones-endorsements.html.
6. *Olivia Dunne's Net Worth in 2025 Is Already Flippin' Stellar*, Parade (Jan. 1, 2025), https://parade.com/celebrities/olivia-dunne-net-worth.
7. The Money Game (2024), https://www.imdb.com/title/tt31048383/ (a documentary series following LSU student athletes as they navigate the NIL era in college sports).

8. Joshua Rogers, *Livvy Dunne Is a Gymnastics Star Worth $9.5m but Couldn't Capitalize on Social Media Popularity Until Major Rule Change*, TALKSPORT (Sept. 11, 2024), https://talksport.com/sport/2044132/livvy-dunne-nil-lsu-money-game-amazon-net-worth/; Maleehah Shakeel, *My Life Changed": Olivia Dunne Breaks Silence on $4 Million Net Worth Ahead of Gymnastics Documentary on Amazon Prime*, ESSENTIALLY SPORTS (Aug. 15, 2024), https://www.msn.com/en-us/sports/other/my-life-changed-olivia-dunne-breaks-silence-on-4-million-net-worth-ahead-of-gymnastics-documentary-on-amazon-prime/ar-AA1oSQyc.
9. Christian Brown, *The 20 Highest Paid Influencers on Instagram in 2024*, GLEWEE (Mar. 5, 2024), https://glewee.com/blog/highest-paid-influencers-on-instagram/.
10. *On3 NIL Valuation*, ON3, https://www.on3.com/nil/rankings/player/nil-valuations/ (last accessed Dec. 30, 2024).
11. *Id.* ("The On3 NIL Valuation is the leading index in the industry that determines the projected annual value (PAV) of college and high school athletes by combining Roster Value and NIL Value. Using a proprietary algorithm, the On3 NIL Valuation establishes a baseline value that helps athletes, schools, and brands negotiate roster contracts and marketing opportunities more effectively.")
12. Shreyahia Chakraborty, *Olivia Dunne Net Worth 2024: from Beach-Nastic Videos to Big Bucks*, INT'L. BUS. TIMES, https://www.ibtimes.com/livvy-dunne-net-worth-beach-nastic-videos-big-bucks-3730004.
13. LSU Sports, *Roster*, Olivia Dunne, https://lsusports.net/sports/gm/roster/player/olivia-dunne/ (last accessed Mar. 15, 2025).
14. Darren Cooper, *Archive: Standout Hillsdale Gymnast Aiming for the Top*, NORTHJERSEY.COM (Apr. 2, 2017), https://www.northjersey.com/story/sports/2017/04/04/archive-standout-hillsdale-gymnast-aiming-top/100037804/.
15. *Id.*
16. LSU Sports, *Roster*, Olivia Dunne, https://lsusports.net/sports/gm/roster/player/olivia-dunne/ (last accessed Mar. 15, 2025).
17. Darren Cooper, *Archive: Standout Hillsdale Gymnast Aiming for the Top*, NORTHJERSEY.COM (Apr. 2, 2017), https://www.northjersey.com/story/sports/2017/04/04/archive-standout-hillsdale-gymnast-aiming-top/100037804/.
18. Oliva Dunne, *My Path to Elite Gymnastics*, LIVVY, https://livvydunne.com/about-me/ (last accessed Mar. 11, 2025).
19. Darren Cooper, *Archive: Standout Hillsdale Gymnast Aiming for the Top*, NORTHJERSEY.COM (Apr. 2, 2017), https://www.northjersey.com/story/sports/2017/04/04/archive-standout-hillsdale-gymnast-aiming-top/100037804/.
20. *Id.*
21. *Id.*
22. *Id.*
23. *Id.*
24. *LSU Gymnast Doubles as Social Media Star*, TIGERTV (Sept. 21, 2020), https://www.tigertv.tv/sports/lsu-gymnast-doubles-as-social-media-star/article_ff643744-fc23-11ea-9b5b-bbbbd2a502ea.html.

25. *Olivia Dunne 2024: Net Worth, Salary, Earnings and Endorsements,* ESSENTIALLY SPORTS, https://www.essentiallysports.com/tag/olivia-dunne/ (last accessed Mar. 11, 2025).
26. *Id.*
27. Oliva Dunne, *My Path to Elite Gymnastics,* LIVVY, https://livvydunne.com/about-me/ (last accessed Mar. 11, 2025).
28. Cara O'Bleness, *10 Things You Don't Know About Olivia Dunne,* SPORTS ILLUSTRATED SWIMSUIT (Nov. 27, 2023), https://swimsuit.si.com/swimnews/10-things-you-dont-know-about-olivia-dunne.
29. Edward Longe & Turner Loesel, *The United States Is the Leader of the Digital Revolution—Pro-Tech Polices Are Key,* James Madison Inst. (Apr. 12, 2024), https://jamesmadison.org/the-united-states-is-the-leader-of-the-digital-revolution-pro-tech-policies-are-key/.
30. *A History of the "Information Age" from the Mid-Twentieth Century,* BREWMINATE (May 14, 2024), https://brewminate.com/a-history-of-the-information-age-from-the-mid-twentieth-century/.
31. *Id.*
32. M. Deutsch & H.B. Gerard, *A Study of Normative and Informational Social Influences upon Individual Judgment,* 51 J. Abnormal & Soc. Psych. 629 (1955).
33. *Id.*
34. Herbert C. Kelman, *Compliance, Identification, and Internalization: Three Processes of Attitude Change,* 2 J. of Conflict Res. 51 (1958).
35. *See generally,* Manuel Castells, THE INFORMATION AGE, VOLUMES 1–3: ECONOMY, SOCIETY AND CULTURE (INFORMATION AGE SERIES) (1999).
36. Penny Redlin, *Your Odds of Getting Rich as a Social Media Influencer,* EDVISORS (June 19, 2024), https://www.edvisors.com/blog/social-media-influencer-pay/.
37. *Id.*
38. *Id.*
39. *Id.*
40. Darren Cooper, *Archive: Standout Hillsdale Gymnast Aiming for the Top,* NORTHJERSERY.COM (Apr. 2, 2017), https://www.northjersey.com/story/sports/2017/04/04/archive-standout-hillsdale-gymnast-aiming-top/100037804/.
41. *LSU Gymnast Doubles as Social Media Star,* TIGERTV (Sept. 21, 2020), https://www.tigertv.tv/sports/lsu-gymnast-doubles-as-social-media-star/article_ff643744-fc23-11ea-9b5b-bbbbd2a502ea.html.
42. Jenna Lemoncelli, *Livvy Dunne Already Planning Next Steps after Becoming $9.5 Million NIL Legend,* N.Y. POST (Sept. 13, 2024), https://nypost.com/2024/09/13/sports/livvy-dunne-planning-next-steps-next-after-becoming-9-5-million-nil-legend/.
43. *Basketball Players, Gymnasts Dominate Top 100 Female Earners,* SPORTS BUS. J. (Sept. 16, 2024), https://www.sportsbusinessjournal.com/Articles/2024/09/16/nil-female-athletes/#:~:text=the%20year%20prior.-,LSU%20gymnast%20Livvy%20Dunne%20is%20the%20only%20female%20athlete%20in,the%20highest%20NIL%20athlete%20valuations.
44. *On3 Women's NIL Valuations,* ON3 (updated Mar. 12, 2025), https://www.on3.com/nil/rankings/player/womens-nil-100/.

45. *Id.*
46. Ananya Panchal, *Olivia Dunne's Net Worth in 2024: A Look at the Highest-Paid Female College Athlete's Earnings,* SISwimsuit (Oct. 17, 2024), https://swimsuit.si.com/financial-fitness-swimsuit/olivia-dunne-net-worth-01j36d6g0xa1.
47. *Olivia Dunne 2024: Net Worth, Salary, Earnings and Endorsements,* Essentially Sports, https://www.essentiallysports.com/tag/olivia-dunne/ (last accessed Mar. 11, 2025). *See* Sports Illustrated (@sportsillustrated), Instagram, https://www.instagram.com/p/CxIuC3HAp5J/ (last accessed Dec. 12, 2024).
48. Olivia Dunne (@livvydunne) Instagram, https://www.instagram.com/p/C3yglrzvUTe/?img_index=1 (last accessed Dec. 12, 2024).
49. Olivia Dunne (@livvydunne) Instagram, https://www.instagram.com/p/TfAMC-QSGk/ (last accessed Dec. 12, 2024).
50. Matt Ryan, *Livvy Dunne Reveals How She Met and Fell for Paul Skenes,* Athlete Lifestyle (Sept. 26, 2024), https://www.si.com/onsi/athlete-lifestyle/news/livvy-dunne-reveals-how-she-met-and-fell-for-paul-skenes.
51. Zach Nagy, *LSU Gymnast Livvy Dunne Reveals She Will Return to Baton Rouge for Fifth Year,* Sports Illustrated (July 8, 2024), https://www.si.com/college/lsu/the-tiger-den/lsu-gymnast-livvy-dunne-reveals-she-will-return-to-baton-rouge-for-fifth-year#:~:text=Dunne's%20decision%20ultimately%20came%20down,renewed%20love%20of%20the%20sport.
52. Carrie McDonald, *Paris Olympics: Simone Biles, Team USA Gymnastics Draw Record Numbers for NBC,* USA Today (Aug. 1, 2024), https://www.usatoday.com/story/sports/olympics/2024/08/01/olympics-gymnastics-nbc-peacock-records/74632783007/.
53. The Money Game (2024), https://www.imdb.com/title/tt31048383/ (a documentary series following LSU student athletes as they navigate the NIL era in college sports).
54. *See* Zach Nagy, *LSU Gymnast Livvy Dunne Reveals She Will Return to Baton Rouge for Fifth Year,* Sports Illustrated (July 8, 2024), https://www.si.com/college/lsu/the-tiger-den/lsu-gymnast-livvy-dunne-reveals-she-will-return-to-baton-rouge-for-fifth-year#:~:text=Dunne's%20decision%20ultimately%20came%20down,renewed%20love%20of%20the%20sport; Arif Islam, *Olivia Dunne Lands "Multimillion-Dollar" NIL Partnership with Passes,* SportsPro (May 2, 2024), https://www.sportspromedia.com/news/olivia-dunne-nil-deal-passes-sponsorship-lsu-ncaa/.
55. *See* Zach Nagy, *LSU Gymnast Livvy Dunne Reveals She Will Return to Baton Rouge for Fifth Year,* Sports Illustrated (July 8, 2024), https://www.si.com/college/lsu/the-tiger-den/lsu-gymnast-livvy-dunne-reveals-she-will-return-to-baton-rouge-for-fifth-year#:~:text=Dunne's%20decision%20ultimately%20came%20down,renewed%20love%20of%20the%20sport.
56. *Id.*
57. Tiana Schoney, *Two Jobs Every College Gymnast Can Get after Their Gymnastics Career,* GMTM, https://gmtm.com/articles/college-gymnastics-didnt-work-out-for-me-so-whats-next (last accessed Mar. 12, 2025).

58. *15 College Football Players Whose Careers Ended Too Soon*, FOX SPORTS (updated Mar. 4, 2020), https://www.foxsports.com/stories/college-football/15-college-football-players-whose-careers-ended-too-soon.
59. Karen Weaver, *College Sports' NIL Era Is Presenting New Challenges for Injured Athletes*, FORBES (Feb. 15, 2023), https://www.forbes.com/sites/karenweaver/2023/02/15/college-sports-nil-era-is-presenting-new-challenges-for-injured-athletes/.
60. Luca Guadagnino, *Challengers* (2024), https://www.imdb.com/title/tt16426418/.
61. *See* Olivia Dunne (@livvy), TIKTOK, https://www.tiktok.com/@livvy?lang=en (last accessed Mar. 12, 2025); Olivia Dunne (@livvydunne) INSTAGRAM, https://www.instagram.com/livvydunne/?hl=en (last accessed Mar. 12, 2025).
62. WWD Staff, *Livvy Dunne's Style through the Years: from Gymnast to Sports Illustrated Swimsuit Model [Photos]*, WWD (Oct. 23, 2024), https://wwd.com/fashion-news/fashion-scoops/gallery/olivia-dunnes-photos-1236389692/.
63. Elise Dopson, *How to Become a Youtuber & Earn in 2025*, DESCRIPT (Mar. 3, 2025), https://www.descript.com/blog/article/how-to-become-a-youtuber.
64. *Feastables*, FEASTABLES.COM, https://feastables.com/ (last accessed Mar. 12, 2025).
65. *PRIME*, DRINKPRIME.COM, https://drinkprime.com/ (last accessed Mar. 12, 2025).
66. Haley Thorpe, *7 Stats that Show Women Dominate Influencer Marketing*, FOHR ALMANAC OF INFLUENCE (Mar. 1, 2023), https://www.fohr.co/articles/7-stats-that-show-women-dominate-influencer-marketing#:~:text=The%20most%20female%2Ddominated%20platform,%25%20female%20and%2031%25%20male.
67. Greg Smith, *Case Study: Leveraging Influencer Marketing with the Kardashians*, HOLLYWOOD BRANDED (Oct. 23, 2019), https://blog.hollywoodbranded.com/case-study-leveraging-influencer-marketing-with-the-kardashians.
68. *Id.*
69. *DASH*, MELROSEAVENUE-SHOP.COM, https://melroseavenue-shop.com/stores/dash.html (last accessed Mar. 12, 2025).
70. *Id.*
71. *Arthur George*, SHOPARTUHURGEORGE.COM, https://www.shoparthurgeorge.com/ (last accessed Mar. 12, 2025).
72. *Kylie Cosmetics by Kylie Jenner*, KYLIECOSMETICS.COM, https://kyliecosmetics.com/ (last accessed Mar. 12, 2025).
73. Courtney Mason, *Every Kardashian-Jenner Family Business Venture*, L'OFFICIEL (updated Mar. 14, 2024), https://www.lofficielusa.com/pop-culture/every-kardashian-family-business-kylie-cosmetics-skims-kkw.
74. Nike, *Jordan Shoes & Sneakers*, NIKE, https://www.nike.com/w/jordan-shoes-37eefzy7ok (last accessed Mar. 12, 2025).
75. *See From an Emmy-Winning AIDS Activist to Librarians Fighting Book Bans: People's 2023 Women Changing the World*, PEOPLE (Mar. 1, 2023), https://people.com/human-interest/women-changing-the-world-2023/.

76. Cara O'Bleness, *2023 SI Swimsuit Model Olivia Dunne Launches the Livvy Fund at LSU, a Historic Move for Funding Women's Sports*, SPORTS ILLUSTRATED (July 6, 2023), https://www.si.com/college/2023/07/06/olivia-dunne-lsu-gymnast-launches-livvy-fund-nil-bayou-traditions.
77. *Id.*
78. *Id.*
79. Angell Wescott, *False Assumptions: Why Title IX Is Not to Blame for Changes in Men's Athletics*, PIT J., https://pitjournal.unc.edu/2023/01/20/false-assumptions-why-title-ix-is-not-to-blame-for-changes-in-mens-athletics/ (last accessed Mar. 12, 2025).
80. *See generally*, Sarah Pruitt, *How Title IX Transformed Women's Sports*, HISTORY (Aug. 16, 2023), https://www.history.com/news/title-nine-womens-sports.
81. *Id.*
82. *Id.*
83. Sierra College, *What Is Title IX?*, SIERRA COLLEGE, https://www.sierracollege.edu/administration/title-ix/#:~:text=What%20is%20Title%20IX?,Report%20a%20Concern (last accessed Mar. 12, 2025).
84. *Id.*
85. *Schools Are Increasing the Gaps Between Men's and Women's Sports Opportunities*, CHAMPION WOMEN (July 17, 2023), https://titleixschools.com/2023/07/17/gender-gap/#:~:text=The%20RAW%20Gap%20in%20the,than%20these%20schools%20provided%20men.
86. *50 Years of Title IX: We're Not Done Yet*, WOMEN'S SPORTS FOUND., https://www.womenssportsfoundation.org/wp-content/uploads/2022/05/Title-IX-at-50-Report-FINALC-v2-.pdf (last accessed Mar. 12, 2025).
87. *Id.*
88. *Id.*
89. Elisa Van Kirk, *Title IX and Its Impact on Opportunities for Women in NCAA Coaching and Administrative Leadership*, SPORT J. (Mar. 13, 2023), https://thesportjournal.org/article/title-ix-and-its-impact-on-opportunities-for-women-in-ncaa-coaching-and-administrative-leadership/.
90. *See* Jenna Lemoncelli, *Livvy Dunne Already Planning Next Steps After Becoming $9.5 Million NIL Legend*, N.Y. POST (Sept. 13, 2024), https://nypost.com/2024/09/13/sports/livvy-dunne-planning-next-steps-next-after-becoming-9-5-million-nil-legend/; *Basketball Players, Gymnasts Dominate Top 100 Female Earners*, SPORTS BUS. J. (Sept. 16, 2024), https://www.sportsbusinessjournal.com/Articles/2024/09/16/nil-female-athletes/#:~:text=the%20year%20prior.-,LSU%20gymnast%20Livvy%20Dunne%20is%20the%20only%20female%20athlete%20in,the%20highest%20NIL%20athlete%20valuations.
91. Vanesha McGee, *NIL Deals Lack Equity for Women College Athletes*, BEST COLLEGES (Feb. 20, 2023), https://www.bestcolleges.com/news/analysis/nil-deals-lack-equity-for-women-college-athletes/#.
92. Sara Fischer, *Newsletter*, AXIOS (Sept. 14, 2024), https://www.axios.com/newsletters/axios-media-trends-tn50-37f5bbc0-720c-11ef-89f8-d9b1cd00d6d3

.html?utm_source=newsletter&utm_medium=email&utm_campaign=newsletter_axiostn50&stream=top.

93. *Id.*
94. Ryan Glasspiegel, *Caitlin Clark Helps Deliver Historic 2.5 Million Viewers in Final Game of Rookie Season*, N.Y. POST (Sept. 26, 2024), https://nypost.com/2024/09/26/sports/caitlin-clark-helps-deliver-historic-tv-ratings-in-final-game-of-rookie-season/#:~:text=During%20the%20regular%20season%2C%20games,to%20Fox%20executive%20Michael%20Mulvihill.
95. Jason Clinkscales, *Caitlin Clark-Angel Reese Matchup Likely to Boost Ion's WNBA Ratings*, SPORTICO (Aug. 30, 2024), https://www.sportico.com/business/media/2024/caitlin-clark-fever-angel-reese-sky-ion-wnba-ratings-1234795393/.
96. Simone Biles (@simonebiles) INSTAGRAM, https://www.instagram.com/simonebiles/?hl=en (last accessed Mar. 12, 2025).
97. Katie Campione, *Simone Biles & Team USA Women's Gymnastics Gold Medal Lead Big Tuesday Olympics Audience for NBCU*, DEADLINE (July 31, 2024), https://deadline.com/2024/07/simone-biles-usa-womens-gymnastics-finals-viewership-olympics-nbc-1236028346/.

4

Bronny James: Eyes on the Prize

For as long as I can remember, Nike's been a part of my family. . . . Getting a chance to team up with them and continue my family's legacy both on the court and in the community is wild. It really means a lot to me.

—LeBron "Bronny" James Jr.[1]

OVERVIEW

LeBron "Bronny" James, Jr., is a study in how outstanding athleticism combined with legacy makes for a winning NIL formula. In July 2023, he joined the USC men's basketball team as a freshman. However, later that month, he suffered a cardiac arrest event that benched him for about five months. On December 10, 2023, he made his collegiate debut for the Trojans. However, he only completed one semester of play before leaving college early, after being selected 55th overall by the Los Angeles Lakers in the 2024 NBA draft. On July 3, 2024, James reportedly signed a four-year contract with the Lakers that is worth $7.9 million.[2] This contract meant that Bronny would be teammates with his father and living basketball legend, LeBron James, making them the first-ever father-son duo to be in the NBA at the same time.

This chapter will discuss how James's famous name, combined with his decision to contract with the NBA after only one year of college, is a winning strategy for a highly talented college basketball athlete. NIL endorsement and NIL collective deals can play a role in a player's decision to continue to play at the collegiate level. However, the money and prestige of playing for a professional team will often outweigh NIL money, glory, and the educational value of remaining on a college team. James's narrative examines three aspects of NIL deals: (1) how top-ranked college athletes who play men's college football or basketball can become instant millionaires from NIL deals with booster-supported collectives; (2) how some players, such as James, decide to become professional league athletes at the earliest possible chance; and (3) how international college athletes are prohibited from contracting NIL deals that constitute employment or labor in the United States. In the end, a lesson from Bronny James is the sooner a player can get a lucrative contract with the NBA or the NFL, the more salary and the NIL money they will enjoy.

JAMES'S NIL DEALS

James inherited more than his famous father's name and genes: his hard work and laser focus on being the best of the best made him the No. 1 recruit when he finished high school. Compared to Livvy Dunne, James had many advantages: being the son of a famous athlete and brand name, the great LeBron James; playing one of the most profitable college sports, men's basketball; and playing a sport where there is a professional team when he graduates and where he can play professionally for a high income and relative longevity. As the son of one of the most entrepreneurial, successful pro athletes, James would certainly have had the best of advisors, including his father, LeBron, to help him navigate NIL deals. Hence, one can assume that he had the support and infrastructure of his father's agents, lawyers, social media consultants, and other professionals needed to succeed. But this did not guarantee success. Just like Dunne, James had to prove himself. That he did, both as an outstanding athlete and as a successful NIL dealmaker.

Similarly to Dunne, James established a social media following early in his career.[3] By the end of high school, he had over 7 million followers on Instagram.[4] His established social media presence along with his legendary family name paid off big when it came to NIL deals. In June 2021, he appeared on the cover of Sports Illustrated.[5] Most importantly, on October 10, 2022, while James was still in high school, Nike announced that it had signed James, Caitlin Clark, Haley Jones, DJ Wagner, and Juju Watkins to NIL endorsement deals.[6] Shortly after signing the Nike deal, James secured another NIL endorsement with Beats by Dre, becoming the first high school athlete to sign with the company.[7] Then, in February 2022, James signed with PSD Underwear, with his own signature collection.[8] It is likely that James's NIL deals, including the one with Nike, may have precluded him from signing a deal with a cooperative to have him play for USC. Consequently, prior to his leaving USC for the Lakers, James had the highest NIL valuation of college athletes in On3's NIL database at $7.2 million.[9] Furthermore, in February 2022, he filed for trademarks on variations of his name: Bronny, BJ Jr., and Bronald.[10]

Needless to say, James's athletic achieves added to his NIL deals. In 2023, James committed to attending USC, where he reportedly received an athletic scholarship to play basketball. His father noted, "UCLA is close to home, but USC feels more like the right place. He can blend in there."[11] While it is not confirmed whether he received an NIL deal to attend USC, his decision to join a high-profile program like USC suggests that NIL opportunities may have played a role in his college choice. However, USC's reputation and connections in the sports and entertainment industries would provide James with valuable NIL opportunities during his time as a college student if he so chose. Further, James expressed an interest in taking advantage of NIL opportunities to capitalize on his personal brand and build his own legacy in the sports world. As a young athlete with a famous last name, James has the potential to attract significant attention and endorsement deals through NIL partnerships, which could further elevate his status as a rising star in basketball.

James's NIL deals are based upon his notoriety, as his famous name is very attractive to brands. As previously mentioned, there are two types of NIL deals: endorsements and collectives. As to NIL deals for endorsements, Livvy Dunne's success in procuring NIL deals reflects her athleticism and her diligent work establishing her brand as a social media influencer. By comparison, James's NIL deals reflect less on his time spent as a social media influencer and more on how his story and family name can sell or promote products and services. His secret sauce is his brand name and superior athletic talent in a world where the best are highly sought-after for the money and notoriety that they bring to a college and the NCAA.

Notwithstanding James's value as a brand endorser, in this chapter, we focus on the second of two types of NIL deals: that with booster-supported collectives. We discuss collectives here because it is their NIL deals that are driving up the value of college athletes, particularly those who are the top talented men who play football or basketball. However, just to be clear, there is no report of James receiving an NIL from any collective for enrolling at USC, although such a deal could have been a private, not public, transaction.

THE RISE OF THE NIL MARKET

The End of NCAA's Control

To understand how James and other college athletes have become NIL millionaires, it is important to explain how college athletes' NIL is an emerging market. Prior to the change in NCAA policy and NIL laws, the market value of the NIL of college athletes was zero dollars. That is because the NCAA prohibited its players from being compensated for their NIL. Players could not be compensated by anyone, including would-be endorsers or their colleges. As the NCAA and its members used their players' NIL to the NCAA's benefit, this greatly devalued the players' NIL. Hence, there was no marketability of college athletes' NIL.

In 2021, the NCAA amended its amateurism rule to permit college athletes to benefit from the value of their NIL. As mentioned, this change resulted in three types of NIL deals. The first is where college athletes are paid by third parties unrelated to their college, such as Nike, for endorsing athletic gear like their shoes. The second is where college athletes are paid by third parties in the form of booster-supported collectives, effectively in consideration for the players' decision to play for a particular college. In 2024, a third type emerged: a few states, including Georgia, Virginia, and Illinois, have enacted laws that allow colleges to pay NIL money *directly* to their athletes without any dollar limitation.[12] These laws prohibit the NCAA and conferences from investigating or punishing colleges and athletes for doing so. There are several other state laws that may passively allow direct pay as well. All these changes in NIL policy were in response to the Supreme Court's decision in *NCAA v. Alston* and the passage of pro-NIL state laws that prohibit the NCAA from enforcing their former strictly restricted amateurism rules. Consequently, these changes meant that the previous non-existent market for college athletes' NIL would quickly result in establishing a market for college athletes' NIL and a sharp increase in the value of NIL.

Collectives and Recruiting Top Talent

One major development in the marketing of college athletes and a contribution to its increased value is the creation of collectives. Collectives are typically organizations founded by and under the control of prominent college alumni and influential supporters, also known as "boosters," who are often wealthy alumni or influential members of the college community. While they promote the enrollment in a particular college, they are not legally affiliated with that college.

> Most collectives are referred to as donor-driven collectives. These collectives take the donated money from boosters and businesses and then help facilitate NIL deals between them and the athletes, resulting in the athletes being paid the donated money for the use of their NILs. Another form of collective is the marketplace collective. These attempts to create a place for athletes and businesses and boosters to meet to develop their own NIL deals. The money donated to these collectives is used to help facilitate these meetings. Finally, there are dual collectives, which perform the functions of both donor-driven and marketplace collectives. Other forms of collectives are beginning to be formed as well, but these three are the most common. School-specific collectives pool funds from a wide swath of donors to help create NIL opportunities for student-athletes through an array of activities.[13]

Collective-based NIL deals are used as a recruiting or retention device, although such practice arguably violates NCAA rules. With these types of NIL deals, players can profit from providing endorsements, selling apparel with their face and name on it, and operating sports camps in consideration for payment by school donors. All such deals must pass the NCAA rule, which prohibits an athlete from being paid money or other compensation to play a sport.[14] In reality, players are being compensated based on their athletic performance and choosing colleges, out of high school or through the Transfer Portal, with money as a major factor.[15]

These collectives are controversial because the ones with more money can recruit the better players. Then there are colleges who believe that the use of collectives to seduce a player to play for a particular school is a violation of NCAA rules or state laws. "We can't promise anybody any money for play," then North Carolina head coach Mack Brown said in February 2024. "Just about every transfer I've talked to was being offered money (from other schools), so it was a little ridiculous."[16] Some NIL critics have asked, "Is it fair that colleges with the boosters that have the most money can recruit the best athletes?"

To further complicate the picture, some collectives have applied for 501(c)(3) nonprofit organizations tax status. If accepted by the IRS, booster donations made to those collectives would be tax deductible. Other collectives are attempting to become 501(c)(7) tax-exempt entities as well. However, the IRS has recently determined that collectives do not qualify for favorable tax treatment.[17]

Among the various collectives throughout the country, there is fierce competition for the top talent in high-revenue collegiate sports, particularly men's football and men's basketball. For example, in 2015, James was only ten years old when colleges began recruiting him, with scholarship offers and letters of interest. His father was incensed and commented, "It should be a violation. You shouldn't be recruiting 10-year-old kids."[18] Notwithstanding, the ability for college athletes to profit off their NIL has become a key factor in recruiting and retaining talented athletes in college sports. College athletic directors, directly or indirectly, use the promise of potential NIL opportunities to attract top recruits. This can include endorsements, sponsorships, appearances, and social media partnerships that allow college athletes to monetize their personal brand while still in college. For example, a school may highlight the success stories of previous athletes who have benefited from NIL deals to entice new recruits to join their program. Hence, colleges indirectly, through collectives, use NIL deals to entice top talent to play for their schools. The best players are being offered top money, while players who are not that good are not being offered money. Consequently, highly-sought-after high school athletes are being recruited in a process that resembles the NFL draft for recruiting their football players.[19]

If one wonders why collectives offer millions of dollars to entice players to join a particular college team, it comes down to one word: money. College men's football and basketball mean big bucks for the top schools.

> The NCAA raked in $1.3 billion in revenue last season and distributed more than half back to Division I members. Television broadcast rights crossed the $4 billion mark in 2022 and continue to grow. There are also ticket sales, alumni donations, licensing and ads, and conference distributions that make college athletics one of the world's biggest businesses. Athletics departments nationwide recently submitted financial reports to the NCAA for the 2023 fiscal year, and the numbers were shocking. Nine programs raked in $200+ million in total operating revenue in 2023, up from five in 2022. Football is the breadwinner. Texas led the nation with $182 million in football revenue last season. Men's basketball brings in the second-most money but pales in comparison. The top-grossing hoops school netted $38 million.[20]

While men's football brings in the most revenue, men's basketball is also a significant money-maker. Every year during March Madness, 68 men's teams compete for the biggest prize in college basketball. They also compete for more than $220 million, which the NCAA distributes via a complex formula that confuses even those who work in college basketball. The NCAA makes about $1.3 billion each year, most of which is generated by March Madness, and it gives much of that revenue back to its member institutions. However, the players play for free. They do not receive a bonus for being on the winning team, nor do they receive a ring, such as what NFL players receive for playing in the Super Bowl.[21] College coaches, on the other hand, can receive substantial financial bonuses for winning. For example, Dan Hurley reportedly received at least $1.8 million in bonuses with the University of Connecticut's ("UConn") 2024 NCAA March Madness national title.[22] "His basic annual pay for this season is $5 million, which placed him seventh in USA TODAY's annual men's basketball coaches' compensation survey."

BRONNY'S EYES ON THE BIG PRIZE: PLAYING FOR THE NBA

Despite the increased financial value in a college athlete's NIL, a high-ranked male athlete can make much more money by playing for a professional league like the NBA. For James, that means a four-year, guaranteed contract worth $7.9 million, with an option to renew. That is a remarkable deal, considering that James suffered cardiac arrest in July 2023 during a USC basketball practice.

What James clearly knows is that even though some college athletes have become NIL millionaires, professional sports is big business where professional sports athletes make more money than many corporate CEOs. While most college NIL deals focus on men's football and men's basketball, professional baseball players are bringing in the highest salaries to play. The latest example is in 2024, when Juan Soto signed a $765 million deal with the New York Mets. In 2023, Shohei Ohtani signed a $700 million-dollar deal with the Los Angeles Dodgers. Skyrocketing league media rights agreements and growing off-field opportunities have already sent athletes' pay soaring in recent years. Additionally, with the infusion of money from Saudi Arabia, some sports salaries, particularly for soccer and golf, are reaching new heights.[23]

With his dad as one of the most highly compensated athletes, James is certainly aware of the top professional players' compensation in terms of annual salaries for their "on field" play. In 2023, the leading salaries were #1 golf giant Phil Mickelson, $104 million; #2 golf genius Dustin Johnson, $102 million; #3 boxer Canelo Álvarez, $100 million; #4 soccer superstar Kylian Mbappé, $100 million; #5 soccer superstar Lionel Messi, $65 million; #6 basketball star Stephen Curry, $48.4 million; #7 soccer superstar Cristiano Ronaldo, $46 million; #8 basketball superstar LeBron James, $44.5 million; and #9 basketball star Kevin Durant, $44.1 million. Notwithstanding, these salaries sometimes pale in comparison to what these superstars make from NIL endorsements, including Cristiano Ronaldo's $90 million a year and LeBron James's $75 million.

Further, James knows the long-term earning potential of a career with the NBA. Take Michael Jordan, who is the undisputed leader when it comes to the highest-paid athletes in history. The basketball legend and former Chicago Bulls star was estimated to have earned a staggering $3.3 billion throughout his career, thanks to his on-court accomplishments, endorsements, and ownership of the Charlotte Hornets. Jordan's enduring popularity and iconic status have cemented his place as one of the greatest athletes of all time.[24]

Consequently, James's decision to cut his college career short was a very smart financial move. Being a basketball superstar, he signed a deal to play for the Los Angeles Lakers after his first year of college. Further, from his high school days, he had already penned significant NIL deals, including with Nike. Consequently, he can and will continue to make money from NIL endorsements as well as from his salary to play for the Lakers. Clearly, with the surname James, there are more big-money NIL deals to come.

DECIDING TO LEAVE COLLEGE FOR A PROFESSIONAL LEAGUE[25]

James's decision to leave college after his first year to join the Lakers raises the question, "When is the best time for a college athlete to decide to stay and continue to play in college or leave to play for a professional team or compete professionally?" The decision to leave college to become a professional athlete arises in several distinct situations. The most common situation is when a player approaches the end of their senior year of college—that is, their fourth year. Such an example is where, during her fourth year at the University of Iowa, Caitlin Clark decided to seek and accept a position with the WNBA. Another situation is when a player might decide to leave college early, that is, prior to their graduation, to take a position with a professional league. Such an example is where Bronny James decided to enter the National Basketball Association ("NBA") draft and left USC after his freshman year to play for the Lakers. Then, there are instances where a college athlete may decide to remain in college for a fifth year and thereby delay becoming a professional athlete. Such an example is where Livvy Dunne decided to remain at LSU for a fifth year and not to move on to professional status. And the fourth situation is where a college athlete remains in college but decides to give up their amateur status by being compensated for some "professional" sport activity, such as competing in golf tournaments for cash prizes.

The question is whether a player should go pro and, if so, when? Before answering that question, it would help to know the benefits and the detriments of leaving college to play for a professional sports team or to compete as a professional athlete. Playing for a professional sports team can be a dream come true for many athletes, but it is important to carefully consider the decision and understand the rules, laws, and potential outcomes before making the move. Here are some key points to consider when deciding whether to stay in college or to become a professional athlete:[26] First, there are a professional league's eligibility rules. That is, different sports have different rules about when an athlete is eligible to join a professional league, often based on the athlete's age and level of education. For example, in the NBA and the National Football League ("NFL"), players must be at least 19 years old and must have completed at least one year of college to be eligible for the draft.[27] In the National Hockey League ("NHL"), players must be at least 18 years old and may leave college at any time to join that league.[28] In Major League Baseball ("MLB"), players can be drafted out of high school, but if they choose to go to college first, they must wait until after their junior year to pay for a professional league.[29] These rules appear to be arbitrary and do not support the importance of what an athlete receives from a college education and experience.

Second, there are financial considerations, as becoming a professional athlete can be a financial windfall for some athletes with the chance to compete at the highest level and the opportunity to make a name for oneself in the professional sports world. To maximize their earning potential, an athlete needs to spend as many of their prime years as possible playing professionally. Further, deciding to become a professional athlete is likely to increase a player's notoriety, which can result in an increased payout in NIL endorsement deals. Every year spent playing college athletics not only reduces the number of years they will spend earning money by playing sports, it also increases the possibility of sustaining a career-ending injury before their professional career even begins. However, it is important to understand the potential risks and rewards. While top draft picks in major sports leagues can earn millions of dollars, many athletes who go pro do not make much money or do not last long in their careers. Additionally, there are usually no guarantees of success or long-term financial stability. By comparison, staying in college can provide a chance to continue developing skills and potentially increase one's value as a professional athlete. Staying in college can provide a chance to continue developing as an athlete and get a degree, which can be valuable in the event of an injury or the end of a sports career.

Third, there are many legal considerations to take into account when deciding whether to go pro or stay in college. For example, if an athlete signs with an agent while still in college, they may jeopardize their eligibility to play college sports. It is important to understand the rules and regulations of the college sports governing body and seek legal advice before making any decisions. Fourth, there is the risk of injury; an athlete must maximize their years playing professionally to protect themselves from the risk of physical injury. If they are injured in college, as was James, who had a heart attack prior to starting his first season, they might not be covered by the university's insurance. However, if they are playing professionally, the league will likely provide medical and disability insurance to cover them for physical injury related to playing their sport.

Fifth, in addition to these eligibility, financial, and legal considerations, there are many personal values for a college athlete to choose to forgo becoming a professional athlete. One consideration is that an athlete, such as Livvy Dunne, might make more money as a college-based social media influencer than they might make as a professional athlete, such as a gymnast. Then, there are some sports for which there are no professional league options or these options do not pay high salaries such as the WNBA. Further, college provides an athlete some unique experiences, such as maturity and growth opportunities, as additional time in college can allow an athlete to mature physically and mentally, potentially improving their performance as a professional. Additionally, staying in college longer might increase one's market value; that is, by further developing skills in college, an athlete could potentially increase their draft position and earning potential when they eventually enter the professional league. Finally, a longer college career can give an athlete time to assess their professional aspirations and make informed decisions about their future.

Hence, as is in the case of James, athletes will likely conclude that, after weighing all the factors, pros and cons, it is better to leave college if given an opportunity to play for a professional league.

NIL AND INTERNATIONAL STUDENT ATHLETES

James chose to cut short his college education to play for the NBA. During his short time in college, he was able to sign lucrative NIL endorsement deals. Unfortunately, there is a group of college students who are legally restricted from participating in U.S.-based NIL deals: These are international student athletes ("ISAs"). Who are ISAs, and why are they denied the right to participate in NIL deals in the U.S.? ISAs are students who are not U.S. citizens and not legal residents of the U.S., but who seek permission from the U.S. government to come to the U.S. to attend college. Consequently, these athletes, like any foreign student who wishes to attend college in the U.S., must apply for and be granted a special visa for legal residency in the U.S., which is an F-1 visa, commonly referred to as a "student visa."[30] This visa grants foreign students the legal right to live in the U.S. on the condition that they are enrolled full-time in an accredited American university.[31]

There is a strong market for ISAs, as there are many foreign athletes interested in attending college in the U.S. and many colleges that desire to enroll foreign students.[32] In 2023, ISAs were reportedly composed of nearly 12.8% of Division I NCAA athletes.[33] In non-revenue sports, such as tennis, foreign athletes made up over 60% of the college players.[34] In the revenue-generating sport of college basketball, foreign students make up 15% of the players.[35] These interesting statistics raise the obvious question: Why and how do ISAs need advocacy when it comes to NIL deals? The answer to that question involves the nature of the F-1 visa and the federal government's restrictions on the ability of foreign students to work while in the U.S.

All visas to enter and stay in the U.S. come with privileges and restrictions. The F-1 visa allows a student to enter the United States as a full-time student at an accredited college, university, seminary, conservatory, academic high school, elementary school, or other academic institution, or in a language training program, at a school authorized by the U.S. government to accept international students.[36] What is important to note, relative to NIL deals in the U.S. for F-1 visa athletes, is that there are limitations on "employment." Specifically, the law provides:

> F-1 students may not work off-campus during the first academic year but may accept on-campus employment subject to certain conditions and restrictions. After the first academic year, F-1 students may engage in three types of off-campus employment: Curricular Practical Training (CPT), Optional Practical Training (OPT) (pre-completion or post-completion), and Science, Technology, Engineering, and Mathematics (STEM) Optional Practical Training Extension (OPT). F-1 students may also be eligible to work off-campus on a case-by-case basis as a result of special situations such as severe economic hardship or special student relief . . .

> any off-campus training employment must be related to their area of study and must be authorized prior to starting any work by the Designated School Official (the person authorized to maintain the Student and Exchange Visitor Information System (SEVIS)) and USCIS.[37]

One might correctly conclude that NIL deals that involve off-campus employment within the U.S., that is, active traditional, social media influencer-based NIL activities, would not be legally permissible. What about NIL deals that involve college collectives, which are boosters who contract with athletes as an inducement to play for a particular college?

This is a big deal, as there are thousands of international student athletes competing in college sports in the U.S., with more than 25,000 NCAA international students currently enrolled and competing at one of the three NCAA division levels.[38] The NCAA provides information and guidance to international student athletes and domestic coaches relative to recruiting those athletes.[39] Sports with the highest rates of international student athletes include tennis, ice hockey, golf, field hockey, soccer, swimming, and water polo.[40] Sports with the lowest rates of international athletes include football, baseball, softball, lacrosse, volleyball, and wrestling.[41]

What can colleges legally do to recruit international student athletes? The simple answer is that international student athletes are eligible to receive athletic and academic scholarships and even some types of financial aid.[42] Full or partial athletic scholarships are offered at the NCAA D1 and D2, National Association of Intercollegiate, and National Junior College Athletic Association levels.[43] However, most athletic scholarships only cover a portion of the school's tuition, room and board, and fees, which means that a student in need would have to seek other financial aid and scholarship opportunities available for high-academic students or other specific criteria.[44] As for academic scholarships, these are typically given to students who have a strong grade point average, high standardized test scores, a high class rank, or have taken challenging coursework or Advanced Placement classes.[45] In addition to academic scholarships, many schools also offer non-academic scholarships to students for such outstanding activities as extracurriculars, leadership roles, and volunteer work.[46] Then, there is financial aid and work-study. While international student athletes are not eligible to receive U.S. federal student aid like grants or loans, some colleges and universities have their own institutional aid they offer to both national and international student athletes based on financial need. Additionally, foreign students are not eligible for Federal Work-Study. That leads to student loans. While international students do not qualify for federal student loans, they may qualify for private loans.

In addition to how a foreign student might finance their education after being accepted into a U.S. college and playing a sport, an international student athlete has a few other obstacles to overcome. They must comply with the NCAA or similar academic and other eligibility requirements. One such eligibility requirement is that the athlete must be compliant with the NCAA's amateurism rules, particularly, relative to NIL, the prohibition on being paid to play a sport, known as "pay to play." While the NCAA's prohibition against its pay-to-play rules is in litigation and may be deemed illegal and unenforceable, the current practice of NIL deal collectives to induce a player to play for a given college for sometimes millions of dollars is ongoing but controversial.

This begs the question: Can and are international student athletes able to contract NIL deals with collectives? The answer to that question is no if the NIL deal is for the players' off-campus labor or employment in the U.S. As previously noted, an international student athlete must obtain an F-1 visa, which, among other things, severely limits their ability to work off-campus. As a result of this limitation in immigration regulations, international student athletes are generally prohibited from participating in NIL deals. That is, because most deals are deemed to be a form of employment and arguably violates the F-1 visa. What would happen if an international student athlete were to sign an NIL deal that violates the F-1 visa employment restrictions? That student could be summarily expelled from the U.S. or at least not allowed to re-enter the U.S. after they leave, as their F-1 visa would be revoked.

However, some argue for loopholes in the immigration laws relative to NIL deals. Although "NIL activities" are not yet expressly addressed by F-1 status regulations, international student athletes in F-1 status must guard against activities that could be misconstrued as unauthorized employment.[47] Only U.S.-based employment activities are regulated under U.S. immigration laws, so international student athletes should strategically seek NIL activities on the international stage and in countries where admissibility and employment authorization are regulated according to the laws of the host country.[48]

Does that mean that an international student athlete is absolutely prohibited from signing an NIL deal? Arguably, it depends on whether the deal requires the athlete to provide labor or constitutes employment. That raises the question: "Are there instances where an NIL deal might not violate the conditions in the provisions of the F-1 visa law?" The General Counsel Office of the University of Oregon presents some excellent examples of how an international student athlete could perhaps benefit from an NIL deal and still maintain their favored student residency status.[49] However, please beware that these legal conjunctures are not actually spelled out as permissible exceptions in U.S. immigration law. These possible, yet unapproved, "loopholes" in the immigration law relative to NIL for international student athletes include (1) where the international student's employment takes place outside of the U.S., such as getting an NIL deal for work in their home countries while visiting home or during academic breaks; (2) where the student endorses a product online without a formal arrangement or cash or in-kind payment or licenses the use of their NIL in their home country with all the revenue going to their parents or some third party; and (3) where the student receives royalties such as licensing the student's NIL to a video game company, which are considered passive income and not "work" in the usual sense, and may not violate U.S. immigration laws.[50]

To date, research shows no reported public instance where the NCAA or U.S. immigration has revoked an international student athlete's F-1 visa for participating in an NIL deal. In fact, there is both public and congressional sympathy for the plight of these students and an appetite to change the F-1 visa employment restriction to permit their participation in U.S.-based NIL deals.[51] Notwithstanding the potential pitfalls, it has been reported that some of the nation's most sophisticated collective management companies have been able to bypass the restrictions of F-1 visa restrictions relative to NIL. One Penn State collective was reportedly able to passively license Canadian athletes' NIL for billboards in their home country.[52]

From a financial perspective, the U.S. would likely benefit economically from permitting international student athletes to participate in NIL deals, particularly those who endorse products. One reason is because the international market for sports (think soccer) is huge and the international market for many products and services far exceeds the U.S. market alone. Besides, the NIL revenue of those international student athletes would likely be taxable and add to the U.S. economy and tax base. It is hard to imagine a reason why this would not be a good idea. Allowing international student athletes to contract NIL deals would also serve as an incentive for those students to attend and play sports at U.S. colleges. Perhaps a person whose father knows the value of being an internationally recognized sports giant, such as Bronny James, would be the perfect advocate for the NIL rights of international student athletes, given the global reach and notoriety of his last name.

NIL POWER SECRET #4: RELISH BRONNY JAMES'S FINANCIAL SAVY BY KEEPING AN EYE ON THE PRIZE

Bronny James is a super-talented, well-connected young man who cut short his college career to maximize his earning potential by entering the NBA draft in his freshman year of college. His power secret is knowing that for an athlete who is good enough, professional sports leagues such as the NBA pay more money than any college NIL deal. He is at the top of the NIL hierarchy because in addition to being a leading social media influencer like Livvy Dunne, he has the potential to become a highly successful, influential professional. This means longevity and notoriety, which is a major draw for NIL deals in athletic gear such as Nike shoes.

Further Reading

Brian Windhorst, LeBron, Inc.: The Making of a Billion-Dollar Athlete (2019).

Bryan Horowitz, *The Griffeys in the House to See Lebron, Bronny Make History*, MLB (Oct. 22, 2024), https://www.mlb.com/news/ken-griffey-jr-and-sr-to-watch-lebron-james-bronny-make-history.

Hanif Abdurraqib, *Bronny James Shoots His Shot*, Men's Health (Oct. 15, 2024), https://www.menshealth.com/fitness/a62490236/bronny-james-interview/.

Janie McCauley, *Dell Curry Cherishes Chance to Call Both Sons' Game as Stephen, Seth Face Off*, NBA (Feb. 24, 2024), https://www.nba.com/news/dell-curry-1st-call-both-sons-game-stephen-seth-face-off.

Ken Griffey, Mark Vancil, & Walter Iooss, Junior: Griffey on Griffey (1997).

Endnotes

1. Pat Benson, *Bronny James Signs NIL Deal with Nike,* SPORTS ILLUSTRATED (Oct. 10, 2022), https://www.si.com/fannation/sneakers/news/bronny-james-signs-nil-deal-with-nike.
2. Dhani Joseph, *Bronny James Signs Multi-Year, Guaranteed Contract with the Los Angeles Lakers: Report,* YAHOO! SPORTS (July 3, 2024), https://sports.yahoo.com/bronny-james-signs-multi-year-guaranteed-contract-with-the-los-angeles-lakers-report-180125058.html. *See also* Shams Charania (@ShamsCharania), X, https://x.com/shamscharania/status/1808521978271207500?s=46&t=LuLzStMNvByXMHfO71 (last accessed Mar. 12, 2025).
3. KJ Smith, *World's Most Influential Teenage Basketball Players,* ON3 (Aug. 18, 2021), https://www.on3.com/news/worlds-most-influential-teenage-basketball-players/.
4. Jack Baer, *Bronny James Rants about Girls and Weed, Gets Smack-Talked by Draymond Green in First Day on Instagram,* YAHOO! SPORTS (May, 29, 2019), https://sports.yahoo.com/lebron-james-bronny-instagram-followers-draymond-green-041030248.html.
5. Sanjesh Singh, *Bronny James Makes First Cover of Sports Illustrated with FaZe Clan,* LEBRON WIRE (June 10, 2021), https://lebronwire.usatoday.com/story/sports/nba/lebron/2021/06/10/bronny-james-makes-first-cover-of-sports-illustrated-with-faze-clan/76770552007/#.
6. Nike Basketball (@nikebasketball), X, https://x.com/nikebasketball/status/1579502094155153409?ref_src=twsrc%5Etfw%7Ctwcamp%5Etweetembed%7Ctwterm%5E1579502094155153409%7Ctwgr%5E51e495d39bdc224d856592c1c7e184af6b89657d%7Ctwcon%5Es1_&ref_url=https%3A%2F%2Fwww.sportingnews.com%2Fus%2Fnba%2Fnews%2Fbronny-james-nil-deals-nike-beats-by-dre-lebron-son%2Fwnbonsmou3k1gmkrk5eixtoq (last accessed Mar. 12, 2025); DJ Dunson, *Why Did Bronny James Pick USC?,* DEADSPIN (May 8 2023), https://deadspin.com/bronny-james-usc-lebron-james-son-college-basketball-1850415722/.
7. Jordan Greer, *Bronny James' NIL Deals, Explained: Nike, Beats by Dre among Brands Teaming Up with Lebron's Son,* SPORTING NEWS (Mar. 28, 2023), https://www.sportingnews.com/us/nba/news/bronny-james-nil-deals-nike-beats-by-dre-lebron-son/wnbonsmou3k1gmkrk5eixtoq.
8. *Id.*
9. Keegan Pope, *Bronny James Tops NIL Valuation Projections from On3,* ON3 (May 6, 2023), https://www.on3.com/nil/news/bronny-james-tops-nil-valuation-projections-from-on3/.
10. Ben Pickman, *LeBron James Jr. Files Three Trademarks for Variety of Names,* SPORTS ILLUSTRATED (Feb. 2, 2022), https://www.si.com/extra-mustard/2022/02/02/bronny-james-files-trademark-names.
11. *See* Dunson, *supra* note 6; Kyle Boone, *Bronny James Commits to USC: Lebron James' Son Chooses to Stay near Father in Southern California,* CBS SPORTS (May 6, 2023), https://www.cbssports.com/college-basketball/news/bronny-james-commits

-to-usc-lebron-james-son-chooses-to-stay-near-father-in-southern-california/; *Breaking Down the Impact of Bronny James' Commitment to USC*, ESPN (May 6, 2023), https://www.espn.com/mens-college-basketball/story/_/id/37528811/the-impact-bronny-james-commitment-play-college-basketball-usc.

12. Email from National College Players Association to author (Sep. 18, 2024, at 1:06:14 PM CDT). "More States Allow Colleges to Pay NIL DIRECTLY to Athletes!"
13. Pete Nakos, *What Are NIL Collectives and How Do They Operate?*, On3 (July 6, 2022), https://www.on3.com/nil/news/what-are-nil-collectives-and-how-do-they-operate/.
14. Steve Ulrich, *How the New Frontier for College Athletics Could Affect Pennsylvania*, Politics PA (Feb. 19, 2025), https://www.politicspa.com/how-the-new-frontier-for-college-athletics-could-affect-pennsylvania/140771/.
15. Andrew Kahn, *Agent Reveals How NIL Really Works in College Sports*, MLive (May 17, 2024), https://www.mlive.com/sports/2024/05/agent-reveals-how-nil-really-works-in-college-sports.html.
16. *See* Pete Nakos, *What Are NIL Collectives and How Do They Operate?*, On3 (July 6, 2022), https://www.on3.com/nil/news/what-are-nil-collectives-and-how-do-they-operate/.
17. Jacob Kaplan M., Nicole Brown, & Trenton Hafley, *Federal Tax / Exempt Organizations Advisory: The IRS's Latest Play on NIL Collectives: Tax-Exempt Status on the Defensive*, Alston & Bird (Oct. 18, 2023), https://www.alston.com/en/insights/publications/2023/10/the-irss-latest-play-on-nil-collectives#:~:text=Chief%20counsel%20for%20the%20IRS,tax%20treatment%20of%20these%20organizations.
18. Myron Medcalf, *LeBron: Stop Recruiting LeBron Jr.*, ESPN (Feb. 25, 2023), https://www.espn.com/nba/story/_/id/12381552.
19. Dalton Hunkle, *The Impact of NIL on High School Athletes*, Method Schools (Oct. 3, 2024), https://www.methodschools.org/blog-2023/the-impact-of-nil-on-high-school-athletes; Jay Bilas, *Why NIL Has Been Good for College Sports. . . . And the Hurdles That Remain*, ESPN (June 29, 2022), https://www.espn.com/college-sports/story/_/id/34161311/why-nil-good-college-sports-hurdles-remain.
20. Grant Hughes, *College Athletics' 25 Powerhouses who Produce the Most Revenue Entering 2024*, 247Sports (June 27, 2024), https://247sports.com/longformarticle/college-athletics-25-powerhouses-who-produce-the-most-revenue-entering-2024-233312519/.
21. Lev Akabas & Eben Novy-Williams, *One Shining Check: The Value of a March Madness Win*, Sportico (Mar. 27, 2024), https://www.sportico.com/leagues/college-sports/2024/march-madness-2024-money-ncaa-units-payouts-1234772616/.
22. Steve Berkowitz, *Dan Hurley Will Receive at Least $1.8 Million in Bonuses with UConn's National Title*, USA Today (Apr. 9, 2024), https://www.usatoday.com/story/sports/ncaab/2024/04/09/uconn-coach-dan-hurley-bonus-championship/73255649007/.

23. Brett Knight, *The World's 10 Highest-Paid Athletes 2023,* FORBES (May 2, 2023), https://www.forbes.com/sites/brettknight/2023/05/02/the-worlds-10-highest-paid-athletes-2023/?sh=515ed8bcb156.
24. *Highest Paid Athletes of all Time Worldwide as of 2023,* STATISTA, https://www.statista.com/statistics/1370671/highest-paid-athletes-ever/ (last accessed Mar. 12, 2025).
25. *Navigating the Decision to Go Pro or Stay in College: A Comprehensive Guide for Student-Athletes,* EDUC. LAWYERS, https://www.educationlawyers.com/blog/student-athlete-go-pro-or-stay-in-college-guide#:~:text=On%20the%20plus%20side%2C%20going,or%20long%2Dterm%20financial%20stability (last accessed Mar. 12, 2025); Cynthia Lally, *Going Pro vs. Getting an Education,* NORTHEASTERN, https://northeastern.digication.com/cynthia_lally/Going_Pro_vs._Getting_an_Education (last accessed Mar. 12, 2025); Herman Davis, *College vs. Pros – Is it Wise for Students to Leave School Early?,* OR. SPORTS NEWS (May 5, 17), https://oregonsportsnews.com/college-vs-pros-is-it-wise-for-students-to-leave-school-early/.
26. *Navigating the Decision to Go Pro or Stay in College: A Comprehensive Guide for Student-Athletes,* EDUC. LAWYERS, https://www.educationlawyers.com/blog/student-athlete-go-pro-or-stay-in-college-guide#:~:text=On%20the%20plus%20side%2C%20going,or%20long%2Dterm%20financial%20 stability (last accessed Mar. 12, 2025).
27. *The Rules of the Draft,* NFL, https://operations.nfl.com/journey-to-the-nfl/the-nfl-draft/the-rules-of-the-draft/#:~:text=Player%20Eligibility%20To%20be%20eligible%20for%20the,start%20of%20the%20next%20college%20football%20season (last accessed Mar. 12, 2025).
28. *Hockey Operations Guidelines,* NHL, https://www.nhl.com/info/hockey-operations-guidelines (last accessed Mar. 12, 2025).
29. *Rule 4 Draft,* MLB, https://www.mlb.com/glossary/transactions/rule-4-draft# (last accessed Mar. 12, 2025).
30. U.S. Citizenship and Immigration Services, *Working in the United States,* USCIS, https://www.uscis.gov/working-in-the-united-states/students-and-exchange-visitors/students-and-employment (last accessed Mar. 12, 2025).
31. *Id.*
32. Noah Henderson, *NIL Confusion Remains for International Athletes,* SPORTS ILLUSTRATED (Nov. 29, 2023), https://www.si.com/fannation/name-image-likeness/news/nil-confusion-remains-for-international-athletes-noah9.
33. *Id.*
34. *Id.*
35. *Id.*
36. U.S. Citizenship and Immigration Services, *Students and Employment,* USCIS, https://www.uscis.gov/working-in-the-united-states/students-and-exchange-visitors/students-and-employment (last accessed Mar. 12, 2025).
37. *Id.*

38. *International Athletes: Your Guide to Getting Recruited in the U.S.*, NCSA, https://www.ncsasports.org/recruiting/how-to-get-recruited/international-athletes#:~:text=they're%20asleep!-,Are%20international%20athletes%20eligible%20for%20scholarships%20and%20financial%20aid%3F,some%20types%20of%20financial%20aid (last accessed Mar. 12, 2025).
39. *Guide to International Academic Standards for Athletics Eligibility 2023–24*, NCAA, http://fs.ncaa.org/Docs/eligibility_center/International_Information/International_Guide.pdf (last accessed Mar. 12, 2025); Next College Student Athlete, *International Athletes: Your Guide to Getting Recruited in the U.S.*, NCSA, https://www.ncsasports.org/recruiting/how-to-get-recruited/international-athletes#:~:text=they're%20asleep!-,Are%20international%20athletes%20eligible%20for%20scholarships%20and%20financial%20aid%3F,some%20types%20of%20financial%20aid (last accessed Mar. 12, 2025).
40. *Guide to International Academic Standards for Athletics Eligibility 2023–24*, NCAA, http://fs.ncaa.org/Docs/eligibility_center/International_Information/International_Guide.pdf (last accessed Mar. 12, 2025).
41. *Id.*
42. *Id.*
43. *Id.*
44. *Id.*
45. *Id.*
46. *Id.*
47. *Can International Student-Athletes Benefit from NIL Agreements?*, Phelps (Nov. 20, 2023), https://www.phelps.com/insights/can-international-student-athletes-benefit-from-nil-agreements.html#:~:text=Therefore%2C%20ISAs%20may%20have%20a,via%20an%20employment%20authorization%20document.
48. *Id.*
49. *Name, Image, and Likeness: International Student-Athletes*, Univ. of Or., https://generalcounsel.uoregon.edu/name-image-and-likeness-international-student-athletes#:~:text=International%20students'%20visas%20limit%20them,above%2Ddescribed%20visa%20employment%20restrictions (last accessed Mar. 12, 2025).
50. *Id. See also* Noah Henderson, *NIL Confusion Remains for International Athletes*, Sports Illustrated (Nov. 29, 2023), https://www.si.com/fannation/name-image-likeness/news/nil-confusion-remains-for-international-athletes-noah9.
51. *Name, Image and Likeness Rights for International Student-Athletes*, change.org, https://www.change.org/p/name-image-and-likeness-rights-for-international-student-athletes?utm_source=share_petition&utm_medium=custom_url&recruited_by_id=afdf5d40-5454-11ec-b913-4df214d0dea1 (last accessed Mar. 12, 2025).
52. *See* Noah Henderson, *NIL Confusion Remains for International Athletes*, Sports Illustrated (Nov. 29, 2023), https://www.si.com/fannation/name-image-likeness/news/nil-confusion-remains-for-international-athletes-noah9.

5

Bryce Underwood: "Pay to Play?": Big Money and Cooperatives

"It's mainly about what I'm trying to get to." "My main goal is the NFL, first draft pick. Money is going to be the last thing I'm thinking about until I get to the league."

—Bryce Underwood[1]

In November 2024, Bryce Underwood was a high school superstar who signed a $10 million NIL deal with a collective relating to his commitment to play football for the Michigan Wolverines in 2025. His narrative is a learning exercise of "what ifs," highlighting the pitfalls that would-be NIL millionaires need to scramble through to make their NIL dreams a reality.

OVERVIEW

In 2024, Bryce Jay Underwood was the number one-ranked quarterback in the national high school class for 2025. On November 21, 2024, he reportedly agreed to a $10 million, four-year NIL deal via the University of Michigan's NIL collective Champions Circle.[2] Champions Circle is a "community of fans, alumni, and supporters whose goal is empowering University of Michigan student-athletes to be the leaders and best through name, image, and likeness."[3] One of its boosters is Larry Ellison, who is a billionaire and co-founder of Oracle and is reportedly the second-richest man in the world.[4] The terms of Underwood's NIL agreement with the Michigan collective were not disclosed. This NIL deal made the news for the huge dollars involved as well as the turnaround in Underwood's decision about where he would matriculate after high school. Underwood had previously committed to LSU with a reported $1.5 million deal.

This chapter focuses on the power of collective NIL deals and exposes the risks that newly minted college millionaires such as Underwood face when signing such a lucrative deal. Some of those risks involve the legal capacity of a minor to sign contracts. Underwood was born on August 19, 2007, which means that he was 17 years old when he agreed to the NIL deal, and therefore, not of legal capacity to sign such a contract in most states. This chapter will also discuss the impact of the Supreme Court's decision against affirmative action and its impact on college admission for African-American college athletes. Underwood is a young African-American male with an outstanding academic record who was offered a scholarship to play football at a top-ranked public university, the University of Michigan.

THE NATION'S BEST HIGH SCHOOL QUARTERBACK

In 2024, Bryce Underwood was a five-star quarterback at Belleville High School. He was an outstanding high school athlete throughout his high school career. He was named the MaxPreps National Freshman of the Year and the Michigan Associated Press Division 1–2 Player of the Year,[5] the MaxPreps National Sophomore of the Year and the Michigan MaxPreps Player of the Year,[6] and awarded the Michigan Gatorade Player of the Year.[7] In his senior year, Underwood was rated as a five-star recruit, the No. 1 quarterback, and the No. 1 overall player nationwide in the class of 2025.[8] Consequently, he received offers from nearly every Division I college, including LSU, Alabama, Ohio State, Florida, Penn State, and Michigan.[9]

One might be curious about Underwood's background.[10] Underwood was born in Detroit, Michigan, and raised in Belleville, Michigan, a small city in Wayne County, a western suburb of Detroit. At 17 years of age, he had developed into a talented athlete, who excelled in basketball, baseball, and football. His parents are Brian and Tasha Underwood, who are both educators. He has two sisters who are also athletes. He has dreams of becoming a doctor, has maintained a 4.0 high grade point average, completed Advanced Placement classes in high school, and was expected to enroll in college in January 2025. He reportedly received scholarship offers from the most prestigious college football programs in the country. Further, he is reportedly a devout Christian who reads the Bible every day, attends church diligently, and is respectful and humble. In a nutshell, he is every college football coach's dream athlete.

GUARANTEED MONEY VS. MILLIONS AT RISK

Now that Underwood has agreed to and signed the University of Michigan NIL deal, is he a guaranteed NIL millionaire? Probably not yet. High school athletes, which includes Underwood, who sign NIL deals should be made aware of risks that might rob them of their millions. Many of these risks can be managed and avoided through guarantees that might be negotiated and agreed to by the parties to the NIL deal contract. Unfortunately, we do not know the specific terms of Underwood's NIL contract, as his deal and those of other NIL millionaires are private and not available to the public. Notwithstanding, some colleges require that their student athlete contracts be disclosed to the college. It is worth noting that, unlike some of the other college millionaires who are highlighted in this book, there are no records of Underwood having signed or received any other NIL deals while in high school. That is perhaps because the state of Michigan prohibits high school athletes from contracting NIL deals that were in effect during their high school years.[11]

Performance-Contingency

In general, contracts that involve the personal performance of one of the parties to the contract are contingent on that person performing some activity or duty. For example, in a contract for Taylor Swift, Beyoncé, or hip-hop artist Kendrick Lamar to perform a concert, payment to them would be contingent upon their actually performing the concert, not for a substitute performer. Similarly, a NIL deal contracted between a college athlete and a college collective is contingent on that athlete actually playing a particular sport for a designated team. For example, Underwood's NIL contract is likely contingent on his actually playing for at least four years as the quarterback for the University of Michigan Wolverines. Hence, Underwood's Michigan NIL deal would be void if he decides to play football for another college or chooses not to play football while attending the University of Michigan. Further, a NIL contract might contain performance-based targets that determine payments, such as paying $20,000 for every touchdown pass or deducting $20,000 for every pass that is intercepted. This raises an important question: What events might derail Underwood's performance and therefore negate or void the payments promised in his NIL deal? One such event might be a disabling physical, mental, or emotional injury, such as a disabling injury resulting from a car accident or from one incurred while playing football in his last year in high school or while in college. Similarly, one might assume that his $10 million deal would not pass on to his estate or be inherited by his heirs were he to die during the four years of his contract. Considering these risks, Underwood would be advised to seek guaranteed payments of his NIL deal, making them not contingent on these types of contingent or disabling events. However, some of his demands for guaranteed payments might not be accepted by the college collective in a negotiation.

Compliance with the Law: Pay to Play?

Another risk to an NIL deal is that the deal must comply with all applicable laws, rules, and regulations. This sounds simple. Just to be clear, if an NIL deal such as Bryce Underwood's does not comply with the applicable laws, it might be invalid. An athlete or their parents who agree to an NIL deal should not presume that deal does in fact comply with regulatory authorities. One might wrongfully assume that the state NIL laws or judicial opinions or even the NCAA or college regulations ensure that NIL deals are legally compliant. Unfortunately, this is not the case. Generally, the NIL state law provides that college athletes can enjoy the right of publicity, which translates into that they can benefit from their NIL. Those NIL laws do not police or guarantee that a particular NIL is either in compliance with the laws of the land or fair to the athlete. Furthermore, those state laws are subject to NCAA regulations under which college athletes agree to comply. Why is this an issue? It is because in 2021, when the NCAA issued its interim policy permitting its players to sign NIL deals, they made two things clear: (1) NIL cannot be compensation for playing for an NCAA team; that is, it must be in consideration for some non-university-related activities such as endorsing a product such as Nike shoes; and (2) NIL cannot be used as a tool to recruit a student to play for a particular school. This is a controversial matter, particularly as it relates to NIL deals with collectives such as the one that Underwood signed with Champions Circle. What authority does the NCAA have over its colleges and players? One answer comes from the Supreme Court's dicta in *NCAA v. Alston*, where the Court noted that the NCAA has the legal authority to regulate its players.[12] However, the NCAA's rules relating to NIL are continuously under review and are being challenged in the courts. Notwithstanding, the NCAA has stated that "schools must adhere to NCAA legislation (or policy) when it conflicts with permissive state laws. In other words, if a state law permits certain institutional action and NCAA legislation prohibits the same action, institutions must follow NCAA legislation."[13]

Further, non-compliance could result in the athlete's disqualification from play. For example, in 2022, a 16-year-old Georgia native, T.A. Cunningham, transferred to a powerhouse Southern California high school in pursuit of NFL dreams.[14] Due to legal technicalities, the junior recruit was benched because of a decision from the state's governing body for high school sports. He was cleared to play halfway through the regular season, although his rating dropped from five to four stars. What should Underwood and all those who are seeking an NIL deal do to protect themselves and their potential deal? They should seek the assistance of a seasoned lawyer who can check the state NIL laws, the NCAA regulations, and their college's rules to ensure that the NIL complies with all laws.

Pay to Play

As presented in a previous chapter, there are three types of NIL deals. The first involves providing services to a third party, such as where a player is compensated for endorsing a product such as Nike shoes. These present issues of fairness and exploitation but do not usually raise

NCAA regulatory concerns. However, some state laws prohibit athletes from endorsing certain types of products and services. In South Carolina, for example, athletes can't endorse "tobacco, alcohol, illegal substances or activities, banned athletic substances, or gambling."[15]

The second type of NIL deal, which has become the greatest source of big-money NIL agreements, involves college collectives. In a nutshell, the reason for the concern is that these agreements conflict with the NCAA's restrictions on "pay to play."[16] Pay to play refers to the NCAA's strict rules against anyone paying and a college student receiving "any compensation or benefits beyond actual and necessary expenses for playing their sport,"[17] not including a scholarship to cover the cost of tuition. Pay to play has long been forbidden under NCAA rules.[18] The point is to prevent anyone from paying an athlete simply for playing their sport and disguising it as an NIL payment. As of 2024, NCAA rules require that any NIL deal be a quid pro quo arrangement. This means that athletes must do something other than simply play a sport in return for the money they are paid. Further, according to the NCAA, an NIL deal cannot be used as an unfair recruiting inducement. According to the NCAA, "Student-athlete NIL agreements should include the expected NIL deliverables by a student-athlete in exchange for the agreed upon-compensation and student-athletes must be compensated only for work actually performed."[19] You might ask, "How can so many high-profile NIL mega-deals involving college collectives be legally compliant if they clearly are designed to serve as a recruitment tool for colleges?" The easy answer to that question is that, notwithstanding their no pay-to-play rule, the NCAA has turned a blind eye to these apparent infractions. That was true until 2023.

Despite its lack of enforcement for pay-to-play arrangements, in 2023, the NCAA began to enforce their no pay-to-play rule where an NIL deal appears to be as compensation for an athlete's playing a given sport. In February 2023, the NCAA published a negotiated resolution with the University of Miami for recruiting violations that occurred in April 2022.[20] They found that the University of Miami women's basketball head coach violated NCAA rules by facilitating an impermissible contact between a booster and two prospective women's basketball players.[21] Then on January 11, 2024, the NCAA announced that a Florida State University ("FSU") assistant football coach violated certain NCAA rules in April 2022 by facilitating an impermissible recruiting contact between a transfer prospect and a booster, where the booster allegedly encouraged the prospect to enroll at FSU and offered an NIL deal as a recruiting inducement, with a value of approximately $15,000 per month.[22] The NCAA claimed that the same assistant coach then violated NCAA ethical conduct rules in February 2023 and November 2023 by allegedly providing false or misleading information about his involvement.[23]

After its investigation, under a negotiated resolution between the NCAA and FSU (the "Negotiated Resolution"),[24] the NCAA and FSU agreed to "Level II" standard penalties; the NCAA imposed a long list of penalties on Florida State, including a two-year probation, a fine of $5,000 plus 1% of the football budget, an assortment of restrictions on its ability to recruit new athletes;[25] and a requirement that FSU dissociate from the booster for three years and dissociate from the NIL collective where the booster served as chief executive officer for one year.[26] Furthermore, during the applicable disassociation period, FSU must refrain from accepting any assistance from the collective and the booster or the booster's business interests that would aid in the recruitment of prospective student-athletes or the support of enrolled student-athletes; however, the collective and any business interest of the booster are expressly permitted to continue working directly with student-athletes for NIL opportunities.[27] The NCAA has previously pursued penalties for violation of its policies, but FSU's Negotiated Resolution is the first significant reported penalty relating directly to NIL collectives and the use of NIL as a recruiting inducement.[28]

Add in another alleged violations, on January 30, 2024, the NCAA reported that it was investigating the University of Tennessee for potential recruiting violations involving its high-profile donor collective, the Volunteer Club.[29] The investigation is looking at potential "major" violations in multiple sports, including possible violations of the NCAA's NIL rules.[30] The penalties against FSU and the current pending investigations signal that the NCAA is currently taking a closer look at potential unfair recruiting inducements tied to NIL, with respect to NIL collectives.[31] Notwithstanding evidence that the NCAA is somewhat serious about enforcing their no pay-to-play rule, there is another twist in the plot. In response to the NCAA's investigation of the University of Tennessee, the attorneys general of Tennessee and Virginia filed a lawsuit in federal court against the NCAA.[32] The lawsuit challenged the NCAA's legal authority to enforce some of their rules including the pay-to-play rule.[33] A federal judge granted a preliminary injunction prohibiting the NCAA from enforcing some of its rules.[34] In response, in February 2024, the NCAA sent a letter to its schools announcing that it was pausing all open enforcement cases "involving third-party participation in NIL-related activities."[35]

Following the *House v. NCAA*[36] decision, there is a third type of NIL deal, in which colleges can now pay their athletes directly to play their sport. To add to the confusion of the future of NIL, in 2025, a federal judge approved a settlement which is predicted to significantly change how the NCAA will regulate NIL deals.[37] In opposition to this proposed settlement, in December 2024, state lawmakers in some 17 states as well as the National College Players Association issued statements highlighting that many universities are prohibited by their states' NIL laws from complying with NCAA and conference NIL restrictions contained in the proposed settlement in the House case.[38] Additionally, in December 2024, in apparent opposition to the proposed settlement as well as the NCAA's no pay-to-play rule, Ohio Governor Mike DeWine signed an executive order allowing Ohio universities to directly pay their athletes NIL.[39] His order makes Ohio the fifth state in 2024 to announce that their athletes can be paid NIL money directly by their colleges; the other states are reportedly California, Georgia, Illinois, and Virginia.[40] Obviously, the landscape of NIL deals is constantly changing and requires that college athletes and their advisors remain vigilant so as to be compliant with all applicable laws, rules, and regulations, even when those laws and rules are apparently in conflict with one another.

Deals Gone Wrong

Notwithstanding the risks inherent with NIL deals, there is the added risk that the deal might fail due to the lack of funding that was promised to a player. Any athlete negotiating an NIL deal, such as Bryce Underwood, should beware and do their due diligence in checking that the deal is for real. That means that the money being promised is actually available and that the person promising the deal has the legal authority to obligate the funds being offered. One can learn from a recent deal gone wrong involving Jaden Rashada.[41] On January 19, 2024, the University of Florida's ("UF") football program was reportedly under NCAA investigation based on a failed NIL deal of former signee Jaden Rashada, a quarterback who contracted with the now-defunct Gator Collective.[42]

In May 2024, Rashada filed a lawsuit against the UF detailing some of his claims.[43] First, in June 2022, Rashada committed to the University of Miami Hurricanes with a $9.5 million promise, which fell through, causing significant career disruptions. In December 2022, Rashada signed a National Letter of Intent with UF. His decision to enroll with UF was contingent on a four-year, $13.85 million NIL deal. However, that deal did not materialize, and Rashada asked for a release from his letter of intent. The lawsuit, among other things, alleges that a UF coach promised Rashada's father a $1 million "partial payment" upon signing, which was never paid. Such a promise would have violated the NCAA's policies. The lawsuit is pending and is a stark reminder that promises of NIL money are not a guarantee of actual payment. A similar claim of an unfulfilled promise of an NIL deal involved University of Nevada, Las Vegas ("UNLV") quarterback Matthew Sluka, who decided to leave an undefeated team. He reportedly was verbally promised a minimum of $100,000 from a UNLV coach and only received $3,000.[44]

In addition to these risks, players seeking NIL deals must be aware of and comply with the disclosure requirements. For example, the NCAA, the states, and many individual colleges require their athletes to report on and disclose their NIL deals to their college. Athletes are required to comply with the relevant state, NCAA, and college-specific NIL rules and, in most cases, to report any NIL deals they enter. According to the NCAA, 20 states currently have such disclosure requirements. On the NCAA front, the disclosure rules are still evolving. In January 2024, NCAA Division I announced new rules that are scheduled to go into effect for member schools on August 1, 2024. They will, for example, require athletes "to disclose to their school's information related to [any] NIL agreement exceeding $600 in value, no later than 30 days after entering or signing the NIL agreement." In addition, "Prospective student-athletes will be required to disclose the same information within 30 days of enrollment."[45] The rules don't require individual athletes to report their NIL deals to the NCAA, but their schools are expected to provide "deidentified" data on them to the NCAA or its designee at least twice a year. The NCAA says it "will use that information to develop an aggregated database so student-athletes can better understand trends in NIL agreements and so the national office and member schools can make informed decisions about NIL-related policy."[46]

In summary, while NIL deals offer college athletes the opportunity to monetize their personal brands, those deals come with several risks. In addition to the ones discussed above, there are others to consider. Athletes may lack the financial literacy to manage large sums of money, leading to poor financial decisions. Further, they can be exploited by unscrupulous agents or companies with unfair contracts. Additionally, the focus on earning money can distract athletes from their academic and athletic responsibilities. Last, NIL deals can create disparities among teammates, potentially causing tension within the team. Some of these risks can be anticipated and guarded against. Others, such as how a mega-deal can lead to tension within a team or even lead to family disharmony, are harder to control. While it is essential that any NIL deal must comply with all applicable laws and NCAA regulations, such compliance requires keen legal acumen as the laws and regulations are in flux. While athletes might be subject to criminal penalties for violating their state laws or potential punishment by their schools, any penalties that the NCAA imposes appear most likely to fall on the schools.

How does Underwood protect himself from the negative impacts of these various risks to his million-dollar fortune? The immediate answer is to hire seasoned professionals, including an attorney, sports agent, financial planner, and tax advisor, who are knowledgeable of contract law, particularly related to college athletes' NIL. These professionals are tasked with understanding the risks in NIL deals and negotiating a deal that provides the best benefits with the greatest guarantees for Underwood and that implements legal and financial strategies that protect Underwood from losses, such as disability and life insurance. Furthermore, as many college recruits like Underwood are minors and still in high school when these NIL deals are negotiated, a player and his family must also be aware of state laws relating to high schoolers' signing NIL deals as well as legal restrictions on the ability of minors to contract.

MINORS AND NIL DEALS[47]

NIL deals rely on contract law as the legal means to establish the relationship, duties, benefits, conditions, and protections in the deal. A fundamental principle of contract law in the United States is "freedom of contract," as each party to a contract is presumed to be a knowledgeable party. In other words, with rare exceptions, the law or government does not patrol contracts and expects each party to obtain legal and financial advice when entering a contract. In fact, NIL law at the state level typically does not provide for protection against exploitation of the players.

One exception to this rule is where a party to a contract is a minor. Minors lack the legal capacity to contract. That being the case, how did Bryce Underwood contract on the NIL deal, as he is a minor? He was born on August 19, 2007, which means he was 17 years old when he contracted with the University of Michigan-affiliated collective. Furthermore, generally, minors cannot own property, which means that Underwood cannot personally "own" or control the millions that derive from his NIL deal.

So how do athletes who are still minors and still in high school contract a NIL deal? The simple answer is the "guardian of the property" or "guardian of the estate" of an athlete who is a minor.[48] That is, a person, often but not always the minor's parents, who has the legal authority and responsibility to oversee the financial affairs of the minor.[49] There is a complication because the NIL deal that relates to where a minor will attend college is arguably under the control of the minor's parents, who are presumably the "guardian[s] of the person."[50] Guardian of the person is a type of guardianship where the guardian manages the personal affairs of a minor, such as medical needs, nutrition, rent, and transportation.[51] Hence, it is often necessary for a court to appoint a guardian of the property to manage the finances of a high school athlete until they reach adulthood, and that does not always mean that the minor's parents will automatically be so appointed.[52]

LIABLE TO PAY TAXES

Another source of legal concern for an athlete and their parents when negotiating a NIL deal is the tax implications and liabilities. Many aspects of college athletics are tax-exempt due to the charitable nature of education.[53] However, the cash and other compensation that a college athlete receives via an NIL deal are subject to federal, state, and local income taxes as well as other tax-related issues such as social security contributions.[54] Consequently, any money, goods, property, or services that a student receives, both monetary and non-monetary, from NIL-related activities must be reported on their federal tax returns and is taxed as ordinary income.[55] This taxation of NIL income applies at the state and local levels as well.[56] Furthermore, it is possible for the IRS to view NIL as property for which there could be taxation for capital gains for its appreciated value.[57] Governments are challenged to determine how NIL, a new virtual asset, should be taxed.[58] Additionally, if NIL is a part of a player's estate when they die, the value of the NIL could be subject to federal and state estate taxes.[59] Another interesting question is whether a person's interest in their NIL could be transferred to a tax-deferred retirement account such as a self-directed Individual Retirement Account.[60] Clearly, a college athlete who has a NIL deal needs to access competent legal, tax, and estate planning advisors.

There are many nuances to the taxation and financial impacts of college athletes' NIL deals, including "the jock tax," self-employment taxes, in-kind compensation, deductions and expenses, estimated tax payments, impact on financial aid, and working with NIL collectives.[61] There are other related tax issues, such as dependency status for a minor athlete's parents' tax returns and the need to file in various states when sponsorship deals involve working in multiple states.[62] Consequently, the tax burden on players' NIL is a huge consideration when deciding whether treating NIL in this way enriches college athletes. Of course, even after paying the taxes owed on their NIL deals, players will hopefully net a financial benefit. That is not always true. If an NIL deal is for a small amount of money, such as $5,000, the negative impact on a student's financial profile might result in disqualification for federal assistance under the Pell Grant program. That could mean that the NIL deal might cost more money than it is worth.

Another NIL related tax issue involves NIL collectives. In the past, NIL collectives have applied for and received tax-exempt status from the IRS, arguing that their NIL contributions were charitable in nature.[63] A collective is usually a group of boosters who organize to provide NIL deals to highly sought-after players to encourage them to play for a particular college.[64] However, in June 2023, the IRS Office of Chief Counsel explained that many organizations that developed and paid NIL opportunities for student-athletes are not eligible for tax-exempt status under IRC § 501(c)(3) "because the private benefits they provide to student-athletes are not incidental, both qualitatively and quantitatively, to any exempt purpose furthered by that activity."[65] That means that some of the revenue that would have gone to the NCAA and its school members—all of whom are tax-exempt, nonprofit entities—would now become taxable. Hence, whereas boosters or collectives who contributed directly to a college or university's athletic program would have received a tax deduction as a charitable donation, those same boosters who form cooperatives to help recruit players via NIL deals have been instructed by the IRS that those NIL funds are not tax deductible.[66] This will likely change how NIL agreements are structured and the status or type of institutions they contract with going forward.[67] It is a reason why there is a push to permit colleges themselves to contract NIL deals directly with their students. That way, boosters can give the NIL money to their colleges and receive a tax deduction for doing so.

BLACK ADMISSIONS IN COLLEGE IN JEOPARDY

As previously mentioned, most NIL college athlete contracts are contingent on enrollment in a particular college and playing a particular sport for that college. This means that an NIL player must be accepted into that college and remain academically eligible to play the sport. Unfortunately, college admission for anyone, particularly at elite colleges, is not guaranteed and has recently come under judicial scrutiny, which will make it more difficult for admission. This should not be an issue for Bryce Underwood. In addition to his athletic achievements, he is a highly accomplished student academically. In his sophomore year of high school, he reportedly had a 4.0 grade point average. Further, he has earned Advanced Placement credits, which will allow him to finish high school and enter college in January 2025.[68] He reportedly is a member of the National Honor Society, the Student Council, and the Chess Club. One would imagine that with his outstanding academic record, his stellar athletic accomplishments, and being an African American, he would be a shoo-in for acceptance into the University of Michigan's undergraduate program. But not so fast!

In June 2023, the Supreme Court (6–2) in *SFFA v. Harvard*[69] held that race-based admission policies at Harvard University and UNC violate the Equal Protection Clause of the 14th Amendment. The ruling requires colleges to amend their admissions policies so they do not discriminate based on an applicant's race. This decision also applies to the recruitment and admission of athletes. Writing for the majority, Chief Justice John Roberts detailed how admissions policies at elite colleges discriminate against Asian American applicants while enhancing the acceptance odds of other categories of applicants, including recruited athletes, legacy children, children of wealthy donors, and applicants from other races.[70] Justice Roberts cited data showing that both Harvard and UNC's admissions programs accept certain categories of applicants at higher rates than other applicants—particularly Asian American applicants—who possess similar academic profiles. For example, UNC's second-highest academic category had admitted 84% of Black applicants compared to 58% of white applicants and 47% of Asian American applicants.[71] Consequently, admissions officers should admit applicants based on academic merit and not for other reasons, including athletic programs. Further, one study showed that white male applicants from affluent families uniquely benefited from such pro-athlete admission practices.[72]

The Court's SFFA decision effectively eviscerates the past practice known as affirmative action, by which colleges sought to level the playing field for Black, Latinx, and Native American applicants by arguably aggressively admitting them. As to race, the SFFA decision bans the upfront use of race as a criterion for admissions nationally, although the Court stated that an applicant's race could be included in their personal statement for admissions consideration.[73] Since the SFFA decision, some colleges have seen a drop in the number of Black students enrolled, following a growing movement against diversity, equity, and inclusion ("DEI") initiatives.[74] One of those schools is the University of Michigan.[75] In fact, even prior to the SFFA decision, the state of Michigan had banned the use of race in college admissions since 2006.[76] So, how does this case relate to college athletes' NIL?

Clearly, one of the conditions to a NIL deal for a college athlete is their enrollment in college. It has been suggested that the SFFA decision will make it more difficult for Black athletes to be enrolled in the most academically selective colleges, such as the University of Michigan.[77] Furthermore, many Black students have reported that they feel unwelcome at their majority-white colleges, especially in "red" states where diversity is under political attack. As to Bryce Underwood, as previously noted, he has a stellar academic record. However, so do many of those who apply to the University of Michigan. Without affirmative action and preference for athletes, his NIL deal, as well as that of other stellar athletes, may not materialize if those athletes are not accepted into their schools of choice. Of course, the SFFA decision does permit an applicant who is an African American to mention in their essay how overcoming racial discrimination was a significant factor in their personal development. Black Americans have come a long way, from a near total ban on admission into elite, formerly white-only colleges until the passage of the Civil Rights Act of 1964. Notwithstanding, challenges continue for Black students on these elite campuses, which makes it difficult for a superstar Black athlete like Bryce Underwood, regardless of the multi-million-dollar NIL deal. Parenthetically, one study estimated that the NCAA owes predominately Black college athletes billions of dollars in generational wealth.[78] Notwithstanding, it will likely take litigation for those athletes to receive any overdue compensation.

THE NEED TO PROTECT PLAYERS IN NIL DEALS

Whether a player signs a mega NIL deal such as Underwood's or is considering signing a small, one-off deal, one should not commit to any such agreement without the advice of competent legal counsel. NIL deals rely on contract law as the legal means to establish the relationship, duties, benefits, conditions, and protections in the deal. A fundamental principle of contract law in the United States is "freedom of contract," which means that each party to a contract is presumed to be a knowledgeable party. In other words, with rare exceptions, the law or government does not patrol contracts and expects each party to obtain legal and financial advice when entering a contract. Added to the deck being dealt against the players, a party contracting a NIL agreement with a college athlete may include a confidentiality or arbitration clause which would preclude an athlete from suing in court. Further, a party contracting with a college athlete could also require that an athlete pay the opposing party's attorney's fees if the athlete challenges their enforceability of the NIL agreement. This reality requires a discussion of NIL deals that go wrong, including deals that exploit college and high school athletes. These bad deals evidence the need to enact laws that protect high school and college athletes from exploitation.

One example of a NIL deal gone sour involves Gervon Dexter, a former UF Gator.[79] He signed a deal with Big League Advance Fund ("BLA"), which required him to pay 15% of his pre-taxed NFL earnings for 25 years in consideration of a one-time payment of $436,485 and a $5,000 contribution to the charity of his choice. Those earnings included,

> without limitation, any wages, salary (including Player's Team Payments), Bonuses (including deferred bonuses), payments made to Player by reason of Player's participation in any playoff game, all-star game, or other championship event, and other compensation whatsoever earned by Player in his services to the Professional Football League or Team of any kind related to or for Player participating in Football Activities, and participating at events during the Extended Term of this Agreement.[80]

In exchange for the payment, Dexter granted BLA a "perpetual, irrevocable, royalty-free, and worldwide license for the duration of the Initial Term to use the player's name, image, likeness, comments, biographical information and/or athletic reputation for the advertisement or publication of BLA, including in social media posts, interviews, online content, press releases, and any other media." Dexter was required to make at least one social media post promoting BLA and its products, autograph as many as 100 items for BLA, make at least two personal appearances, and provide BLA with at least one VIP invitation to the NFL draft and draft-related events that he hosted. Dexter later signed a four-year, $6.72 million contract with the Chicago Bears, meaning he would owe BLA about $1 million over the lifetime of that deal. He is now suing in federal court to void the agreement, arguing that the deal does not conform with Florida's NIL law and the state's athlete agent statute.

Exploitation of college and high school athletes comes in many forms and often constitutes fraud or misrepresentation. The problem is once an athlete signs an exploitive NIL contract, it is presumably binding and very difficult and costly to undo. There are tons of unfair NIL deals being pitched to these athletes. One such agreement, which has been pitched to basketball players, is to promote a New Jersey company on Instagram, TikTok, and other social media sites.[81] On one page, without any mention of who owns the student's intellectual property rights or defines the meaning of net profits, the players are legally assigning all their NIL rights to an unknown person for unknown compensation.[82] In another contract that was shopped to college football players, a Texas apparel company proposed keeping at least 40% of the revenue from merchandise sales and included revenue-sharing for any future profit-generating deals, including autograph signings or sponsorships, effectively turning the company's relationship with the athlete into that of an agent and a client.[83] Any NIL deal should be of limited duration and not obligate the player forever. An IP license gives a company the right to use a student's social media posts forever and allows the licensee to recycle those posts without increasing the athlete's royalties, even if they go pro and their market value rises. Hence, a college athlete's NIL deal should terminate when that athlete is no longer a student (for example, when they graduate), at the discretion of the college athlete. Few states have enacted laws that protect college and high school athletes from some of these exploitative agreements. For example, Texas prohibits students from signing NIL agreements that outlast their college careers. Apparently, so does the state of Florida, although its provisions may not effectively protect Gervon Dexter.

A related problem is a player who relies on a NIL agent.[84] Professional football agents must register with the player's association, pass a legal examination, and cap their commission at 3%. By contrast, the most an NIL agent who represents a high school or college athlete must do is pay an application fee to the state, and there is no limit on their commission rate. U.S. Senator Tommy Tuberville of Alabama and former Senator Joe Manchin of West Virginia have introduced federal legislation that would require such agents to register with the Federal Trade Commission. Further, NCAA president Charlie Baker is seeking to establish a way to certify agents either through federal laws or on their own.[85]

To date, there is general agreement that college and high school athletes need protection from exploitation in NIL deals. Notwithstanding, they are sheep being slaughtered by the wolves. The regulatory bodies are doing very little to protect the players.[86] On August 1, 2024, the NCAA Division I Council unanimously adopted New NIL Protections.[87] These are designed to protect college athletes by promoting the sharing and centralization of information related to NIL deals, such as contract terms and trustworthy service providers. The policy lists four specific protections, including (1) a "voluntary registration process for NIL service providers (e.g., agents and financial advisors)" so student-athletes are better able to make informed decisions as they select service providers; (2) student-athletes will be required to disclose to their schools the terms included and information related to NIL agreements (e.g., description of services rendered, contract term length, compensation and payment structure, and contact information for involved parties and service providers) exceeding $600 in value, no later than 30 days after entering into or signing an agreement ("The schools will deidentify and provide the data to the NCAA, and such data will be used by the NCAA to "develop an aggregated database."); (3) the NCAA will develop "a template contract and recommended contract terms" and educate student-athletes on contractual obligations; and (4) the NCAA will develop a plan to "provide ongoing education and resources to support student-athletes on policies, rules and best practices pertaining to NIL."[88] The last two provisions, which are to develop a template NIL contract and to educate players on NIL deals, seem promising. However, they will do very little to prevent fraud or exploitative NIL deals. As long as the general rule of law is freedom of contract, which puts the burden on every party to a contract to protect their own interest, it is incumbent on players and their families to be diligent and become knowledgeable about the pitfalls of NIL deals. Such protection against exploitation requires the enrollment of a seasoned-NIL contract lawyer.

NIL POWER SECRET #5: SCRAMBLE WITH BRYCE UNDERWOOD THROUGH THE NIL PITFALLS

In November 2024, Bryce Underwood had a very special reason to celebrate Thanksgiving. He had just agreed to a $10 million NIL deal, which involves him playing for the University of Michigan Wolverines football team after he graduates from high school in 2025. This NIL deal raises questions of "pay to play" as well as the lack of legal protections of young athletes, both relevant to NIL deals. While several college athlete NIL millionaires are members of very affluent, well-resourced families, many of them are first-generation college students whose families are less fortunate, particularly some who are African Americans.

As NIL deals are facilitated via contract law, where the rule is "freedom of contract," the government seldom interferes to ensure that NIL deals are fair and do not exploit the players. Where those players are minors, the law protects them by requiring that a "guardian of the property" be appointed whose job is to safeguard minors from financial exploitation and safeguard their property, including in NIL deals. In addition, NIL can be fraught with risks, which requires knowledgeable professional consultants, including lawyers, to navigate. Fortunately, some states and the NCAA are taking measures to protect players, particularly minors, from exploitation in NIL deal. However, real protection does not exist, which requires that athletes and their parents who are negotiating NIL deals are best advised to seek the counsel of a seasoned NIL lawyer.

Consequently, the secret lesson one can learn from Bryce Underwood's multi-million-dollar NIL deal is to manage the risks that can be deal breakers: (1) stay physically and emotionally healthy by avoiding injury or mental breakdown; (2) practice sound judgment so as not to get benched, suspended, or expelled from school for drugs, grades, bad behavior, or betting; (3) be business savvy so as to avoid exploitation, recognizing that not every NIL deal is a fair deal; (4) value and pursue your educational goals and do not squander your learning opportunities; and (5) comply with the law, rules, and regulations by being aware of and complying with them, particularly the tax laws.

Bryce Underwood has hit the NIL jackpot, landing a $10 million, four-year NIL deal to join the University of Michigan's football team. His power secret is scrambling through the pitfalls of a NIL Mega Deal. As he agreed to become the newest NIL college millionaire, his journey through the pitfalls is just beginning. He has declared that he has two goals: to be a star quarterback for an NFL team and to become a doctor. Notwithstanding, he and other multi-millionaire college athletes must manage several risks that can result in them losing their hard-earned fortunes.

Understanding the risks inherent with college athlete NIL deals will alert players and their families to the importance of enrolling in the professional resources needed to achieve their goals. Doing so can result in millions of dollars and can provide a lifetime of revenue, even after a player has graduated from college. A college athlete who is not resourced with competent professional services, including legal, accounting, taxation, physical and emotional support, and academic support, is like going skydiving without a parachute. You will fall flat on your face.

Further Reading

Austin Meek, *Five Pressing Michigan Football Questions: Could Bryce Underwood Start Right Away*, ATHLETIC, N.Y. TIMES (Mar. 17, 2025), https://www.nytimes.com/athletic/6206996/2025/03/17/michigan-football-bryce-underwood-spring-practice/.

Dylan Sanders, *7 High School Football Players at or Nearing Seven Figures in NIL Money Already*, SPORTS ILLUSTRATED (Nov. 8, 2024), https://www.si.com/fannation/name-image-likeness/nil-news/7-high-school-football-players-at-or-nearing-seven-figures-in-nil-money-already.

Trent Knoop, *Report: Michigan Football QB Bryce Underwood to Make the Cover of NCAA Football 26 Video Game*, SPORTS ILLUSTRATED (Mar. 12, 2025), https://www.si.com/college/michigan/football/michigan-football-quarterback-bryce-underwood-on-cover-of-ncaa-football-26-video-game.

Endnotes

1. Pete Nakos, *Nation's No. 1 Recruit Bryce Underwood Focused on LSU, NFL Instead of NIL Payday*, On3 (June 3, 2024), https://www.on3.com/nil/news/nations-no-1-recruit-bryce-underwood-focused-on-lsu-tigers-football-nfl-instead-of-nil-payday/.
2. Morgan Moriarty, *Bryce Underwood NIL Money, Explained: What to Know About Michigan's "Champions Circle" Behind $10.5m Recruiting Flip*, MSN, https://www.msn.com/en-us/sports/other/bryce-underwood-nil-money-explained-what-to-know-about-michigans-champions-circle-behind-105m-recruiting-flip/ar-AA1uANo5?ocid=BingNewsSerp.
3. *Id.*
4. *Id. See also* Lisa Scherzer, Alex Schiffer, & Dennis Young, *Oracle Billionaire Larry Ellison Funded Michigan's NIL Stunner*, Front Off. Sports (Nov. 23, 2024), https://frontofficesports.com/larry-ellison-michigan-nil-bryce-underwood/.
5. Stephen Spiewak, *Bryce Underwood of Belleville Named 2021 MaxPreps National Freshman of the Year*, CBS Sports (Jan. 7, 2022), https://www.cbssports.com/high-school/football/news/bryce-underwood-of-belleville-named-2021-maxpreps-national-freshman-of-the-year/.
6. Jared Purcell, *Bryce Underwood Shines again in D1 Title Game as Belleville Football Claims Back-To-Back Titles*, MLive.com (Nov. 26, 2022), https://www.mlive.com/highschoolsports/2022/11/bryce-underwood-shines-again-in-d1-title-game-as-belleville-football-claims-back-to-back-titles.html.
7. *Belleville High School Student-Athlete Named Gatorade Michigan Football Player of the Year*, Gatorade (Jan. 3, 2024), https://playeroftheyear.gatorade.com/poy/assets/writable/81551/2024_FB_BUnderwood.pdf.
8. Manny Navaro & Ari Wasserman, *QB Bryce Underwood, No. 1 Prospect in Class of 2025, Commits to LSU*, N.Y. Times (updated Nov. 21, 2024), https://www.nytimes.com/athletic/5183047/2024/01/06/bryce-underwood-commits-lsu/.
9. Austin Meek, *Can Michigan Keep Bryce Underwood Home? Meet the Next Big Quarterback Recruit*, Athletic, N.Y. Times (July 24, 2023), https://www.nytimes.com/athletic/4710395/2023/07/24/bryce-underwood-college-football-recruiting-michigan/.
10. Deepika Verma, *Bryce Underwood Age: Height, Wiki, Parents, Biography, Girlfriend, Net Worth, Education & Facts*, Wiki Celebs, https://www.wikicelebs.com/bryce-underwood-wiki/ (last accessed Mar. 12, 2025).
11. Jeremy Crabtree, *Where Is NIL Prohibited for High School Athletes?*, On3 (July 22, 2024), https://www.on3.com/nil/news/where-is-nil-name-image-likeness-prohibited-for-high-school-athletes-hs-football-basketball/.
12. *See NCAA v. Alston*, 141 S. Ct. 2141, 2169 (2021), at 2168 (Kavanaugh, J., concurring).
13. National Collegiate Athletic Association, *Untitled Question and Answer Document*, NCAA, https://mc97gsxn49y6wmpf4p2n764zq7z1.pub.sfmc-content.com/2ezhyl105pc (last accessed Mar. 12, 2025).

14. Kit Ramgopal, Kenzi Abou-Sabe, & Gabe Gutierrez, "*There's No Rules. It's Crazy": New Money in NCAA Recruiting Leaves Elite Athletes Ripe for Exploitation*, NBC NEWS (Nov. 27, 2022), https://www.nbcnews.com/news/us-news/star-high-school-athletes-can-now-profit-nil-deals-rcna51075.
15. LegiScan, "Bill Text: SC S0685, https://legiscan.com/SC/text/S0685/2021.
16. College Athlete Advantage, *Understanding NCAA Rules & Eligibility: A Comprehensive Guide for Aspiring College Athletes*, COLLEGE ATHLETE ADVANTAGE (Nov. 18, 2024), https://collegeathleteadvantage.com/blog-details/Understanding%20NCAA%20Rules%20%20Eligibility:%20A%20Comprehensive%20Guide%20for%20Aspiring%20College%20Athletes.
17. Sharon Morioka, *The Business of College Sports*, U. MICH. LAW QUADRANGLE (Spring/Summer 2023), https://quadrangle.michigan.law.umich.edu/issues/springsummer-2023/business-college-sports#:~:text=The%20NCAA%20rules%20underneath%20are%2C%20one%2C%20no,linkage%20between%20the%20payments%20and%20their%20performance.
18. *Id.*
19. National Collegiate Athletic Association, *Untitled Question and Answer Document*, NCAA, https://mc97gsxn49y6wmpf4p2n764zq7z1.pub.sfmc-content.com/2ezhy1105pc (last accessed Mar. 14, 2025).
20. Negotiated Resolution, University of Miami (Florida) – Case No. 020161, NCAA (Feb. 24, 2023), https://ncaaorg.s3.amazonaws.com/infractions/decisions/FEB2023D1INF_COIPublicReportUniversityMiamiFL.pdf.
21. *Id.*
22. This case was resolved through the NCAA's negotiated resolution process instead of a formal hearing because FSU, NCAA enforcement staff, and the assistant coach agreed on the violations and the penalties. "Negotiated resolutions may not be appealed and do not set case precedent for other infraction cases." Meghan Durham Wright, *NIL-Related Recruiting Violation Occurred in Florida State Football Program*, NCAA (Jan. 11, 2024), https://www.ncaa.org/news/2024/1/11/media-center-nil-related-recruiting-violation-occurred-in-florida-state-football-program.aspx.
23. *Id.*; Negotiated Resolution, Florida State University—Case No. 020169, NCAA (Jan. 12, 2024), https://ncaaorg.s3.amazonaws.com/infractions/decisions/Jan2024D1INF_FloridaStateNegotiatedResolution.pdf.
24. This case was resolved through the NCAA's negotiated resolution process instead of a formal hearing because FSU, NCAA enforcement staff, and the assistant coach agreed on the violations and the penalties. "Negotiated resolutions may not be appealed and do not set case precedent for other infractions cases." Meghan Durham Wright, *NIL-Related Recruiting Violation Occurred in Florida State Football Program*, NCAA (Jan. 11, 2024), https://www.ncaa.org/news/2024/1/11/media-center-nil-related-recruiting-violation-occurred-in-florida-state-football-program.aspx.
25. *Id.*

26. *Id.*; Negotiated Resolution, Florida State University—Case No. 020169, NCAA (Jan. 12, 2024), https://ncaaorg.s3.amazonaws.com/infractions/decisions/Jan2024D1INF_FloridaStateNegotiatedResolution.pdf.
27. *Id.*
28. Dan Murphy, *NCAA Penalizes FSU Football; Assistant Gets 3-Game Ban for Violations,* ESPN (Jan. 11, 2024), https://www.espn.com/college-football/story/_/id/39289391/ncaa-penalizes-florida-state-football-nil-rule-violations.
29. Michael S. Schmidt, David A. Farenthold, & Billy Wiltz, *NCAA Inquiry Takes on Growing Role of Booster Groups,* N.Y. Times (Jan. 30, 2024), https://www.nytimes.com/2024/01/30/us/ncaa-tennessee-booster-group-violation.html.
30. Pat Forde, *Sources: Tennessee Under Potential NCAA Investigation for NIL Violations in Multiple Sports,* Sports Illustrated (Jan. 30, 2024), https://www.si.com/college/2024/01/30/sources-tennessee-under-ncaa-investigation-for-nil-violations-in-multiple-sports.
31. Christopher P. Conniff *et al., NIL Round-Up: New NCAA DI Student-Athlete Protections, Policy Proposals, Enforcement Actions, and the Current State of NIL,* Ropes & Gray (Feb. 15, 2024), https://www.ropesgray.com/en/insights/alerts/2024/02/nil-round-up-new-ncaa-di-student-athlete-protections-policy-proposals-enforcement-actions.
32. Teresa M. Walker & Ralph D. Russo, *Judge Hands NCAA Another Loss, Says Compensation Rules Likely Violate Antitrust Law, Harm Athletes,* AP (Feb. 23, 2024), https://apnews.com/article/tennessee-ncaa-lawsuit-nil-7ecfad9c88f8c8baa7e0f4bb00f22ec9.
33. *Id.*
34. *Id.*
35. *Id.*
36. 545 F. Supp. 3d 804 (2021).
37. *House v. NCAA, Hubbard v. NCAA,* and *Carter v. NCAA* have been consolidated into one case. *See* Michelle Brutlag Hosick, *Settlement Documents Filed in College Athletics Class-Action Lawsuits,* NCAA (July 26, 2024), https://www.ncaa.org/news/2024/7/26/media-center-settlement-documents-filed-in-college-athletics-class-action-lawsuits.aspx.
38. Noah Henderson, *State Senators Release Statement Opposing NIL Revenue Sharing Settlement,* Sports Illustrated (Dec. 5, 2024), https://www.si.com/fannation/name-image-likeness/nil-news/state-senators-release-statement-opposing-nil-revenue-sharing-settlement.
39. Ohio Exec. Order No. 2024–08D (Nov. 18, 2024); https://content.govdelivery.com/attachments/OHIOGOVERNOR/2024/11/18/file_attachments/3074880/EO.pdf.
40. *See* Noah Henderson, *State Senators Release Statement Opposing NIL Revenue Sharing Settlement,* Sports Illustrated (Dec. 5, 2024), https://www.si.com/fannation/name-image-likeness/nil-news/state-senators-release-statement-opposing-nil-revenue-sharing-settlement.
41. Joe Sabin, *Rashada Lawsuit Highlights NCAA's Failures in NIL Era,* Forbes (Oct. 2024), https://www.forbes.com/sites/joesabin/2024/06/17/rashada-lawsuit

-highlights-ncaas-failures-in-nil-era/; ESPN Staff, *Jaden Rashada-Florida NIL Lawsuit: What to Know, What Comes Next,* ESPN (May 21, 2024), https://www.espn.com/college-football/story/_/id/40190447/jaden-rashada-florida-gators-nil-lawsuit-next.

42. Mark Long, *Florida Is under NCAA Investigation A Year after a Failed NIL Deal with QB Signee Jaden Rashada,* AP (Jan. 19, 2024), https://apnews.com/article/florida-ncaa-investigation-jaden-rashada-c8d1cc38838a43f8e216ef7ca2cb464a; Mark Schlabach, *NCAA Investigating Gators for Jaden Rashada Recruitment,* ESPN (Jan. 19, 2024), https://www.espn.com/college-football/story/_/id/39345170/ncaa-investigating-gators-jaden-rashada-recruitment.
43. *See* Joe Sabin, *Rashada Lawsuit Highlights NCAA's Failures in NIL Era,* FORBES (Oct. 2024), https://www.forbes.com/sites/joesabin/2024/06/17/rashada-lawsuit-highlights-ncaas-failures-in-nil-era/; ESPN Staff, *Jaden Rashada-Florida NIL Lawsuit: What to Know, What Comes Next,* ESPN (May 21, 2024), https://www.espn.com/college-football/story/_/id/40190447/jaden-rashada-florida-gators-nil-lawsuit-next.
44. Max Olson, *QB Matthew Sluka Leaving UNLV: What We Know and What's Next,* ESPN (Sept. 25, 2024), https://www.espn.com/college-football/story/_/id/41438443/qb-matthew-sluka-unlv-rebels-nil-dispute-next.
45. Meghan Durham Wright, *Division I Council Approves NIL Disclosure and Transparency Rules,* NCAA (Jan.10, 2024), https://www.ncaa.org/news/2024/1/10/media-center-division-i-council-approves-nil-disclosure-and-transparency-rules.aspx.
46. Associated Press, *NCAA Pausing NIL Investigations in Wake of Tennessee Case,* ESPN (Mar. 1, 2024), https://www.espn.com/college-football/story/_/id/39633142/ncaa-pausing-nil-investigations-wake-tennessee-case.
47. *See NIL College Rules,* ON3, https://www.on3.com/nil/laws/college/ (last accessed Dec. 10, 2024); Braly Keller, *High School NIL: State-By-State Regulations for Name, Image and Likeness Rights,* OPENDORSE (Sept. 16, 2024), https://biz.opendorse.com/blog/nil-high-school/.
48. *See generally,* Cornell Law School, *Guardian of the Person,* CORNELL L. SCHOOL, https://www.law.cornell.edu/wex/guardian_of_the_person (last accessed Mar. 14, 2025); Angel M. Murphy, *What Is a Guardian of the Property?,* AM. BAR ASSOC. (Aug. 26, 2020), https://www.americanbar.org/groups/senior_lawyers/resources/voice-of-experience/2010-2022/what-guardian-property/.
49. A guardian of the property acts as a fiduciary for people who cannot pay their bills, cannot file their taxes, cannot manage checkbooks, and a fiduciary makes sure that the accounting is done correctly. Usually, the court appoints an attorney from the court-approved list to serve in this role. *See* Angel M. Murphy, *What Is a Guardian of the Property?,* AM. BAR ASSOC. (Aug. 26, 2020), https://www.americanbar.org/groups/senior_lawyers/resources/voice-of-experience/2010-2022/what-guardian-property/. A similar arrangement to manage the financial affairs of an adult who is deemed unable to manage their own finances is called a conservatorship. The most notable such court-ordered arrangement involved Britney Spears. *See* "Framing Britney Spears: Critics and fans welcome 'rigorous' documentary," BBC News (Feb. 8, 2021).

50. *See* Cornell Law School, *Guardian of the Person*, CORNELL L. SCHOOL, https://www.law.cornell.edu/wex/guardian_of_the_person (last accessed Mar. 14, 2025).
51. *Id.*
52. *Id.*
53. 26 U.S.C. § 141. The 1969 Tax Reform Act created universities' tax-exempt status by developing Section 501(c)3 of the Internal Revenue Service (IRS) Code: to support public goods such as education and philanthropy. Section 501(c)3 stipulates that every religious, charitable, scientific, literary, or educational organization in the United States that fits certain requirements is a private foundation and, therefore, qualifies for tax benefits. *Id. But see C. F. Mueller Co. v. Commissioner of Internal Revenue*, 190 F.2d 120, 120 (3d Cir. 1951), where the Third Circuit Court of Appeals found that even indirect connection to non-academic profits made by certain revenues is taxable under the unrelated income business taxes (UBIT). "The Mueller case, when applied to college sports, highlights that even universities that reinvest athletic-related funds into academics are not entitled to claim tax exemption for their revenue from athletics. The crux of this decision directly applies to college sports, as these revenues, even if reinvested in an academic form, are taxable." Ethan Lewis, *University Exploitation of the 501(C)3 Tax Status*, COLUM. UNDERGRAD. L. REV. (May 21, 2022), https://www.culawreview.org/journal/the-college-tax-scam-addressing-university-exploitation-of-the-501c3-tax-status; Scott Hodge, *The Big Business of Tax-Free College Sports*, TAX FOUND. (Aug. 21, 2023), https://taxfoundation.org/blog/college-sports-tax-free-revenue/.
54. *See* Memorandum from the Off. of Chief Couns. of the Internal Revenue Serv. to the Dir. of EO Rulings & Agreements (May 23, 2023), https://www.irs.gov/pub/lanoa/am-2023-004-508v.pdf; Internal Revenue Service, Name, Image and Likeness (NIL) Income (page last reviewed or updated: Apr. 23, 2025), https://www.irs.gov/businesses/small-businesses-self-employed/name-image-and-likeness-income ("If you are a student-athlete and you receive any monetary or financial gain, in cash or non-cash, from a transaction in which you benefit from the use of your name, image or likeness, that gain is Name, Image and Likeness (NIL) income. . . . Student-athletes are generally considered independent contractors for tax purposes and receive Forms 1099 if their income is $600 or more from one source. . . . NOTE: Income or benefits you received as a student-athlete must be included in taxable income on the FAFSA (Free Application for Federal Student Aid) application and could impact the amount of financial aid granted. Pell grants are based on other factors but can also be impacted by NIL income"). *See also,* Carlos J. Hornbrook, *Student Athletes Need to Know the Potential Tax Implications of the Name, Image, Likeness Rules in College Football*, 42 ABA TAX TIMES 11 (June 11, 2023), https://www.americanbar.org/groups/taxation/resources/tax-times/archive/student-athletes-potential-tax-implications-name-image-likeness-rules/.
55. *See* 26 U.S.C.S. § 64; Rebecca Lake, *NIL Deals and Tax Implications: A Guide for College Athletes*, INVESTOPEDIA (May 30, 2024), https://www.investopedia.com/nil-deals-tax-implications-8599929; *Student-Athletes Involved in Name Image Likeness*

(NIL) Agreements Should Be Aware of Their Tax Obligations, TAXPAYER ADVOC. SERV. (Dec. 7, 2023), https://www.taxpayeradvocate.irs.gov/news/nta-blog/nta-blog-student-athletes-involved-in-nil-agreements-should-be-aware-of-their-tax-obligations/2023/12/. (Explaining that such reportable"income" include free products or services that an athlete receives in exchange for endorsing a brand or business; fees earned through student-focused activities, such as signing autographs or making promotional appearances; compensation from brand ambassadorship or sponsorship deals, including brand marketing conducted on social media channels; fees paid for public speaking engagements; money earned from appearances in televised advertisements; ad revenue generated through a YouTube channel, blog, or podcast that the student owns; royalties or fees earned through a licensing or merchandising agreement; and licensing via non-fungible tokens (NFTs)).

56. *See How Do State and Local Individual Income Taxes Work?*, TAX POL'Y CTR. (updated Jan. 2024), https://www.taxpolicycenter.org/briefing-book/how-do-state-and-local-individual-income-taxes-work (last accessed Mar. 14, 2025).
57. *See generally*, The Investopedia Team, *Can You Realize Capital Gains on Intangible Property?*, INVESTOPEDIA (Aug. 23, 2022), https://www.investopedia.com/ask/answers/032715/can-you-realize-capital-gains-intangible-property.asp.
58. For example, relative to cryptocurrencies, such as Bitcoin, the IRS views them as property, which trigger tax events when used as payment or cashed in. "When you realize a gain—that is, sell, exchange, or use crypto that has increased in value—you owe taxes on that gain." Joe Liebkind, *Cryptocurrency Taxes: How They Work and What Gets Taxed*, INVESTOPEDIA (updated Nov. 16, 2024), https://www.investopedia.com/tech/taxes-and-crypto/.
59. *See generally*, Raquel Sportel, *Intellectual Property Assets in Estate Planning*, PORTER WRIGHT (July 7, 2022), https://www.porterwright.com/media/intellectual-property-assets-in-estate-planning/.
60. *See* Carlos J. Hornbrook, *Student Athletes Need to Know the Potential Tax Implications of the Name, Image, Likeness Rules in College Football*, 42 ABA TAX TIMES 11 (June 11, 2023), https://www.americanbar.org/groups/taxation/resources/tax-times/archive/student-athletes-potential-tax-implications-name-image-likeness-rules/.
61. *Id.*
62. *Name, Image, Likeness and the Tax Implications of Paying College Athletes*, H&R BLOCK, https://www.hrblock.com/tax-center/income/nil-student-athletes/ (last accessed Mar. 14, 2025).
63. *Name, Image, and Likeness (NIL) Collectives*, TAXPAYER ADVOC. SERV. (updated Nov. 19, 2024), https://www.taxpayeradvocate.irs.gov/get-help/general/nil/nil-collectives/.
64. *See generally*, David Ubben & Tess DeMeyer, *What Is NIL, How Has It Changed College Sports and Why Are Schools Under Investigation?*, ATHLETIC, N.Y. TIMES (Feb. 2, 2024), https://www.nytimes.com/athletic/5245564/2024/02/02/nil-explained-ncaa-name-image-likeness-investigation/. ("Collectives are organizations that fundraise via large and small donors with the intent to direct that money to a school's athletes

through NIL deals. . . . One of the NCAA's first pieces of official NIL guidance, sent to schools in May 2022, stated that collectives count as boosters and are subject to the same, long-applied recruiting rules. In short, collectives cannot be involved in recruiting, and they can't entice a recruit to sign with a particular school with the promise of payment.")

65. *See* Memorandum from the Off. of Chief Couns. of the Internal Revenue Serv. to the Dir. of EO Rulings & Agreements (May 23, 2023), https://www.irs.gov/pub/lanoa/am-2023-004-508v.pdf.
66. *Id.*
67. *See generally*, KRISTI DOSH, THE ATHLETE'S NIL PLAYBOOK: THE COMPLETE GUIDE TO OWNING AND PROFITING FROM YOUR NAME, IMAGE, AND LIKENESS (2025).
68. Deepika Verma, *Bryce Underwood Age: Height, Wiki, Parents, Biography, Girlfriend, Net Worth, Education & Facts*, WIKI CELEBS (Dec. 17, 2022), https://www.wikicelebs.com/bryce-underwood-wiki/.
69. 600 U.S. 181 (2023).
70. *Id.*
71. *Id.*
72. *See* U.M. Jayakumar, W.C. Kidder, E. Comeaux, & S. Thaxton, *Race and Privilege Misunderstood: Athletics and Selective College Admissions in (and Beyond) the Supreme Court Affirmative Action Cases, 70* UCLA L. REV. DISCOURSE 230–264. *See also* Kirsten Hextrum, *Special Admission: How College Sports Recruitment Favors White Suburban Athletes* (2021).
73. Bernard Mokam, *After Affirmative Action Ban, They Rewrote College Essays with a Key Theme: Race*, N.Y. TIMES (updated Jan. 21, 2024), https://www.nytimes.com/2024/01/20/us/affirmative-action-ban-college-essays.html#:~:text=But%20the%20ruling%20also%20allowed,race%2C%20like%20grit%20or%20courage.
74. Aatish Bhatia, Ben Blatt, Francesca Paris, Alicia Parlapiano, & Eve Washington, *What Happened to Enrollment at Top Colleges after Affirmative Action Ended*, N.Y. TIMES (Jan. 15, 2025), https://www.nytimes.com/interactive/2025/01/15/upshot/college-enrollment-race.html#.
75. Katherine Managan, *Where DEI Efforts Are Ambitious, Well Funded, and Taking Fire from All Sides*, CHRON. OF HIGHER EDUC. (June 20, 2023), https://www.chronicle.com/article/where-dei-efforts-are-ambitious-well-funded-and-taking-fire-from-all-sides.
76. Jacquelyn Elias & Nick Perez, *How Enrollment Changed in States That Banned Race-Conscious Admissions*, CHRON. OF HIGHER EDUC. (June 22, 2023), https://www.chronicle.com/article/race-conscious-admission-bans.
77. Michael McCann, *SCOTUS College Race Ruling May Impact Athlete Recruiting*, SPORTICO (June 29, 2023), https://www.sportico.com/law/analysis/2023/scotus-affirmative-action-decision-college-athletics-1234727874/.

78. Ramogi Huma, Ellen J. Staurowsky, & Roy H. Park, *How the NCAA's Empire Robs Predominantly Black Athletes of Billions in Generational Wealth* (July 30, 2020), https://drive.google.com/file/d/1z97vhcjErrHIvuO3Nu2wUWbG90bFKnm_/view.
79. Mark Schlabach, *Florida Legislator Says Bears DT Gervon Dexter's NIL Deal Violated Law*, ESPN (Sept. 5, 2023), https://www.espn.com/college-football/story/_/id/38335229/florida-legislator-says-bears-dt-gervon-dexter-nil-deal-violated-law.
80. *Id.*
81. Nicole Sadek & Ronnie Greene, *College Athletes Lured by NIL Deals, Exploited by Fine Print*, Bloomberg Law (July 18, 2023), https://news.bloomberglaw.com/antitrust/college-athletes-lured-by-nil-deals-exploited-by-fine-print.
82. *Id.*
83. *Id.*
84. *Id.*
85. *See generally*, Bill Carter, *The Case for Certifying NIL Agents: Protecting Student Athletes in a New Era*, Sports Bus. J. (Oct. 2024), https://www.sportsbusinessjournal.com/Articles/2024/10/01/carter-nil-corner.
86. *See* Christopher P. Conniff *et al.*, *NIL Round-Up: New NCAA DI Student-Athlete Protections, Policy Proposals, Enforcement Actions, and the Current State of NIL*, Ropes & Gray (Feb. 15, 2024), https://www.ropesgray.com/en/insights/alerts/2024/02/nil-round-up-new-ncaa-di-student-athlete-protections-policy-proposals-enforcement-actions.
87. *See* Meghan Durham Wright, *Division I Council Approves NIL Disclosure and Transparency Rules*, NCAA (Jan. 10, 2024), https://www.ncaa.org/news/2024/1/10/media-center-division-i-council-approves-nil-disclosure-and-transparency-rules.aspx.
88. *Id.*

6

Arch Manning: Playing the Long Game to Brand Dynasty

The beauty of it for us, here's a guy whose NIL value of whatever it is – and this guy's grandpa won't let him take NIL money. . . . It is a pretty good message from Archie.

—The University of Texas at Austin head coach Steve Sarkisian, reporting that Arch Manning's grandfather has advised Arch not to sign NIL deals prematurely[1]

OVERVIEW

Archibald "Arch" Manning is a college football superstar who possesses the secret sauce of NIL deals. He currently plays as an American football quarterback for the University of Texas at Austin ("UT") Longhorns. Like Dunne, James, and Underwood, Manning was an outstanding, highly decorated athlete while in high school. Unlike Dunne, the Princess of Social Media, Manning has consciously minimized social media interaction. Like James, Manning is a legacy player. In joining UT, Manning became the third generation of Mannings to star as a quarterback in the SEC. He is the nephew of former NFL quarterbacks Peyton and Eli Manning, who are both Super Bowl champions, and the grandson of Archie Manning, who also was a star NFL quarterback. His father is Cooper Manning, who is the older brother of NFL legends Peyton and Eli Manning, and works as a television host. The Manning family has amassed a multi-million-dollar fortune due to their sports-related legacy.[2] In 2024, Arch's net worth was reportedly around $1 million,[3] while his NIL market valuation is one of the top ten in the nation.[4] As of July 21, 2025. Arch Manning was ranked No. 1 in NIL valuation, with a $6.8 million value and 430,000 Instagram followers.[5]

This chapter highlights the wisdom of Manning's decision to (1) set his sights on the mega-millions of dollars that come from playing the long game of sharing in the Manning family brand dynasty; (2) defer high school NIL and college endorsement deals, despite his high valuation and significant social following; and (3) seek to increase his favorability or attractive marketability, including his decision not to seek a transfer after he was the backup quarterback, which evidences his loyal nature, a positive market trait.

MANNING'S LONG GAME OF BRAND DYNASTY, A LIFETIME OF MEGA-MILLIONS

Manning's outstanding high school record and family name made him one of the top college athletes in NIL valuation.[6] However, his family must have advised him on the importance, both mentally and financially, of keeping his eye on the long game, which is brand dynasty.[7] Brand dynasty refers to a brand in which a series of persons aka brand heirs, embody the brand persona, which enhances market recognition and increases the wealth of the family members.[8] As applied to Manning, his highest and best value is the legacy of one of football's most iconic families, who have gone beyond their football successes to make them nationally-recognized television personalities. One example of their broad appeal is Peyton Manning hosting the *Country Music Awards* each year from 2022 to 2024.[9]

Manning was an outstanding, highly decorated football quarterback at Isidore Newman School in New Orleans. He ranked No. 5 in the nation in the 2023 class. He received an extensive list of sport awards while in high school. For example, as a freshman, he was awarded MaxPreps National Freshman of the Year honors. He was a four-time all-state honoree and earned All-America status. In 2022, he was selected to participate in the U.S. Army Bowl and was named the Bobby Dodd National Back of the Year.[10] Due to his high school record, his expected college successes, and his future NFL and career prospects, Manning has been and continues to be listed in the top five in NIL valuation.[11] Notwithstanding, Manning held back from signing any NIL deals while in high school, and, as of 2024, only signed two small NIL deals while in college. Additionally, there are no reports of his having signed an NIL collective to play for UT.

Why would he not do what so many other high-ranked NIL-valued college and high school athletes have done? That is, to cash in now for his share of the NIL billions? Perhaps the answer is that he is seeking a much better deal, one that shares in the Manning brand dynasty. Further, he might have been advised that negotiating an NIL before he reached his market value peak, which is after he is drafted into the NFL, would likely mean taking a discounted payout against his future earnings. Additionally, as discussed previously, third-party NIL deals are not always great deals financially, and NIL deals with college collectives are frowned upon by the NCAA and could result in disqualification from playing college football and being tainted as a rule violator. Ultimately, what Manning knows and is his power secret is not to undervalue his future earning potential as a brand dynasty beneficiary.

What is the value of brand dynasty, its future value, and how does that relate to college NIL deals? To answer that question, one needs to review how much money the most highly compensated professional athletes are being paid and their net worth. First, there is a lot of money for superstars just for playing their sport. One example in December 2023, superstar pitcher and designated hitter, Shohei Ohtani, contracted a $700 million, ten-year deal to play baseball for the Los Angeles Dodgers of MLB.[12] A year later, in December 2024, the New York Mets announced a 15-year contract for $765 million, to retain home-run slugger Juan Soto, with $75 million upfront and an additional nearly $47 million draw over the next nine months.[13]

Notwithstanding, several professional athletes are billionaires and make more money from NIL endorsements than they make from playing their sport.[14] The top two are international soccer superstars, each with phenomenal social media followings. At the top of the list is Cristiano Ronaldo's annual income, reportedly totaling $136 million, with on-field income of $46 million and off-field income of $90 million.[15] He has 850 million followers across Facebook, Instagram, and Twitter, more than any other athlete in the world.[16] Next on the list is Lionel Messi, with $130 million in annual income, with on-field income of $65 million and off-field income of $65 million.[17] Number four on the list is LeBron James, with a total annual income of $119.5 million, with $44.5 million from on-field income and a whopping $75 million in off-field income, who became the first active athlete to be certified a billionaire by Forbes in June 2023.[18]

Clearly, many of the richest sports superstars earn more of their money from brand endorsements rather than from playing their sport.[19] Basketball phenom Steph Curry's 2013 deal with Under Armour is reportedly the largest shoe contract of all time, expected to exceed $1 billion.[20] In 2003, international soccer superstar Cristiano Ronaldo signed a lifetime endorsement deal with Nike that is projected to exceed $1 billion, in addition to endorsements with other name brands including Herbalife, EA Sports, and American Tourister.[21] As of 2008, superstar golfer Tiger Woods is reportedly worth more than $1.5 billion, with only 10% coming from prize money.[22] Twenty-time Grand Slam tennis giant Roger Federer had a 20-year deal with Nike worth $150 million and has signed a $300 million ten-year deal with the Japanese designer Uniqlo.[23] Another international soccer superstar, Lionel Messi, earns $27 million per year from his 2006 lifetime endorsement of Adidas products.[24] In 2015, one of the greatest sports figures, LeBron James, re-signed a minimum $1 billion lifetime deal with Nike, which is reportedly possibly the largest NIL endorsement.[25]

What is more amazing is that many superstar athletes and non-sport social media influencers make substantially sums of money for their online presence.[26] For example, brands with large budgets that want to reach millions of people via one post look to celebrities who have a substantial number of online followers. They have paid insane money per post. The top celebrities with the highest average price per post on Instagram only include Cristiano Ronaldo ($3.2 million), Lionel Messi ($2.6 million), Selena Gomez ($2.5 million), Kylie Jenner ($2.3 million), Dwayne Johnson ($2.3 million), Ariana Grande ($2.2 million), Kim Kardashian ($2.1 million), Beyoncé Knowles ($1.9 million), Khloe Kardashian ($1.8 million), Justin Bieber ($2.7 million), Kendall Jenner ($1.7 million), Taylor Swift ($1.6 million), Jennifer Lopez ($1.5 million), Virat Kohli ($1.4 million), Nicki Minaj ($1.3 million), and Kourtney Kardashian ($1.3 million).[27] In addition, social media content creators are operating in a growth industry, which is estimated to be worth $250 billion in 2024 and predicted to swell to nearly $500 billion by 2027.[28]

This leads to a discussion of brand dynasty and highlights the brand powerhouse family of the Kardashian-Jenner ("K-J") clan. Looking above at the list of the top Instagram average payments per post, the K-J family has five in the top 20! In 2020, their combined net worth was $3 billion.[29] Each member of the family, which includes Kris Jenner, Caitlyn Jenner, Kourtney Kardashian, Kim Kardashian, Khloe Kardashian, Rob Kardashian, Kendall Jenner, and Kylie Jenner, reportedly has a net worth above $10 million.[30] Kim K. alone has a staggering net worth of $1.7 billion.[31] That is what I call a brand dynasty! Is there a similar brand dynasty in the sports world? There are two sports families that come to mind. One is LeBron and Bronny James. The other one is the Mannings. Their reported combined total net worth of the five Manning athletes in 2023 totaled nearly half a billion dollars.[32] Peyton Manning is reportedly among the richest NFL players in the world, with a net worth of $300 million.[33] He endorses many major brands including Reebok, Buick, ESPN, DirecTV, Papa Johns Pizza, and Sony.[34]

When one considers the enormous wealth that derives from brand dynasty, one can see the wisdom of Arch Manning's decision not to rush into NIL deals. Consequently, his family must have advised him on the importance, both mentally and financially, of focusing on the long game, which is brand dynasty. From his high school days, Manning's family reportedly advised him to avoid media interviews and to decline premature NIL deals and college scholarship offers. He had a private account on Instagram, allowing only friends and coaches to follow him, including Ole Miss head coach Lane Kiffin. "They've shut down everything," said one member of the local media, "but the attention is going to come."[35] In his college search, he visited several top college football powerhouses in the South, including the University of Mississippi ("Ole Miss"), his grandfather's and father's alma mater.[36] His uncle Peyton attended and was a superstar at the University of Tennessee. On December 21, 2022, after he signed a letter of intent to play for UT, he made his Internet account public.[37]

Relative to NIL deals, Manning has generally avoided them with a few small exceptions. [38] In July 2023, prior to Manning starting his first college game, he signed an NIL partnership deal with Panini America, the collectibles company, to create trading cards featuring Manning, along with his exclusive autographs.[39] This was Manning's first publicly known NIL agreement since entering college. The multi-year agreement's financial details were not disclosed, but the proceeds from the auction of Manning's first Panini trading card would reportedly be directed to Central Texas children's nonprofits, the company said. Panini reportedly planned to produce and sell cards autographed by Manning, starting with a special one-of-one Prizm black autographed card, which will be auctioned off on the Panini website.[40] In 2024, Manning signed a second NIL deal, for which he reportedly received $50,000 to $60,000 from EA Sports for taking part in an advertisement for its 2024 college football video game, which included his receiving a copy of the game and $600.[41] Notwithstanding these third-party NIL endorsement deals, Manning's UT coach disclosed that Manning did not receive any NIL deals relating to his decision to attend UT.[42] In 2025, Manning reportedly signed a UT NIL deal with Vuori, a clothing company, and that he has NIL deals with Red Bull and Uber. The report also suggests that he has an NIL deal with UT's collective, the Texas One Fund, although that is unconfirmed.[43] Previously noted, as of July 23, 2025, he was ranked No. 1 in NIL valuation, with a $6.8 million value and 430,000 Instagram followers, based on On3's proprietary NIL algorithm of NIL-deal data, performance, influence, and exposure.[44]

In summary, Arch Manning's decision to shy away from NIL deals reveals a broader strategy, which is that he is patiently waiting for better deals, ones that shares in the Manning brand dynasty. Further, he might have been advised that negotiating an NIL before he reached his market value peak (which is after he is drafted into the NFL) would likely mean taking a discounted payout against his future earnings. Additionally, as discussed previously, third-party NIL deals are not always great deals financially, and NIL deals with college collectives are frowned upon by the NCAA and could result in disqualification from playing college ball and being tainted as a rule violator. Ultimately, what Manning knows and is his power secret is not to undervalue his future earning potential as a brand dynasty beneficiary. In addition to minimizing NIL deals while in college, Manning avoided NIL deals while a high school student.

MANNING'S DECISION TO REFRAIN FROM NIL DEALS WHILE IN HIGH SCHOOL

Another aspect of Manning's NIL power secret involves his decision to avoid high school NIL deals, despite his high valuation and significant social media following. This leads to a discussion of high school

NIL deals and the question of whether a high school athlete and their families can or should accept an NIL deal. Let's address the first most important question: "Does the law permit high school athletes to contract NIL deals?" One might assume that the answer is yes, as college athletes are now permitted to benefit from their NIL. Unfortunately, that is not the case in every state, because NIL rights for college or high school athletes are currently a privilege granted or denied by state governments and/or NCAA rules, which vary state by state. The current NIL rules related to college and to high school athletes apply via state law and/or NCAA rules. Due to the potential of having a patchwork of so many NIL rules, the NCAA has been seeking federal legislation addressing this patchwork of NIL rules.

The NCAA allows member institutions to recruit and sign high school athletes who have participated in NIL activities while the student was in high school. Within the fifty states and the District of Columbia, many states permit high school athletes to sign NIL deals.[45] According to one survey, in 2024, there are seven states that prohibit such deals, including Alabama, Hawaii, Indiana, Michigan, Mississippi, Ohio, and West Virginia, with North Carolina prohibiting NIL deals for public schools but permitting NIL deals for private schools.[46] A separate survey states that there are an additional four states that prohibit high school deals, including Montana, South Carolina, Wisconsin, and Wyoming.[47] For some states, it is not clear whether such deals are permitted, which means a student contracts a NIL at their risk of losing eligibility or even facing fines or other penalties.[48] Even in states that "permit" high school NIL deals, those deals are still highly regulated. For example, in June 2024, the state of Florida permitted NIL deals for high school students but aims to protect against recruiting and high-school-oriented collectives focused on retaining talent at the high school level.[49] Consequently, each state's law needs to be evaluated and strictly complied with to ensure that an NIL deal is permitted and compliant. What would happen to a high school athlete if they knowingly or unknowingly contracted orally or in writing a non-compliant or illegal NIL deal? One answer is that the student could lose eligibility and be suspended, which could negatively impact their eligibility to play at the college level. Other penalties might include fines or loss of national awards. In addition to these career-threatening precautions relating to legal compliance, there are many financial and reputational risks in doing an NIL that turns out to be exploitative, illusory, or illegal.[50]

Notwithstanding the financial risk and compliance issues, many high-school athletes desire to become social media influencers or brand ambassadors, seeking to amass millions, such as their peers who are social media personalities and who are not athletes. For example, Charli D'Amelio, aged 20 in 2024, reportedly amassed a $23 million fortune as a top TikTok creator, with deals with Prada, Amazon, and other brands.[51] Then there is another non-athlete TikTok creator, Khabane Lame, who, at 24 years old, has 11.1 million subscribers and has had over 3.6 billion views, with a reported net worth of $40 million and 2024 income of $17 million.[52] One wonders how a state might prohibit a high school athlete from seeking to become a social media influencer.

From the start of the NIL revolution, where it was permitted, high school athletes have landed many highly lucrative NIL deals. In 2021, California was the first state to embrace high school athletes' right to monetize their NIL.[53] As a result, several athletes transferred from schools in other states and enrolled in California high schools.[54] For example, in 2022, Jada Williams moved with her mother from a Kansas City suburb to San Diego and reportedly made a six-figure annual salary from endorsement deals with Spalding, Move Insoles, Lemon Perfect, and Gym Shark while playing for La Jolla Country Day School.[55] Several high school athletes, across various sports, have signed NIL deals, including with Nike.[56] Some of these young athletes include women's soccer sensations Alyssa and Gisele Thompson, who, in May 2022, were the first high school athletes to sign an NIL deal with Nike.[57] In October 2022, Bronny James signed an endorsement deal with Nike, along with other high school basketball superstar DJ Wagner.[58] In 2024, Mia Brahe-Pedersen was the first prep track and field athlete to sign an NIL deal with Nike.[59] Also in 2024, Anna Frey, a high school junior who is a tennis phenom and has a massive social media following, partnered with FILA and HEAD.[60] In 2023, she had reported net worth of $1 million.[61]

Like everything in life, there are pros and cons to allowing high school athletes to sign NIL deals. Clearly, there are good reasons and legal arguments as to why high school athletes should have the legal right to monetize their NIL, as is the legal right of high school students who are not athletes. Allowing these athletes to do so would allow them to earn money, find fame, gain exposure, build their personal brand, and create wealth for themselves and their families. So, what is the reluctance in many states that prohibit young athletes from these opportunities or choose not to play sports?[62] Some argue concerns over distraction from academics, potential conflicts of interest, mental health problems in high school teens, and the stress of managing school, sports, and an enterprise. Further, they are vulnerable to unscrupulous dealmakers seeking to take advantage of inexperienced, underrepresented teens. Additionally, there is the fear that talented players would transfer from a state that prohibits NIL deals into a state that does, which would add tension with resident athletes. Then there are several issues relating to the need to protect high school athletes from exploitation, such as the opportunity for exploitation of minors who may, directly or through their parents, sell out their future value for a deep discount to a greedy third party or inexperienced or greedy sports agent. There is also the legal argument against signing an NIL deal while in high school, which is whether such an action violates or puts in jeopardy a student's compliance with NCAA regulations or state NIL laws.

Arch Manning, a highly recruited high school quarterback, apparently did not sign any NIL deals while in high school, possibly due to his focus on academics and maintaining his amateur status for college athletics. Currently, 38 states and the District of Columbia allow athletes to participate in NIL deals without forfeiting the ability to play high school sports.[63] Yet, there are still 12 state associations that prohibit high school athletes from contracting an NIL deal or losing their eligibility to play.[64] Notwithstanding, even where a state permits NIL deals, the devil is in the details, requiring a legal opinion to be in compliance with the state laws. For example, the Florida rule permitting NIL deals has many restrictions, the violation of which could result in the athlete being disqualified or sanctioned. Some of these restriction include that an athlete: (1) cannot hire a registered agent to manage their athletic career, other than for the purpose of advising on NIL-related matters; (2) must negotiate any NIL activities independent of their school, school district, or the Florida High School Athletic Association (FHSAA); and (3) are prohibited from monetizing their NIL with the use of their school's uniform, equipment, logo, name, proprietary patents, products, or copyrights associated with an FHSAA member school or school district, either in public, print, or social media platforms.[65] Athletes are also encouraged to seek legal counsel and tax advice when considering NIL activities, and the district promised to provide all the educational tools for athletes and families to participate in NIL.[66] Further, Florida high schools and boosters are prohibited from offering NIL deals to recruit athletes from other schools.[67] Additionally, high school athletes who transfer in season will not be allowed to secure an NIL agreement for that season unless granted a Good Cause Exemption from the district.[68]

Hence, as the NCAA rules apparently prohibit pay-to-play NIL deals, it is risky for a high school student to do so without the benefit of a legal opinion. As many high school superstars are from lower-income families, it is especially important for them to hire good, seasoned, and honest legal counsel and accounting advice, and to not let a sudden influx of money lead to irrational, harmful decisions.

Another upset to high school NIL deals is the legal status or incapacity of a minor to contract. Contract law holds that a person who is under the age of majority by state law, usually 21 years old (although that age varies by state law), lacks the legal capacity to contract. That means that an athlete who is under age, whether in high school or in college, must solicit the aid of their legal guardian(s). That guardian is usually the student's parents. Legally, a minor must have a parent or legal guardian sign the NIL deal on their behalf. The contract must also comply with state laws regarding minors entering contracts.

Parents play a crucial role in guiding and supporting their minor child in navigating NIL opportunities. They can help ensure the deals are in the best interest of the athlete and comply with legal requirements. However, there is also a potential for parents to exploit their child's talent for personal gain, so it is important for parents to act in the best interest of the athlete. This might lead to a conflict of interest, where a parent(s)'s financial interest, such as making a quick buck, is not in the best interest of the minor athlete. This might result in the minor requesting that a court assign a "guardian of the property" who would have legal control over the property and contracts of the athlete.

Many high school athletes, following the lesson from Manning, have refrained or are refraining from signing NIL deals while in high school, despite the potential financial and endorsement opportunities those deals offer. Many high school and even college athletes have decided, are deciding, or may decide to refrain from pursuing or signing NIL deals for several distinct reasons. Some find NIL deals too risky and may choose to avoid potential violations of NCAA rules or eligibility issues that could jeopardize their athletic careers. Perhaps those reluctant players recognize that NIL deals are highly regulated, that NIL laws vary from state to state, and that federal legislation and litigation may change the nature of NIL deals. Further, the NCAA has specific rules and regulations governing NIL activities for college athletes. Or perhaps some athletes who refrain from NIL deals have weighed the cost to benefit and are aware that for most college athletes, particularly those who are not star football, basketball, or baseball players, pursuing NIL deals is too costly in time and money. In fact, most NIL deals are not the multi-million dollar deals we read about, as most college NIL deals are under $10,000 a year.[69] Or perhaps those players, particularly those who play high-profile sports like football, know that the odds of them being recruited to the NFL are very slim, as the league only hires 300 athletes each year out of thousands of college players. They may decide to focus their time and attention on their education and non-sports related career goals.

In addition to participating in intercollegiate sports, most college students attend college for reasons other than making money while they are in college and so might not be interested in pursuing NIL deals. Not all college athletes may be interested in or comfortable with leveraging their NIL for endorsement deals or sponsorships. Further, some athletes may simply prefer to maintain a low profile and avoid the spotlight that comes with NIL opportunities. Then there is the challenge of time management. Balancing the demands of being a college athlete with academic coursework, training sessions, and competitions can be challenging. Some athletes likely feel that they do not have the time or resources to actively pursue and manage NIL deals on top of their existing commitments.

Overall, the decision to refrain from NIL deals is a personal one and can be influenced by a variety of factors, including athletic priorities, NCAA regulations, personal values, lack of interest, time constraints, and uncertainty about the future. Each college and high school athlete may have their own reasons for choosing whether to pursue NIL opportunities. However, high school athletes, unless they have significant online social media followers, should not get too excited about landing an NIL deal. In reality, less than 1% of the nearly 8 million high school athletes in the nation sign lucrative NIL deals.[70] Consequently, high school athletes and their families who are considering entering an NIL deal should enlist the assistance of credible, honest, knowledgeable professionals, including a sports agent, a lawyer, an accountant, a financial planner, and a life coach.[71]

PURSUING BRAND DYNASTY THROUGH POPULARITY

The third aspect of the "Manning" strategy toward achieving brand dynasty involves the development of Arch's "favorability." Favorability is akin to likability or popularity, which means how a person is perceived by the public. Often used to rate the popularity of a U.S. presidential candidate during national elections, a person's favorability translates into market value. As previously mentioned, in 2025, Manning had the highest ranking in the NIL valuation, with a $6.8 million value and 430,000 Instagram followers.[72] Just to be clear, a valuation does not mean that Manning has been paid $6.8 million in NIL deals, as some news reporters have misrepresented. A valuation means the amount of money a person's NIL should be worth in the marketplace.[73] One factor in that valuation is a player's popularity or favorability. During his first year at UT, Manning has exhibited certain personality traits that are endearing him to the public, which should mean a multi-million-dollar deal when he enters the NFL draft in 2026. His positive image, and, therefore increased NIL valuation, are likely the result of his carefully considered decisions. Three decisions have apparently added to his favorability. These include decisions (1) to refrain from receiving NIL money to play for UT; (2) to accept being a backup quarterback; and (3) to stay with UT and pass on transferring to another school via the Transfer Portal.

Relative to Manning's decision to refrain from seeking or accepting NIL money to play for UT, he has shown that he is focused on the long game of brand dynasty. Caveat, it is possible that Manning is receiving NIL money from a UT collective but nothing to that effect has been publicly announced. Considering that some of his peers, such as Bryce Underwood, are signing NIL deals for $10 million or more, Manning certainly could have negotiated such a multi-million-dollar deal with UT or one of its competitor teams. By deciding to pass on such a NIL deal, Manning added positives to his image and marketability. First, he has shown his understanding of the long-term financial benefits of patiently waiting for the even bigger bucks that will likely come from the NFL draft, brand endorsements, and national favorability. Second, he has sent a message to prospective brand businesses that he is not desperate for money, and, therefore, his endorsements will not come cheap. Third, he is enhancing his image is presenting himself as a team player, a humble person, and loyal, which are all positive traits in the eyes of the consuming public and attractive to many businesses. Overall, Manning appears to be comfortable in his own skin and understands his destiny as the next Manning to join the brand dynasty.

How might Manning's brand dynasty pay off? It already has. On September 14, 2024, with the injury of its starter, superstar quarterback Quinn Ewers, Manning came off the bench to be recognized as a hero, saving the team from a pending loss.[74] While he was benched, he had the luxury of learning the UT playbook and avoided injury. By not seeking to transfer to another college, he has likely earned the respect of his coaches and the camaraderie of his teammates. Furthermore, with the Manning name, he is already the darling of the national sports commentators, many of whom are close friends with their Manning family colleagues. He is already being described by the media as a "normal guy" who is a college superhero.[75] One notable national college football writer and analyst put it this way: "Texas quarterback Arch Manning will be a better QB than Ohio State's Julian Sayin, Alabama's Jalen Milroe, Nebraska's Dylan Raiola, and Oklahoma's Jackson Arnold. At least, that's the idea when considering just how much attention Manning draws given his last name."[76] Moreover, the media loves a good story, particularly one featuring the Manning dynasty. This is evidenced by the media coverage over the issue of whether Arch would seek to transfer from UT. For example, one source has speculated on whether Manning will seek a transfer from UT.[77] Notwithstanding, Manning appears to be loyal to UT, which also endears him to the public.[78]

Manning has developed a popular, all-American image. One YouTube media interview shows an Arch Manning who is humble, poised, and self-assured. He describes how he had his teammates over for gumbo with his family while they were playing in New Orleans for the Sugar Bowl.[79] Most importantly, he seems to be embracing the Manning brand dynasty strategy, which is for him to be highlighted as a future No. 1 draft pick. Achieving that goal comes with a multi-million-dollar, multi-year, guaranteed contract. One should note that Manning is already the source of speculation to replace some aging or free agent players like Russell Wilson, who signed a one-year deal with the Steelers in 2024 after the Denver Broncos released their former five-year, $242 million quarterback.[80] Added to this, Manning understands the importance and the value of protecting and promoting the Manning brand and legacy for future Mannings: these are his sister May who plays volleyball at the University of Virginia and his brother Heid who plays center on Isidore Newman High School's football team.[81] Mannings forever!

NIL POWER SECRET #6: PLAY ARCH MANNING'S LONG GAME TO MULTI-MILLIONS

Arch Manning is in an envious position as a legacy college athlete. He is the youngest college athlete who is the up-and-coming heir to America's first football dynasty, the Manning family, whose former football players have a combined net worth of over half a billion dollars.

His narrative and NIL power secret are to be cautious, patient, and loyal. He has cautiously avoided short-sighted NIL deals that might discount his true value and diminish his overall brand. He has also cautiously avoided injury, which might improve his chances of playing in the NFL. He has patiently waited for his turn to shine at UT, starting out as the second-string quarterback. Furthermore, he is showing the well-regarded virtue of loyalty by not jumping ship for a better deal at another university via the Transfer Portal. His narrative is a unique one because, like Bronny James, he is a member of a sports dynasty that he can inherit and contribute to. That legacy goes beyond sports and will likely include being a nationally recognized spokesperson, commentator, or podcast blogger following the lead of the $100 million podcast deal of the Kelce Brothers dynasty with Amazon's Wondery.[82]

Further Reading

Aaron Raley, *Is EA Sports Leaving Texas QB Arch Manning off Cover of College Football 26?*, Sports Illustrated (Mar. 13, 2025), https://www.si.com/college/texas/football/is-ea-sports-leaving-texas-qb-arch-manning-off-cover-of-college-football-26-01jp8by9j1rr.

Arch Manning Stays Grounded under Red Bull's Wings, Boardroom (Jan. 30, 2025), https://boardroom.tv/arch-manning-red-bull-texas-longhorns-football-nil/.

Lars Anderson, The Mannings: The Fall and Rise of a Football Family (2016).

Mark Ribowsky, In the Name of the Father: Family, Football, and the Manning Dynasty (2018).

Endnotes

1. Trey Luerssen, *Arch Manning's NIL Status—Power Plays, Charity and Controversy*, Longhorns Wire (Aug. 24, 2024), https://longhornswire.usatoday.com/2024/08/24/arch-mannings-nil-status-controversy-texas-longhorns/.

2. Chris Ndetei, Peris Walubengo, & Kevin Omuya, *The Manning Family's Net Worth: Who Is the Wealthiest Manning?*, YEN (updated Jan. 20, 2025), https://yen.com.gh/facts-lifehacks/201291-manning-family-net-worth-who-wealthiest-manning/.
3. *Arch Manning—Texas NIL Deals, Net Worth, Player Information*, College Net Worth (Dec. 20, 2024), https://www.collegenetworth.com/arch-manning-texas/.
4. *On3 NIL Valuations*, On3 (updated July 23, 2025); Mustafa Gatollari, *What Are Arch Manning's NIL Earnings, and Will They Go Up after His Explosive Five-Touchdown Game?*, MSN (Sept. 19, 2024), https://www.on3.com/nil/rankings/player/nil-valuations/; https://www.msn.com/en-us/sports/nfl/what-are-arch-manning-s-nil-earnings-and-will-they-go-up-after-his-explosive-five-touchdown-game/ar-AA1qP5GJ; SK Desk, *How MuchIs Arch Manning Nil Deal Worth in 2025?*, sportskeeda (Jan. 9, 2025), https://www.sportskeeda.com/college-football/arch-manning-nil-deal-worth.
5. *Id.*
6. *Id.*
7. Zach Ragan, *Arch Manning Details Relationship with Peyton and Eli; Reveals How often He Talks with His Famous Uncles*, AZ Sports (Dec. 31, 2023), https://atozsports.com/nashville/arch-manning-news-peyton-eli-texas-tennessee-ole-miss-football/.
8. Eric Arnould, *Brand Dynasty: Managing Charismatic Legitimacy over Time*, Taylor & Francis (Sept. 15, 2022), https://www.tandfonline.com/doi/full/10.1080/0267257X.2022.2120059; Joshua Frick, *What Legacy Brands Can Teach Business Leaders*, Forbes (Apr. 23, 2024), https://www.forbes.com/councils/forbesbusinesscouncil/2024/04/23/what-legacy-brands-can-teach-business-leaders/.
9. Teddy Ricketson, *Why Peyton Manning Is Hosting the 2024 CMA Awards with Luke Bryan and Lainey Wilson*, Sporting News (Nov. 20, 2024), https://www.sportingnews.com/us/nfl/news/why-peyton-manning-hosting-2024-cma-awards/4041b8caa356d4b706c7dce8.
10. *Arch Manning—Texas NIL Deals, Net Worth, Player Information*, College Net Worth (Dec. 20, 2024), https://www.collegenetworth.com/arch-manning-texas/.
11. *See On3 NIL Valuations*, On3 (updated July 22, 2025); Mustafa Gatollari, *What Are Arch Manning's NIL Earnings, and Will They Go Up After His Explosive Five-Touchdown Game?*, MSN (Sept. 19, 2024), https://www.on3.com/nil/rankings/player/nil-valuations/; https://www.msn.com/en-us/sports/nfl/what-are-arch-manning-s-nil-earnings-and-will-they-go-up-after-his-explosive-five-touchdown-game/ar-AA1qP5GJ; SK Desk, *How Much Is Arch Manning Nil Deal Worth in 2025?*, sportskeeda (Jan. 9, 2025), https://www.sportskeeda.com/college-football/arch-manning-nil-deal-worth.
12. Justin Birnbaum, *With His $700 Million Deal, Shohei Ohtani Is Set to Become MLB's All-Time Earnings Leader*, Forbes (updated Dec. 9, 2023), https://www.forbes.com/sites/justinbirnbaum/2023/12/09/with-his-700-million-deal-shohei-ohtani-is-set-to-become-mlbs-all-time-earnings-leader/.
13. Dan Freedman, *Juan Soto's $765 Million Contract with the Mets Has a Ton of Extras*, Forbes (Dec. 14, 2024), https://www.forbes.com/sites/danfreedman/2024/12/14/juan-sotos-765-million-contract-with-the-mets-has-a-ton-of-extras/.

14. Brett Knight, *The World's 10 Highest-Paid Athletes 2023,* FORBES (May 2, 2023), https://www.forbes.com/sites/brettknight/2023/05/02/the-worlds-10-highest-paid-athletes-2023/?sh=515ed8bcb156.
15. *Id.*
16. *Id.*
17. *Id.*
18. *See* Brett Knight, *The World's 10 Highest-Paid Athletes 2023,* FORBES (May 2, 2023), https://www.forbes.com/sites/brettknight/2023/05/02/the-worlds-10-highest-paid-athletes-2023/?sh=515ed8bcb156.
19. Alex de Crespigny, *6 Largest Athlete Endorsement Deals in the Modern Era,* MAN OF MANY (updated Aug. 28, 2023), https://manofmany.com/entertainment/sport/athlete-endorsement-deals.
20. *Id.*
21. Ahiza Garcia, *Cristiano Ronaldo Is the Third Athlete to Sign Nike "Lifetime" Deal,* CNN BUS. (Nov. 9, 2016), https://money.cnn.com/2016/11/09/news/companies/cristiano-ronaldo-nike-lifetime-contract/.
22. Tod Leonard, *Tiger Woods Reaches Another Mind-Blowing Milestone: $1 Billion in Net Worth, According to Forbes,* GOLF DIGEST (June 10, 2022), https://www.golfdigest.com/story/tiger-woods-reaches-1-billion-dollars-in-net-worth-according-to-forbes.
23. Scott Allen, *Roger Federer, a Longtime Nike Endorser, Begins Wimbledon Title Defense in Uniqlo Gear,* WASH. POST (July 2, 2018), https://www.washingtonpost.com/news/early-lead/wp/2018/07/02/roger-federer-a-longtime-nike-endorser-begins-wimbledon-title-defense-in-uniqlo-gear/.
24. *See* Alex de Crespigny, *6 Largest Athlete Endorsement Deals in the Modern Era,* MAN OF MANY (updated Aug. 28, 2023), https://manofmany.com/entertainment/sport/athlete-endorsement-deals.
25. Darren Rovell, *Lebron James Signs Lifetime Nike Deal,* ESPN (Dec. 7, 2015), https://www.espn.com/nba/story/_/id/14314807/lebron-james-signs-life-deal-nike.
26. *20 of Instagram's Highest Paid Stars in 2024,* INFLUENCER MARKETING HUB (July 22, 2024), https://influencermarketinghub.com/instagram-highest-paid/.
27. *Id.*
28. Steven Bertoni, *The Creator Economy Is Growing Fast—and Growing Up,* FORBES (updated Mar. 4, 2025), https://www.forbes.com/sites/stevenbertoni/2024/10/28/top-creators-2024-the-influencers-turning-buzz-into-billions/.
29. Allen Lee, *Who Is the Richest Kardashian? Ranking all their Net Worths,* MONEY, INC. (July 30, 2022), https://moneyinc.com/richest-kardashian/.
30. *Id.*
31. Mehera Bonner, *Wondering Who the Richest Kardashian Is? Here's a Ranking of their Family's Net Worths,* COSMOPOLITAN (Feb. 8, 2025), https://www.cosmopolitan.com/entertainment/celebs/a60856506/who-is-richest-kardashian-family-net-worth/.
32. *See* Chris Ndetei, Peris Walubengo, & Kevin Omuya, *The Manning Family's Net Worth: Who Is the Wealthiest Manning?,* YEN (updated Jan, 20, 2025), https://yen.com.gh/facts-lifehacks/201291-manning-family-net-worth-who-wealthiest-manning/.

33. *Id. See also* Dan Western, *The 50 Richest NFL Players in the World*, WEALTHY GORILLA (Jan. 1, 2024), https://wealthygorilla.com/richest-nfl-players/.
34. *Id.*
35. Ross Dellenger, *All Eyes on Arch Manning to Extend Family's QB Dynasty*, SPORTS ILLUSTRATED (Feb. 11, 2022), https://www.si.com/high-school/2020/02/11/arch-manning-next-generation-eli-peyton.
36. Steve Wiltfong, *Arch Manning Begins June Visit Swing this Weekend at Clemson*, 247SPORTS (June 4, 2021), https://247sports.com/article/arch-manning-clemson-visit-dabo-swinney-brandon-streeter-166099600/; James Parks, *No. 1 2023 Recruit Arch Manning Set to Visit 4 Schools*, COLLEGE FOOTBALL HQ (Sept. 21, 2021), https://cfb-hq.com/2021/09/21/college-football-recruiting-arch-manning-georgia-visits-sec-schools/; Tyler Calvaruso, *Arch Manning Finishes June with Trips to Alabama and Georgia*, MSN (June 28, 2021), https://www.msn.com/en-us/sports/ncaafb/arch-manning-finishes-june-with-trips-to-alabama-and-georgia/ar-AALxUg4; Ethan Sears, *Arch Manning Makes Surprise Recruiting Visit to University of Virginia*, N.Y. POST (Apr. 9, 2022), https://nypost.com/2022/04/09/arch-manning-makes-surprise-visit-to-university-of-virginia/.
37. Pete Thamel, *QB Arch Manning, No. 1 Recruit in 2023 Class, Commits to Texas*, ESPN (June 23, 2022), https://www.espn.com/college-football/story/_/id/34136486/qb-arch-manning-no-1-recruit-2023-class-commits-texas; Arch Manning (@ArchManning) X, https://x.com/archmanning/status/1540005818619334656 (last accessed Mar. 14, 2025); Meghan Overdeep, *It's Official: Arch Manning Signs Letter of Intent, Commits to Texas*, SOUTHERN LIVING (Dec. 21, 2022), https://www.facebook.com/SouthernLiving/posts/in-his-four-years-at-isidore-newman-high-school-arch-broke-elis-school-record-fo/10159270895206463/; Sam Khan Jr., *Arch Manning Commits to University of Texas*, ATHLETIC, N.Y. TIMES (June 23, 2022), https://www.nytimes.com/athletic/4174824/2022/06/23/arch-manning-commits-to-university-of-texas/.
38. RJ Young, *Reggie Bush and Arch Manning: A Lesson in NIL and the Right to Choose*, FOX SPORTS (Apr. 25, 2024), https://www.foxsports.com/stories/college-football/reggie-bush-and-arch-manning-a-lesson-in-nil-and-the-right-to-choose.
39. Pete Nakos, *Texas Quarterback Arch Manning Inks First NIL Deal in Multi-Year Partnership with Panini*, ON3 (July 25, 2023), https://www.on3.com/nil/news/texas-quarterback-arch-manning-inks-first-nil-deal-in-multi-year-partnership-with-panini/.
40. *Panini America Signs Arch Manning to First NIL Partnership with Exclusive Autograph Trading Card Agreement with Charitable Component*, PANINI, https://docs.google.com/document/d/1Ls3R_ytDO2bWKzJsNJnlCLITKbeSIjyc/edit#heading=h.30j0zll (last accessed Mar. 14, 2025).
41. Cam Smith, *EA Sports' Arch Manning NIL Deal Is Steal of the Year (For EA Sports)*, SPORTING NEWS (July 9, 2024), https://www.sportingnews.com/us/ncaa-football/sec/news/ea-sports-arch-manning-nil-deal-steal-year-ea-sports/1a8687cfee4a24b10ee9ce1d#:~:text=As%20reported%20everywhere%2C%20the%20youngest,to%20the%20resurrected%20video%20game. *See Gatollari*, *supra* note 4.

42. David Cobb, *Texas QB Arch Manning Took 'Zero Money from NIL' Despite High-Profile Commitment, Says Steve Sarkisian,* CBS Sports (Apr. 27, 2023), https://www.cbssports.com/college-football/news/texas-qb-arch-manning-took-zero-money-from-nil-despite-high-profile-commitment-says-steve-sarkisian/.
43. Trey Luerssen, *Already No. 1 NIL Earner in College Sports, Arch Manning Inks New Clothing Deal* (April 9, 2025), https://longhornswire.usatoday.com/story/sports/college/longhorns/football/2025/04/09/no-1-nil-earner-arch-manning-signs-big-new-deal/83015741007/.
44. *See On3 NIL Valuations,* On3 (updated July 22, 2025); Mustafa Gatollari, *What Are Arch Manning's NIL Earnings, and Will They Go Up After His Explosive Five-Touchdown Game?,* MSN (Sept. 19, 2024), https://www.on3.com/nil/rankings/player/nil-valuations/; https://www.msn.com/en-us/sports/nfl/what-are-arch-manning-s-nil-earnings-and-will-they-go-up-after-his-explosive-five-touchdown-game/ar-AA1qP5GJ; SK Desk, *How Much Is Arch Manning Nil Deal Worth in 2025?,* sportskeeda (Jan. 9, 2025), https://www.sportskeeda.com/college-football/arch-manning-nil-deal-worth.
45. *See NIL College Rules,* On3, https://www.on3.com/nil/laws/college/ (last accessed Dec. 10, 2024); Braly Keller, *High School NIL: State-By-State Regulations for Name, Image and Likeness Rights,* Opendorse (Sept. 16, 2024), https://biz.opendorse.com/blog/nil-high-school/. Rick Sutter, *Current High School NIL Rules in Each of the 50 States (Plus D.C.),* USA Today (July 25, 2024), https://www.usatodayhss.com/story/sports/high-school/2024/07/25/high-school-nil-rules-in-each-of-the-50-states-plus-d-c/76246939007/.
46. *Id.*
47. *NIL High School Rules,* On3, https://www.on3.com/nil/laws/high-school/ (last accessed Mar. 14, 2025).
48. *See* Rick Sutter, *Current High School NIL Rules in Each of the 50 States (Plus D.C.),* USA Today (July 25, 2024), https://www.usatodayhss.com/story/sports/high-school/2024/07/25/high-school-nil-rules-in-each-of-the-50-states-plus-d-c/76246939007/.
49. Florida High School Athletic Assoc., *Board of Directors Meeting—Agenda Item,* FHSAA (June 3–4, 2024), https://fhsaa.com/documents/2024/5/29/35_38.pdf.
50. Brandon Allison, *NIL Pros and Cons | the College Game Is Changed Forever,* SportsEpreneur (Mar. 29, 2024), https://sportsepreneur.com/nil-pros-and-cons/.
51. Elizabeth Heubeck, *High School Athletes Can Profit from Brand Deals: What that Means for Schools,* Educ. Week (Aug. 6, 2024), https://www.edweek.org/leadership/high-school-athletes-can-profit-from-brand-deals-what-that-means-for-schools/2024/08.
52. *Khaby Lame Net Worth,* Celebrity Net Worth, https://www.celebritynetworth.com/richest-celebrities/richest-comedians/khaby-lame-net-worth/ (last accessed Mar. 14, 2024).
53. California Interscholastic Federation, *CIF Constitution and Bylaws,* https://www.cifstate.org/governance/constitution/index, Ca. Interscholastic Federation (last accessed Mar. 15, 2025).

54. *High School Athletes Are Getting Major Endorsement Deals following State Law Changes,* CBS News (Nov. 30, 2022), https://www.cbsnews.com/news/high-school-athletes-nil-deals-name-image-likeness-six-figures/.
55. *Id.*
56. Darian Kelly, *Nike's NIL Deals: Full List of Nike High School and College Athletes,* Bus. of College Sports (July 21, 2023), https://businessofcollegesports.com/name-image-likeness/nikes-nil-deals-full-list-of-nike-high-school-and-college-athletes/.
57. *Id.*
58. *Id.*
59. *Id.*
60. Kenneth Teape, *High School Tennis Star Signing Two Worldwide NIL Deals with Major Companies,* MSN (Nov. 22, 2024), https://www.msn.com/en-us/sports/other/high-school-tennis-star-signing-two-worldwide-nil-deals-with-major-companies/ar-AA1uApHG?ocid=BingNewsSerp.
61. Andy, *Anna Frey Biography,* Biography World (Oct. 24, 2024), https://thebiographyworld.com/anna-frey-biography/.
62. William Murphy & Ian Alves, *Point-Counterpoint: Should High School Athletes Get NIL Deals?,* Sentinel (Mar. 2, 2024), https://www.thesentinel.com/communities/point-counterpoint-should-high-school-athletes-get-nil-deals/article_ae5997aa-d8e7-11ee-9e98-9372f10a6ae2.html; https://sportsepreneur.com/nil-pros-and-cons/.
63. Jeremy Crabtree, *Florida State Board of Education Approves NIL Deals for High School Athletes,* On3 (July 24, 2024), https://www.on3.com/nil/news/florida-state-board-of-education-approves-nil-deals-for-high-school-athletes/.
64. Jeremy Crabtree, *Where Is NIL Prohibited for High School Athletes?,* On3 (July 7, 2024), https://www.on3.com/nil/news/where-is-nil-name-image-likeness-prohibited-for-high-school-athletes-hs-football-basketball/.
65. *See* Jeremy Crabtree, *Florida State Board of Education Approves NIL Deals for High School Athletes,* On3 (July 24, 2024), https://www.on3.com/nil/news/florida-state-board-of-education-approves-nil-deals-for-high-school-athletes/.
66. *Id.*
67. *Id.*
68. *Id.*
69. Troy Brock, *College Athletes' Average NIL Earnings Shockingly Low Despite Headline Deals,* Sports Illustrated (Dec. 30, 2024), https://www.si.com/fannation/name-image-likeness/nil-news/college-athlete-average-nil-earnings-shockingly-low-despite-headline-deals.
70. *See* Elizabeth Heubeck, *High School Athletes Can Profit from Brand Deals: What That Means for Schools,* Educ. Week (Aug. 6, 2024), https://www.edweek.org/leadership/high-school-athletes-can-profit-from-brand-deals-what-that-means-for-schools/2024/08.
71. Robert Boland, *NIL in High School: A Parents' Guide,* Culture in Sports (Sept. 13, 2022), https://cultureinsports.com/nil-in-high-school-a-parents-guide/; David Hitz, *Choosing Your Course: A Handbook for Securing NIL Contracts in High*

School Athletic, ATHLETE NARRATIVE (Apr. 3, 2024), https://athletenarrative.com/blog/choosing-your-course-a-handbook-for-securing-nil-contracts-in-high-school-athletics/#:~:text=High%20school%20athletes%20should%20learn,deals%20for%20using%20their%20image.

72. *See On3 NIL Valuations*, ON3 (July 22, 2025); Mustafa Gatollari, *What Are Arch Manning's NIL Earnings, and Will They Go Up After His Explosive Five-Touchdown Game?*, MSN (Sept. 19, 2024), https://www.on3.com/nil/rankings/player/nil-valuations/; https://www.msn.com/en-us/sports/nfl/what-are-arch-manning-s-nil-earnings-and-will-they-go-up-after-his-explosive-five-touchdown-game/ar-AA1qP5GJ; SK Desk, *How Much Is Arch Manning Nil Deal Worth in 2025?*, SPORTSKEEDA (Jan. 9, 2025), https://www.sportskeeda.com/college-football/arch-manning-nil-deal-worth.
73. *Id.*
74. Max Olson, *Behind the Scenes of Arch Manning's First Start at Texas*, ESPN (Sept. 22, 2024), https://www.espn.com/college-football/story/_/id/41371734/texas-qb-arch-manning-first-start-scenes. *See* Mustafa Gatollari, *What Are Arch Manning's NIL Earnings, and Will They Go Up After His Explosive Five-Touchdown Game?*, MSN (Sept. 19, 2024), https://www.on3.com/nil/rankings/player/nil-valuations/; https://www.msn.com/en-us/sports/nfl/what-are-arch-manning-s-nil-earnings-and-will-they-go-up-after-his-explosive-five-touchdown-game/ar-AA1qP5GJ.
75. Kevin Borba, *Texas QB Arch Manning Says He's Just a "Normal Guy" Amid Media Frenzy*, ATHLON SPORTS (Dec. 31, 2023), https://athlonsports.com/college-football/big-12/texas-qb-arch-manning-says-hes-just-a-normal-guy-amid-media-frenzy.
76. RJ Young, *Can Texas QB Arch Manning Live Up to the Expectations That Come with His Name?*, FOX SPORTS (Apr. 3, 2024), https://www.foxsports.com/stories/college-football/can-texas-qb-arch-manning-live-up-to-the-expectations-that-come-with-his-name.
77. Sarah Effress, *Will Arch Manning Transfer? What Texas QB Has Said About Staying with Longhorns for 2025*, SPORTING NEWS (Jan. 8, 2025), https://www.sportingnews.com/us/ncaa-football/news/arch-manning-transfer-texas-qb-longhorns-2025/4d65a3bd65d8628f4c5c2414; Evan Massey, *NIL Star and Texas Longhorns Quarterback Projected to Eye 2025 Transfer Move*, SPORTS ILLUSTRATED (Dec. 3, 2024), https://www.si.com/fannation/name-image-likeness/nil-news/nil-star-and-texas-longhorns-quarterback-projected-to-eye-2025-transfer-move.
78. Zach Bachar, *Arch Manning Explains Decision Not to Transfer from Texas with Quinn Ewers Being QB1*, BLEACHER REPORT (July 8, 2024), https://bleacherreport.com/articles/10127588-arch-manning-explains-decision-not-to-transfer-from-texas-with-quinn-ewers-being-qb1.
79. Austin American-Statesman, *10 Minutes with Arch Manning: Texas QB Answers Questions at Longhorns Media Day Before CFP Semifinal*, YOUTUBE (Dec. 30, 2023), https://www.youtube.com/watch?v=g3KOZ54_stE; Luke Easterling, *When Will Arch Manning Be Eligible for the NFL Draft?*, ATHLON SPORTS (Oct. 14, 2024), https://athlonsports.com/nfl/arch-manning-nfl-draft-eligible-texas-longhorns-college-football.

80. Jonathan Adams, *Texas Star Arch Manning Could Eventually Replace Former $242 Million Pro Bowl QB*, MSN (Nov. 30, 2024), https://www.msn.com/en-us/sports/nfl/texas-star-arch-manning-could-eventually-replace-former-242-million-pro-bowl-qb/ar-AA1v2YQs?ocid=BingNewsVerp; *See* Easterling, *supra* note 78.
81. Teddy Ricketson, *Arch Manning's Family Tree: Meet Texas QB's Dad, Mom and His Relation to Peyton, Eli Manning*, SPORTING NEWS (Jan. 8, 2025), https://www.sportingnews.com/us/ncaa-football/news/arch-manning-family-tree-texas-qb-dad-mom-peyton-eli-manning/ee0b22a52cc6221017ac3eaa.
82. Conor Murray, *Jason and Travis Kelce Sign Reported $100 Million Podcast Deal with Amazon's Wondery*, FORBES (Aug. 27, 2024), https://www.forbes.com/sites/conormurray/2024/08/27/jason-and-travis-kelce-sign-reported-100-million-podcast-deal-with-amazons-wondery/.

7

Shedeur Sanders: Maximizing One's Value

I definitely love NIL, but it's pros and cons to it though. Cons is like you gotta, you gotta like, don't feel like you made it already. You know, when you able to get whatever you want at anytime in life, like, a lot of things don't really interest you no more. So you gotta really get down to the core of what makes you happy.

—Shedeur Sanders[1]

OVERVIEW

Shedeur Sanders possesses both stellar athletic talent and charisma. In December 2024, he had a projected NIL valuation of $6.5 million, the highest of any college athlete, with a social media following of over 2 million people.[2] Consequently, he is earning millions of dollars in NIL deals, including landing a Nike endorsement deal, reportedly the first for a college football player.[3]

Sanders has a unique narrative and teaches an invaluable lesson. His career trajectory is as meteoric as his athletic performance is record-breaking. He is a young Black man, born and raised in Texas, who set athletic records and broke through NIL barriers during his first two years of college at Jackson State University ("Jackson State"), which is a Historically Black College or University ("HBCU"). In 2022, Sanders made a strategic decision to transfer to the University of Colorado ("Colorado"), where he became their lead quarterback. In December 2024, Sanders was predicted to be the No. 1 draft pick in the 2025 NFL draft due to his phenomenal leadership and quarterbacking skills.[4] Reflecting his success, in 2024, his estimated net worth was reportedly $3 million.[5]

Sanders's love of the game of football, combined with his athletic skills, power of positivity, and resilience in overcoming obstacles, has led him to fame and fortune. This chapter illustrates how his love of the game resulted in outstanding athletic achievements and lucrative NIL deals. It further demonstrates how Sanders incorporated the power of positivity to achieve his goals. Notwithstanding positivity, Sanders's success has also required grit and resilience, particularly as he battled through severe physical injury and exhibited the courage to face future injury, which is endemic to playing football. His story is one for the ages.

LOVE OF THE GAME

One road to college NIL millions is perhaps both the easiest and the hardest: knowing what really matters to you. In plain language, discovering why God put you on planet Earth and knowing what your role is in glorifying God. Such a discovery is often very elusive, often requires going down painful paths, and, for many people, ends up in frustration and failure. For Shedeur Sanders, the journey demanded knowing what matters, what makes you happy, and what value you bring to others. It included both planned and unexpected twists and turns, much like so many of the NIL college millionaires described in this book. What follows next illustrates how Sanders navigated through key decision-making points in his life to achieve sports fame and NIL fortune.

A Meteoric Rise to Stardom

Sanders's journey to becoming a college NIL millionaire started off relatively slowly but shot up like a powerful rocket ship to NIL million-dollar deals. He was born in Tyler, Texas, and attended Trinity Christian School in Cedar Hill, Texas. Similar to the other NIL college millionaires that are showcased in this book, Sanders was an outstanding athlete in high school.[6] He had a four-star rating as a top-10 prospect in Texas, where he reportedly ended his high school career with 12,498 passing yards and 166 passing touchdowns, for an average of 3,124 yards and 42 touchdowns each season.[7] Consequently, in 2020, he reportedly received over 25 athletic scholarship offers, including from Alabama, Florida State, LSU, and Oregon. He initially committed to play for coach Willie Taggart at Florida Atlantic University ("Florida Atlantic") in Boca Raton.[8]

During the next two years, 2020–2022, Sanders's college athletic career would exhibit how his love of the game of football, married with the guidance of his mentor and father, Deion Sanders, led to two unpredicted, life-changing career moves. The first came in the winter of 2020–2021, when Sanders decided to bypass playing for Florida Atlantic and instead enrolled at Jackson State, where his father had been named their head football coach.[9] If he were not attuned to his destiny and being faithful to his love of the game, he might have resented that move. That is because for the spring 2021 season, he was ruled ineligible to play, as that football season had replaced the fall 2020 season due to the COVID-19 pandemic.[10] In his truly humble and always willing to learn and grow personality, Sanders reflected on being sidelined for his first college season: "The thing that was a blessing was that I was able to see what the teams were doing to us as an offense . . . I really gained a lot of knowledge just sitting back watching."[11]

In the fall of 2021, his freshman year at Jackson State, Sanders's athletic career reached the next level of success. In his first college season, he played with consistent, stellar, record-breaking performance, passing for 3,231 yards, with 30 touchdowns and only eight interceptions.[12] This led to one of what would be many subsequent breakout moments: being named the Southwestern Athletic Conference ("SWAC") Freshman of the Year.[13] Further, to add to his national recognition, he received the Jerry Rice Award as the most outstanding freshman in the NCAA Division I Football Championship Subdivision, becoming the first player from an HBCU to win the award.[14]

Sanders continued to perform at the highest level in his second season at Jackson State, where he completed 70.6% of his pass attempts for 3,732 yards, with 40 touchdowns and only six interceptions. He left his mark at Jackson State, establishing himself as one of the best players in college football.[15] He broke Jackson State records with 40 passing touchdowns and 344 completions. In his two years as the starting quarterback, he completed 616 of 901 passes for 6,983 yards and 70 touchdowns with just 14 interceptions, while adding 157 yards and nine rushing touchdowns. Consequently, he was named the SWAC Offensive Player of the Year,[16] another milestone in his athletic career.

This would lead to the second of the most significant decision moments in Sanders's career. In December 2022, with his playing for Jackson State in the 2022 Celebration Bowl, Sanders entered the NCAA Transfer Portal, which allowed him to seek offers to transfer from Jackson State and play for a different school.[17] His decision to seek a transfer likely resulted from the announcement that his mentor and father, Deion Sanders, had accepted the head football coach's position at Colorado.[18] Consequently, Sanders transferred to Colorado and was named as its starting quarterback for fall 2023.[19] While his award-winning performance at Jackson State was his breakout moment, Sanders's talents were about to be challenged on the big stage, as Colorado was then a member of the highly competitive NCAA Pac-12 Conference, and announced that it would be joining the lucrative Big 12 Conference.[20]

Sanders's mettle was going to be tested in two ways, one as to his athletic abilities and the other being the strength of his character. Certainly, it was stressful to be moving from a low-profile football conference at Jackson State to a high-profile starting quarterback position at Colorado. In addition, prior to his playing for Colorado, some critics claimed that his being named as the starting quarterback was undeserved and was merely a part of the negotiated terms by his father to become the head football coach at Colorado.[21] Notwithstanding the enormous pressures he must have felt, Sanders would rise to the occasion and show the critics wrong. In his first game at Colorado, he broke a school passing record, having completed 38 of 47 pass attempts for 510 yards.[22] In addition, he broke several other Colorado records with his stellar play.[23] He started and played in 11 games during the 2023 season and was 298 of 430 (.693) for 3,230 yards and 31 touchdowns with just three interceptions.[24] He was the only quarterback nationally with more than six touchdowns; he had 11, with no interceptions in the fourth quarter when he was 67 of 92 (.728) passing for 1,039 yards with those 11 touchdowns and no interceptions.[25] Over the 2023 football season, he finished the season with 3,230 passing yards, 27 passing touchdowns, only three interceptions, and four rushing touchdowns, in 11 out of 12 games, as he sustained an injury that precluded his playing in the last game of the season.[26] Consequently, his 2023 stellar performance was evidenced with several coveted national college football awards, including being named by the Associated Press as the Pac-12 Newcomer of the Year, among other awards.[27]

During his second year at Colorado, which was the 2024 football season, Sanders showed consistency in his record-breaking performance and was again celebrated with national player awards.[28] He finished that season with 4,134 in passing yards, 37 touchdowns, and only 10 interceptions.[29] With outstanding athletic performance comes coveted national awards. Consequently, in December 2024, he was named the Big 12 Offensive Player of the Year for 2024.[30] Further, he was a highly regarded contender for the Heisman Trophy.[31] In December 2024, he was named the All-Big 12 Conference's Offensive Player of the Year.[32] In December 2024, he also won the Johnny Unitas Golden Arm Award, given annually to the top upperclassman quarterback in college football, judged on accomplishments on the field as well as on their character, scholastic achievement, and leadership qualities.[33]

NIL Fortune

With fame, such as record-breaking, award-winning athletic performance, comes NIL fortune. This is certainly true for Sanders. As previously mentioned, he has over 2 million social media followers, with the highest NIL valuation in On3's December 2024 report.[34] Further, it clearly pays to be a superstar for one of the leading teams in a top NCAA football conference, the Big 12. However, unlike some of his contemporaries, such as Olivia Dunne and Bryce Underwood, Sanders's NIL deals were slow to come. There are none reported while he attended high school; perhaps, at that time, NIL law was just being developed to grant players their right to benefit from their NIL.

Just to be clear, a NIL deal is a private transaction between a player and a third party, not the players' college, although some states require the player to report their NIL deals to their college. As a result, we must rely on various news sources to piece together what deals any college athlete has. Further, those reports are sometimes inaccurate and typically do not provide any details on the deals, such as for how much money and under what terms. With that in mind, the following information as to Sanders's NIL deals is what has been collected from various published reports.[35]

Booster-Collective NIL Deals

Recall that there are different types of NIL deals, one of which is a booster-collective deal. In that type of NIL deal, college boosters, who are often wealthy, influential alumni and community leaders, pool funds to contract services with a given player to induce them to play for a particular school. These types of deals compose the greatest percentage of NIL deals,[36] yet are controversial because they arguably violate the NCAA rule against pay-to-play.[37] Further, many have criticized these deals for their tremendous cost to colleges and because they create an unlevel playing field between rich schools and those not so. Again, as NIL deals are private transactions, we do not know if they exist, and, if so, their terms. Obviously, many of these collective deals are made public when they are announced to the public, such as in the case of Bryce Underwood's deal with a University of Michigan-related collective.[38] Further, some have been made public because of deals gone bad or are subject to lawsuits or NCAA investigations.[39]

Relative to Sanders and booster-collective NIL deals, there are no reports that claim that Sanders had signed any NIL endorsement deals while in his high school, unlike Bryce Underwood, who signed an NIL deal while a high school student. That is likely because the laws that allow players to benefit from their NIL were just being enacted. In addition, there are no reports that Sanders received any NIL deals to play for the Jackson State Tigers. Like many schools of every background that have few, if any, wealthy alumni and other boosters, Jackson State is on a different, unequal playing field compared to well-funded schools like Colorado or Michigan when it comes to booster-collective NIL deals.[40] However, there are reportedly a few (yet growing number of) HBCUs that have collectives of boosters who are enticing athletes to play for them,[41] such as South Carolina State University.[42]

Compared to Jackson State, Colorado boosters have lots of collective money to transact NIL deals that entice a player to play there.[43] One news report, showing deals from July 2021 to July 2024, concluded that "most of the NIL money paid to Colorado football players has come from big brands . . . plus the school's collective and SMAC Productions. No program's athletes have come close to earning as much."[44] In March 2024, Colorado announced a new collective, the 5430 Alliance, which is a "unified, streamlined NIL collective that will support 350 Colorado student-athletes across all 11 sport programs."[45] Colorado noted that this is only one of several programs to assist their college athletes with NIL opportunities, others include "the Buffs NIL Exchange, where businesses can work directly with CU athletes to facilitate NIL deals tailored for them, as well as player merchandise opportunities through the Colorado NIL Store and the Fanatics Player Merchandise."[46]

While Colorado has lots of NIL dollars to spend, it is unclear whether Sanders signed any NIL deals with a collective to play for Colorado, as such a deal is not a public document. However, one news source reported that Sanders had an NIL deal with 5430 Alliance, a collective for Colorado athletics.[47] Notwithstanding, in 2023, Sanders reportedly jokingly stated that he would stay and play an additional year at Colorado for $10 million.[48]

Brand Endorsement NIL Deals

Another type of NIL deal involves brand endorsements, such as promoting Nike shoes. As to this type of NIL deal, Sanders had some notable success, despite playing for an HBCU, such member schools noticeably have not received much attention when it comes to brand endorsement deals.[49] Just to explain and better understand the importance of Sanders having received millions of NIL dollars while playing for Jackson State. Like many schools with various racial compositions, NIL deals often reflect the amount of media revenue a school receives and the national profile of its athletes. Relative to HBCUs, in September 2023, the Biden-Harris Administration reported that HBCUs have been underfunded by more than $13 billion over the past three decades.[50] This discrepancy, documented in letters to 16 state governors, highlighted the significant resource disparities between HBCUs and predominantly white institutions.[51] Such a tremendous, historic underfunding of HBCUs has resulted in unequal athletic programs and facilities.

As for HBCUs, the paucity of NIL deals for their students mirrors the many notable, yet disproportionate representation of HBCU students who eventually play for professional leagues, such as the NFL. On the one hand, HBCUs have a rich legacy of producing NFL talent, providing a critical source for NFL talent. Schools such as Florida A&M University, Grambling State University, and Jackson State have NFL Hall of Famers, including Deacon Jones (South Carolina State University and Mississippi Valley State University), Pro Football Hall of Famer; Steve McNair (Alcorn State University), Most Valuable Player quarterback and NFL star; Walter Payton (Jackson State), running back for the Chicago Bears; Jerry Rice (Mississippi Valley State), widely considered the greatest wide receiver in NFL history; and Shannon

Sharpe (Savannah State University), Hall of Fame tight end and prominent sports commentator.[52] However, with coaches like Deion Sanders (previously at Jackson State), some HBCUs are reversing this trend by attracting top talent. Notwithstanding, many highly talented Black athletes never reach HBCUs or transfer later, as many of them, like Sanders, are heavily recruited and attend elite, white private and public high schools throughout the country.[53] Additionally, as in the case with Sanders, some HBCU athletes transfer to larger Division I schools for greater exposure, better facilities, and higher chances of making it to the NFL. Despite these challenges, players from HBCUs have shown exceptional resilience and endurance, thriving in the NFL against the odds. They continue to provide opportunities for NFL hopefuls, and with greater attention to their programs, the number of players making it to the professional level could grow, along with their NIL deals.

Shedeur Sanders is one of the few HBCU athletes who garnered significant NIL deals, having signed NIL endorsement deals worth over $1 million during his time at Jackson State. In September 2021, while still playing for Jackson State, Sanders reportedly signed an NIL brand endorsement deal with Beats by Dre, a consumer audio products manufacturer that was founded in 2006 by hip-hop artist, record producer, music executive, and actor Dr. Dre and record company executive Jimmy Lovine.[54] Further, in December 2021, Sanders reportedly signed an NIL deal with Tom Brady's apparel company, Brady.[55] Additionally, in January 2022, Sanders reportedly signed an NIL deal with Gatorade, becoming the first player from an HBCU to do so.[56]

With his transfer to Colorado in December 2022 and his award-winning performance there, Sanders's NIL deals have grown exponentially. Although the dates of the signing of the following deals are uncertain, they appear to have been signed after he transferred to Colorado. On August 28, 2024, while a celebrated senior at Colorado, Sanders reportedly secured a significant footwear and apparel deal with Nike,[57] which is allegedly Nike's first NIL deal with a college football player.[58] In addition, he reportedly has NIL deals with Mercedes-Benz, Under Armour, Google, AT&T, Smoothie King, Topps, PLB Sports and Entertainment, Oikos, Active Black, KFC, Urban Outfitters, and other brands.[59] In addition to his existing NIL deals, Sanders stated that he is particularly interested in a NIL partnership with luxury Swiss watch brand Audemars Piguet, a product that he has already endorsed for free on his online social media postings.[60] Further, putting his toe into the world of entertainment, in May 2024, Sanders released a music single, "Perfect Timing," singing about money and luxurious items, mentioning a Mercedes Maybach and an Audemars Piguet watch.[61]

In a related and eye-catching NIL news report, in 2024, Sanders reportedly gifted his offensive lineman, Jordan Seaton, a luxurious Mercedes Maybach, with a price tag nearing $200,000, to thank Seaton for his impeccable offensive-line protection that season.[62] Sanders clearly has a promising sports and NIL future. In 2024, he was predicted to be the No. 1 draft pick in the 2025 NFL draft and could land a contract worth over $40 million dollars.[63]

Hence, Sanders's love of the game of football has resulted in outstanding athletic achievements and lucrative NIL deals. However, love of the game alone will not ensure NIL success. Beyond a mission, a would-be NIL college millionaire needs to adopt Sanders's power of positivity.

POWER OF POSITIVITY

Knowing what makes you happy is the foundation for building a successful, meaningful, and fulfilling career, including for NIL college millionaires. However, understanding why God put you on the planet does not guarantee success. It takes more than knowing one's mission in life, their reason for living. To achieve one's mission, one must embrace the power of positivity. Positivity is the engine that powers one through the hard work needed and the adversity encountered along the way to success. Sanders's positivity is evidenced in his use of two key, distinct strategies: finding the right mentor and emulating the greatest of all time in one's profession. What follows is how Sanders embraced positivity through following the advice of a mentor and emulating the best of the best in his profession to achieve his career goals.

A Righteous Mentor

Once a person becomes self-aware of their mission in life, what really matters, it is critical to identify and enlist the guidance of a righteous mentor. Before describing the process of doing so, let's understand what is meant by a "righteous mentor." What I refer to as a righteous mentor is a person who has experience with their profession but also has the wisdom and integrity that promote positive values such as community, teamwork, faith, and family.

Perhaps, most importantly, from the start and throughout his career, Sanders has been coached and mentored by a legendary athlete and righteous mentor: his father, Deion Sanders, aka "Coach Prime." Incidentally, Deion won two Super Bowls, was enshrined in the Pro Football Hall of Fame, and played MLB, where he hit more than .500 in a World Series for the Atlanta Braves while playing with a broken bone in his foot.[64] This father-son, coach-mentor relationship is unique in sports history and is a hallmark of Sanders's success. It is an example of another father-son sports legacy, that of the golf phenom Tiger Woods and his son Charlie.[65] Sanders's special father-son nurturing relationship became obvious during his high school years at Trinity Christian School in Cedar Hill, Texas, where he benefitted from his father's mentorship as the school's offensive coordinator.[66] This special mentor relationship continued as the dynamic duo moved to Jackson State and, two years later, as they transferred to team up at Colorado. Clearly, Sanders's success was facilitated by his following the sage advice of his father-mentor. He obviously made the right choice when he chose to follow his father's lead.

Hence, Sanders, who became self-aware of his mission in life, then enrolled and followed the advice of a righteous mentor, who was his father and football coach, Deion Sanders. He also sought to emulate the best of the best in his profession.

The GOATs

In addition to following the advice of a righteous mentor, a would-be college NIL millionaire should study the career journeys of the Greatest of All Time ("GOATs") in their profession and emulate their best traits and learn from their weaknesses.

Sanders, with his multifaceted skills as a quarterback, has arrived on the college football scene during the era of the "super quarterback." A super quarterback is one who is highly versatile, who can scramble, rush, and tackle, as well as pass extraordinarily. Not to be misunderstood, over the years, the NFL, in its many years of operation, has seen some spectacular quarterbacks, including Tom Brady, Joe Montana, Peyton

Manning, Johnny Unitas, Otto Graham, and Drew Brees, who topped the NFL's 2019 "top 25 quarterbacks of all time" list.[67] Not surprisingly, there were only two Black quarterbacks on that list: Russell Wilson, who was listed at #18, and Warren Moon, who was listed at #22.[68] However, times have changed since 2019.

In 2024, Patrick Mahomes broke into the #4 spot on the USA Today's "10 greatest NFL quarterbacks of all time" list.[69] His rise to prominence began the era of what has been referred to as the "Mahomes Effect."

> The Mahomes Effect is the wide acceptance by coaches and players at every level of quarterbacks playing the position like Mahomes: free, wild, and even crazy at times.[70] Improvisation is now an accepted part of playing the position. If you can't throw sidearm, throw no-look, or throw a wrench in the opposition's plans with a split-second decision, you are not of this era. . . . The entire football mentality has changed to embrace what is called "off schedule" plays. That's the hip, industry term these days. "On schedule" is taking a three-, five-, or seven-step drop while surveying the field before ripping a throw. Off schedule is entertaining and fun—there's that word again—basically a football painting by abstractionist Jackson Pollock. Making it up as you go can be brilliant.[71]

With the ESPN 2024 NFL season leaders, a new breed of quarterback has emerged.[72] They are further examples of how the game has evolved, the role of the super quarterback. At the top of the list is Buffalo Bills' Josh Allen, followed by Baltimore Ravens' Lamar Jackson, Cincinnati Bengals' Joe Burrow, Washington Commanders' Jayden Daniels, Arizona Cardinals' Kyler Murray, and, of course, Kansas City Chiefs' Patrick Mahomes.[73] Parenthetically, six out of the top ten are African Americans. Clearly, over the last 20 years, there has been a rise in the Black quarterback. This revolution reached a new height with Super Bowl LVII, which marked the first time that both Super Bowl starting quarterbacks were Black: Patrick Mahomes started for the Kansas City Chiefs, while Jalen Hurts started for the Philadelphia Eagles.[74] So, what's the point? Not too long ago, there was a dearth of Black quarterbacks who played for the NFL.[75] Some Black leaders called foul and expressed their frustration and belief that this was due to racism.[76]

Notwithstanding, as college football has evolved, the role of the quarterback has expanded. As a result, currently, coaches are looking to the super quarterback, one who can run, block, and pass to win games, regardless of their skin color. Apparently, Sanders has studied the many quarterbacking styles of these super quarterbacks. When he was asked which NFL professional quarterback he most admired, he often spoke about how Tom Brady had been a mentor and noted that he saw similarities between their attributes.[77] By the way, there are reports that Sanders's admiration of Brady is mutual.[78]

In summary, Sanders, who became self-aware of what matters in his life and followed the advice of a righteous mentor, then studied and emulated the best qualities of the most accomplished professional NFL quarterbacks. Consequently, even with knowing one's mission in life and utilizing positivity, a would-be NIL college millionaire needs one additional character trait to succeed. That is grit, which is the perseverance and resilience to overcome adversity, particularly physical injury.

OVERCOMING ADVERSITY

In addition to knowing what makes you happy and embracing positivity, a would-be college NIL millionaire must have the grit to overcome adversity. College athletes, particularly ones who play football, are susceptible to the pain and disruption that come from sports-related physical injury. Some of those injuries can be serious, that is, life-threatening or debilitating. This truth compels us to examine how likely it is for a college athlete, particularly one who plays intercollegiate football, to be injured for sport-related activity. How might such a player respond to such an injury? And what effect does a severe injury have on a player's NIL deals?

This discussion explores several related topics: the physical risk of injury that college athletes, particularly football players, face; how physical injury, particularly suffered during postseason bowl games, can negatively impact a college football player's career, including their NIL deals; and how these matters are playing out for Sanders. Using Sanders's experience with a severe injury that shortened his 2023 football season, we examine what it means to have the grit needed to overcome adversity. His resilience and courage to play a sport that is fraught with the risk of severe physical injury is a lesson in what it takes to be a college NIL millionaire and how physical injury might negatively affect NIL deals.

Injuries, Resilience, and Courage

Unfortunately, physical injury is part and parcel of college sports, particularly football. A study by the Centers for Disease Control and Prevention ("CDC") estimated that there were about 210,700 injuries on average per year among the roughly 478,900 NCAA college athletes, between 2009 and 2014.[79] College sports, particularly football, can be especially dangerous to the physical and emotional health and wellbeing of the students. One study reported that 34 NCAA football players have died during football activities in the past 18 years; 27 nontraumatic deaths were reported in 2017, while six players died from trauma to the head or neck over the same time period.[80] Equally tragic, serious injuries that require securing long-term treatment, determining insurance coverage if available, and negotiating with health care providers are left to the resources and responsibility of the players, with possible few exceptions for the most sought-after players.[81] Consequently, anyone who plays college football should make themselves familiar with the incidence of physical injury, which can be life-threatening or debilitating. Notwithstanding, one study shows that college football players greatly underestimate the high level of concussion and other severe injuries due to participating in a sport.[82]

Further, reactions to injury, specifically season- or career-ending, can manifest in many different ways for college athletes, including depression, anxiety, and suicidal ideation.[83] In addition to being sidelined by injury, a college athlete, not limited to football, can experience near-death illness, such as the heart attack that Bronny James experienced.[84] Furthermore, it has been documented that college football players are encouraged to withstand pain, including through the use of prescription and non-prescription drugs, in order to continue to play for their college teams without compensation.[85] However, despite the risk, college athletes, particularly football players, can and do experience personal growth after an injury.[86]

This reality, that college football players do sustain multiple injuries, can have profound life-changing effects on their health and on their careers. That raises the question, "How, if at all, does physical injury negatively affect a NIL college millionaire's financial future?"

Sanders's Injuries and Resilience: Love of the Game

Like many who love to play the sport, Sanders has sustained many physical injuries while playing football. He was no novice to football-related physical injury, and how it might negatively affect his ability to play. During his college career, Sanders experienced and sustained many physical injuries while playing football. One injury resulted in his being benched and not allowed to play in the last game of the regular season.[87] It was during the 2023 season at Colorado when he sustained a fractured back injury.[88] During the offseason, he worked hard to rehabilitate and recover from the injury.[89] Despite his injury, Sanders subsequently excelled in the 2024 football season.[90] His 2024 season has reportedly created a lasting record for Colorado: "3,926 passing yards, 35 touchdowns, and a completion percentage of 74.2%. His efficiency and consistency have been unmatched, placing him in elite company alongside past Heisman finalists like Dwayne Haskins, Joe Burrow, and C.J. Stroud. Sanders's leadership and playmaking have been responsible for 82% of Colorado's offensive output, a school and Big 12 record."[91] In recognition of his success, he was awarded the 2024 Johnny Unitas Golden Arm Award, which, as previously mentioned, an honor given annually to the nation's top senior or upperclassman quarterback who demonstrates excellence in character, academics, and athletics.[92]

As a result of his resilience and devotion to his team, Sanders continues to perform at the highest level, earning the respect of sport commentators who proclaimed that he would be the No. 1 pick in the 2025 NFL draft. However, in college football, one severe injury does not guarantee against future injuries. In October 2024, Sanders reportedly injured his left hip flexor during Colorado's game against the University of Cincinnati and received treatment from Colorado's medical staff on the sidelines.[93] In November 2024, he reportedly avoided a knee injury from a late hit from University of Kansas defensive end Dean Miller who came crashing into Sanders's knees.[94] The hit sent Sanders flipping through the air, landing awkwardly on his neck.[95]

One would imagine that Sanders recognized the issue of how physical injury, particularly in a postseason bowl game, could negatively affect a players' financial wellbeing. As he and other college athletes were approaching the end of the normal football season with bowl games, he decided to take the risk to his future professional NFL and NIL earnings in deciding to play in the Alamo Bowl, which was held on December 28,

2024.[96] Along with his teammates, Sanders decided to risk injury during the bowl game, despite his history of injury. Incidentally, Sander's teammate and Heisman Trophy winner, Travis Hunter, suffered a lacerated liver that kept him out of three games in 2023 and a shoulder injury that knocked him out of a game in October 2024.[97] Perhaps the two superstars felt some comfort in playing in the bowl game after their coach, Sanders's father Deion, announced that Colorado had obtained a record amount of insurance coverage to protect them in case they were injured in the Alamo Bowl.[98] One report noted that, according to legal insider Darren Heitner, the belief is that Shedeur Sanders and Travis Hunter each had coverage for over $18 million.[99] Notwithstanding, insurance coverage does not guarantee that an athlete will not sustain injury that might end their sports career or even their life.

Contrary to many star players who decided not to play in bowl games because they were transferring to another college or preparing for the 2025 NFL draft, Sanders chose to play in the Alamo Bowl. In doing so, he faced possible injury and, worse, a somewhat embarrassing loss to Brigham Young University, which some believe may have negatively impact his ranking in the upcoming 2025 NFL draft.[100] When asked why he put his health, NFL salary, and NIL value on the line by playing in the Alamo Bowl, he said his reason for doing so was simple:

> I'll say it's about the team, and it's about everything I stand for. You know, it is about equality . . . I got to play with my receivers. I've got to be able to play with the team, the O-line, everything like that because we may not ever have a chance to play again together on the same team.[101]

That raises the question: how, if at all, does physical injury negatively affect an NIL college millionaire's financial future?

Injury and NIL Deals

An NIL deal, whether for a product endorsement, such as a Nike deal, or a deal with a booster-sponsored collective to play for a particular college, is predicated upon an athlete actually playing a given sport, such as Shedeur Sanders playing as a quarterback for Colorado. So, what happens to an NIL deal when a player cannot play their given sport, temporarily or permanently, due to a severe sport-related injury? The legal answer is to look to the specific terms of the NIL deal's contract. What if the NIL contract has a term that makes payments to a player contingent upon that player actually playing a given sport for an entire four-year period while in college, such as a deal with collective A to play for college A? If the NIL contract expressly provides for its termination upon the athlete being injured and unable to play due to that injury, then the deal could be canceled and the player would not receive any further compensation. On the other hand, it is possible that a NIL contract, such as a product endorsement with Nike, is not so stark in terms of termination?

An NIL deal with an athlete who has a strong social media following, like Livvy Dunne, might include a condition that allows the other party, such as Nike, to cancel or modify payments if the athlete suffers a severe injury. This does not mean that the deal is terminated as, an athlete might increase their social media following because they are injured, such as when Simone Biles decided to drop out of the 2020 Tokyo Olympic Games due to mental health concerns and a condition called the "twisties."[102] Notwithstanding her decision to pull out of the games, Biles came back stronger and more popular in the 2024 Summer Olympics in Paris to win four more Olympic medals: three gold in team, all-around, and vault, and one silver in floor exercises.[103] Therefore, a physical injury, even a severe one, does not mean a fatal blow to a college athlete's NIL deals, but such injuries are likely to negatively affect both NIL deals and NFL salary, depending on the terms of the players' contracts.

Relative to physical injury and NFL contracts, college athletes are particularly leery about how playing in a postseason bowl game might negatively risk their NFL careers due to the possibility of injury.[104] This was true for the 2024 bowl game season, where a long, impressive list of players decided to forgo playing in a bowl game, either because they are seeking to transfer to another college via the Transfer Portal or in preparation for the 2025 NFL draft.[105] Relative to financial risk that might result from bowl game injuries, there are several examples of college football players who experienced significant salary reductions due to injuries sustained during bowl games.[106] For example, in 2003, University of Miami running back Willis McGahee was projected to be a top draft pick before he severely injured his left knee in the 2003 Fiesta Bowl against Ohio State.[107] This injury cost him dearly as he slipped to the 23rd pick in the draft and received a less than expected $7 million contract for five years, plus incentives.[108] Other examples include when

Notre Dame linebacker Jaylon Smith fell in the draft after injuring his knee in the 2016 Fiesta Bowl, as did Michigan tight end Jake Butt, who injured his own knee in the Orange Bowl that same year.[109]

Faced with the possibility of losing the benefits of their NIL deals due to physical injury, what can a college athlete do to protect their financial interest in an NIL deal? There are three options. The first, unlikely one, is not to get injured. The second is to negotiate in a NIL contract a clause that guarantees payment that is not subject to actually playing such as due to an injury, which is defined in the contract. The third is to purchase insurance to compensate a player due to an injury, such as a disability policy or personal performance policy. As to the latter, in the entertainment world, a performer, such as Taylor Swift, who does not appear and perform for any reason would result in millions of dollars in lost revenue for the promoter and the performer.[110] Fortunately, there is a specialty insurance market to insure such a risk, with Lloyd's of London as one source of such a policy, which is very expensive due to potentially high payout.[111]

Going back to the decision by college football players to play or forgo playing in a postseason bowl game prior to entering the NFL draft the following year, purchasing insurance does not guarantee full reimbursement of financial losses.[112] Relative to the three examples already mentioned, Willis McGahee, who was injured in the 2003 Fiesta Bowl; Jaylon Smith, who was injured in the 2016 Fiesta Bowl; and Jake Butt, who was injured in the 2016 Orange Bowl, all were reportedly insured.[113] However, none were fully reimbursed for their financial losses, according to reports.[114] In Butt's case, he was due to collect $543,000 from his insurance but fell so far in the draft that he ultimately lost $2.8 million because of the injury.[115] In McGahee's case, he took out a $2.5 million policy shortly before the bowl game but could only collect on it if he never played football again, but he did not collect because he returned to play in 2004 and played 10 seasons in the NFL.[116]

Hence, such disability or personal performance insurance, if available, is expensive and contains a lot of conditions and exceptions. Further, payments may fall short of the actual loss. What advice should one give to a college athlete relative to protecting their financial interests, particularly in an NIL deal, when they are injured and cannot play? Current or future NIL college millionaires should include a guarantee clause in their NIL contracts so that they may still get paid even if they are injured. It also helps for them to secure additional insurance on top of what the NCAA provides as well as diversify their income streams so that they are not solely reliant on sports and NIL. Furthermore, a college athlete should consult with a seasoned insurance coverage and claims attorney to purchase a comprehensive policy that includes actual coverage of the risk that might result in a loss in market value as to a player's future salary or their NIL value.[117]

Relative to injuries and NIL value, Shedeur Sanders loves playing football, has suffered injuries, and has worked diligently to recover from injuries. His resilience evidences his commitment to play through injury, which unfortunately is a real, dangerous aspect of college football. His perseverance through his injury, recovery, and phenomenal season following his injury is a testimony to his greatness and physical and psychological integrity. It is also a sobering reminder of the dangers that college athletes face each day as they pursue their dreams, particularly those who play football. Sanders's NIL power secret is his love of the game and fortitude and resilience to recover from physical injuries and courage to play knowing that doing so could greatly diminish or possibly end his football career and NIL deals.

Hence, Sanders's success, in addition to love of the game and positivity, possesses the required grit and resilience, particularly as he battled through severe physical injury and exhibited the courage to face future injury. Sanders teaches us many important lessons relative to what it takes to be a NIL college millionaire.

NIL POWER SECRET #7: SAVOR SHEDEUR SANDERS'S LOVE OF THE GAME

Shedeur Sanders is a phenomenal athlete with a huge social media following and multi-million-dollar NIL deals. Most importantly, he teaches us that the road to being an NIL millionaire needs to begin and end with self-awareness and knowing what really matters. Like so many other NIL college millionaires, who have earned more money than they might have imagined, he asked the question, what in your life really matters? Put in another way, what are your values, and what motivates you once you have achieved high levels of performance, wealth, and fame? In his words, "What makes you happy?" For Shedeur Sanders, the answer is captured in four simple words: love of the game.

Further Reading

Deion Sanders, ELEVATE AND DOMINATE: 21 WAYS TO WIN ON AND OFF THE FIELD (2024).

Eric Edholm, *Shedeur Sanders Landing Spots: Seven Teams Most Likely to Pick Colorado QB in 2025 NFL Draft*, NFL (Feb. 19, 2025), https://www.nfl.com/news/shedeur-sanders-landing-spots-seven-teams-most-likely-to-pick-colorado-qb-in-2025-nfl-draft.

Shedeur Sanders Is Being Called "Arrogant" After the NFL Combine. Is That Fair?, FOX SPORTS (Mar. 4, 2025), https://www.foxsports.com/Stories/Nfl/Shedeur-Sanders-Being-Called-Arrogant-After-Nfl-Combine-Fair.

Endnotes

1. Robert Griffin III (@RGIII) X, https://x.com/RGIII/status/1837147717551702188?ref_src=twsrc%5Etfw%7Ctwcamp%5Etweetembed%7Ctwterm%5E1837147717551702188%7Ctwgr%5Ef9e01692037654456cb05b3a8c000aceb6aab19c%7Ctwcon%5Es1_&ref_url=https%3A%2F%2Fathlonsports.com%2Fcollege%2Fcolorado-buffaloes%2Fshedeur-sanders-money-contract-salary-nil-deals-how-much-make (last accessed Mar. 15, 2025).
2. On3 NIL Valuations, On3.com (July 22, 2025), https://www.on3.com/nil/rankings/player/nil-valuations/.
3. On3 (On3sports) X, https://x.com/On3sports/status/1828832319920345321 (last accessed Mar. 15, 2025); FRONT OFFICE SPORTS (@FOS) X, https://x.com/FOS/status/1828832106254102714 (last accessed Mar. 15, 2025); *Shedeur Sanders Pens Huge NIL Deal with Nike that Will Help Establish His Legacy*, MARCA (Aug. 28, 2024), https://www.marca.com/en/ncaa/2024/08/28/66cf6ca546163fbf198b457c.html.
4. *See supra* note 2.
5. Nate Duffett, *Shedeur Sanders' Net Worth in 2024 from NIL Deals*, YARD BARKER (Aug. 29, 2024), https://www.yardbarker.com/college_football/articles/shedeur_sanders_net_worth_in_2024_from_nil_deals/s1_17125_40814652; Svetozar Pavlovic, *NCAA Football: How Much Is Shedeur Sanders' NIL Deal Worth? Colorado Buffaloes QB's Valuation*, AS (Sept. 22, 2024), https://en.as.com/ncaa/ncaa-football-how-much-is-shedeur-sanders-nil-deal-worth-colorado-buffaloes-qbs-valuation-n-2/; Farouk Yusuf, *Shedeur Sanders NIL Deals: What Is the Current Valuation of Coach Prime's Son? Current Deals, Net Worth, and More*, SPORTSKEEDA (Nov. 3, 2023), https://www.sportskeeda.com/college-football/shedeur-sanders-nil-deals-what-current-valuation-coach-prime-s-son-current-deals-net-worth.

6. *2024 Football Roster*, CUBUFFS.COM, https://cubuffs.com/sports/football/roster/shedeur-sanders/17232 (last accessed Mar. 15, 2024).
7. *Where Did Colorado QB Shedeur Sanders Play in High School?*, COLLEGE FOOTBALL NETWORK (Sept. 7, 2024), https://collegefootballnetwork.com/colorado-qb-shedeur-sanders-high-school/#:~:text=While%20Sanders'%20familial%20lineage%20certainly,top%2D10%20prospect%20in%20Texas.
8. *Id.*
9. *Id.*
10. Rashad Milligan, *Shedeur Sanders Watched Jackson State's Spring Football Season from the Sideline. He Called it a 'Blessing'*, MISS. CLARION LEDGER (July 20, 2021), https://www.clarionledger.com/story/sports/college/jackson-state/2021/07/20/jackson-state-shedeur-sanders-deion-son-excited-college/8009678002/.
11. *Id.*
12. *Shedeur Sanders Player Stats*, ESPN, https://www.espn.com/college-football/player/stats/_/id/4432762/shedeur-sanders (last accessed Mar. 15, 2025).
13. Craig Haley, *Jackson State QB Shedeur Sanders Wins 2021 FCS Jerry Rice Award*, NCAA (Dec. 20, 2021), https://www.ncaa.com/news/football/article/2021-12-13/jackson-state-qb-shedeur-sanders-wins-2021-fcs-jerry-rice-award.
14. *Id.*
15. *See 2024 Football Roster*, CUBUFFS.COM, https://cubuffs.com/sports/football/roster/shedeur-sanders/17232 (last accessed Mar. 15, 2024).
16. *SWAC Announces Football Postseason Honors*, SWAC (Nov. 29, 2022), https://swac.org/news/2022/11/29/swac-announces-football-postseason-honors.aspx.
17. Max Olson, *What Happened to Deion Sanders' Colorado Castoffs? Revisiting a Record-Setting Exodus*, ATHLETIC, N.Y. TIMES (updated Aug. 24, 2024), https://www.nytimes.com/athletic/5449961/2024/04/29/deion-sanders-colorado-transfer-portal-2023/?utm_medium=social&utm_campaign=twhq&source=twitterhq.
18. Joseph Zucker, *Deion Sanders Says Son Shedeur Will Be Colorado's QB after Leaving Jackson State*, BLEACHER REPORT (Dec. 4, 2022), https://bleacherreport.com/articles/10057619-deion-sanders-says-son-shedeur-will-be-colorados-qb-after-leaving-jackson-state.
19. *Id.*
20. Pete Thamel & Heather Dinich, *Colorado Board Unanimously Approves Move from Pac-12 to Big 12*, ESPN (July 27, 2023), https://www.espn.com/college-football/story/_/id/38083687/colorado-board-unanimously-approves-move-pac-12-big-12.
21. *See* Max Olson, *What Happened to Deion Sanders' Colorado Castoffs? Revisiting a Record-Setting Exodus*, ATHLETIC, N.Y. TIMES (updated Aug. 24, 2024), https://www.nytimes.com/athletic/5449961/2024/04/29/deion-sanders-colorado-transfer-portal-2023/?utm_medium=social&utm_campaign=twhq&source=twitterhq.
22. *Shedeur Sanders*, SPORTS REFERENCE CFB, https://www.sports-reference.com/cfb/players/shedeur-sanders-1/gamelog/2023/ (last accessed Mar. 15, 2025).
23. *See 2024 Football Roster*, CUBUFFS.COM, https://cubuffs.com/sports/football/roster/shedeur-sanders/17232 (last accessed Mar. 15, 2024).
24. *Id.*

25. *Id.*
26. *Id.*
27. *Id.*
28. *Id.*
29. *See Shedeur Sanders Player Stats*, ESPN, https://www.espn.com/college-football/player/stats/_/id/4432762/shedeur-sanders (last accessed Mar. 15, 2025).
30. Mike Kadlick, *Colorado's Shedeur Sanders, Travis Hunter Sweep Big 12 Player of the Year Awards,* SPORTS ILLUSTRATED (Dec. 5, 2024), https://www.si.com/college-football/colorado-shedeur-sanders-travis-hunter-sweep-big-12-player-of-the-year-awards.
31. Mike Fitzpatrick, *Colorado Two-Way Star Travis Hunter Wins Heisman Trophy as College Football's Top Player,* AP (Dec. 14, 2024), https://apnews.com/article/heisman-trophy-travis-hunter-colorado-c76c411ca04108018eefb18beaa649fe (his teammate Travis Hunter who was awarded the Big 12 Defensive Player of the Year for 2024, having received 80.14% of possible points, the 11th-highest in Heisman Trophy history).
32. *2024 All-Big 12 Football Teams and Awards Announced,* BIG 12 SPORTS (Dec. 5, 2024), https://big12sports.com/news/2024/12/5/2024-all-big-12-football-teams-and-awards-announced.aspx.
33. Johnny Unitas Golden Arm Educational Foundation, Inc., *Shedeur Sanders Wins the 2024 Johnny Unitas Golden Arm Award® Presented by A. O. Smith,* GOLDENARMFOUNDATION.COM, https://goldenarmfoundation.com/2024/11/shedeur-sanders-wins-the-2024-johnny-unitas-golden-arm-award-presented-by-a-o-smith/ (last accessed Mar. 15, 2025).
34. *See On3 NIL Valuations*, ON3 (updated Mar. 15, 2025); Mustafa Gatollari, *What Are Arch Manning's NIL Earnings, and Will They Go Up After His Explosive Five-Touchdown Game?,* MSN (Sept. 19, 2024), https://www.on3.com/nil/rankings/player/nil-valuations/; https://www.msn.com/en-us/sports/nfl/what-are-arch-manning-s-nil-earnings-and-will-they-go-up-after-his-explosive-five-touchdown-game/ar-AA1qP5GJ; SK Desk, *How Much Is Arch Manning Nil Deal Worth in 2025?,* SPORTSKEEDA (Jan. 9, 2025), https://www.sportskeeda.com/college-football/arch-manning-nil-deal-worth.
35. *NIL Deals for Shedeur Sanders,* ON3, https://www.on3.com/db/shedeur-sanders-107068/nil-deals/ (last accessed Mar. 15, 2025).
36. *NCAA Takes Aim at Booster-Backed "Collectives" and Their NIL Deals,* DAVIS GILBERT (June 22, 2022), https://www.dglaw.com/ncaa-takes-aim-at-booster-backed-collectives-and-their-nil-deals/.
37. *Id.*
38. Kenneth Teape, *Michigan Wolverines Received NIL Funding from Billionaire to Land Bryce Underwood,* SPORTS ILLUSTRATED (Nov. 25, 2024), https://www.si.com/fannation/name-image-likeness/nil-news/michigan-wolverines-received-nil-funding-from-billionaire-to-land-bryce-underwood.
39. Seth M. Corwin, *NIL Deal Gone Wrong: Former University of Florida Recruit Sues Head Football Coach & NIL Collective,* MCLANE MIDDLETON (June 3, 2024), https://www

.mclane.com/insights/nil-deal-gone-wrong-former-university-of-florida-recruit-sues-head-football-coach-nil-collective/.

40. The Associated Press, *Prospect of Player Pay Adds Wrinkle for HBCUs, Where Big NIL Deals Are Still Taking Root,* ANDSCAPE (Aug. 21, 2024), https://andscape.com/features/prospect-of-player-pay-adds-wrinkle-for-hbcus-where-big-nil-deals-are-still-taking-root/.
41. *Id.*; Rise HBCU, RISEHBCU.COM, https://www.risehbcu.com/memberships#:~:text=We%20are%20the%20second%20HBCU%20NIL%20collective,to%20providing%20HBCU%20student%20athletes%20NIL%20opportunities (last accessed Mar. 15, 2025).
42. HBCU Gameday Newswire, *HBCU in the Heart of SEC Country Announces NIL Collective,* HBCU GAMEDAY (Apr. 30, 2024), https://hbcugameday.com/2024/04/30/hbcu-in-the-heart-of-sec-country-announces-nil-collective/.
43. Albert Samaha & Emily Giambalvo, *At Colorado, Getting NIL Money Means Keeping Close to Coach Prime,* WASH. POST (Oct. 21, 2024), https://cubuffs.com/news/2024/3/26/general-cu-athletics-partners-with-new-5430-alliance-nil-collective.
44. *Id.*
45. *CU Athletics Partners with New 5430 Alliance NIL Collective,* CUBUFFS.COM (Mar. 26, 2024), https://cubuffs.com/news/2024/3/26/general-cu-athletics-partners-with-new-5430-alliance-nil-collective, *Buffs4Life NIL Collective—Colorado Buffaloes Collective,* ON3, https://www.on3.com/db/shedeur-sanders-107068/nil-deals/ (last accessed Mar. 15, 2025). ("MARCH 26, 2024, UPDATE: With the launch of the 5430 Alliance, the Buffs4Life NIL Collective will no longer be operating. Buffs4Life will fold all of its operations into the new 5430 Alliance, which replaces the previously launched 5430 Foundation. PREVIOUS INFORMATION: The Buffs4Life Foundation is a 501(c)(3) organization that provides financial assistance and mental health resources for former Colorado athletes. In late October 2022, it announced the creation of the Buffs4Life NIL Collective to support current Colorado athletes through NIL opportunities. Prior to the launch of the Buffs4Life NIL Collective, the only collective or membership-based community designed to support Colorado athletes was the Boulder NIL Club, which is backed by the company YOKE. Buffs4Life NIL Collective's website says, 'A tax-deductible financial contribution to the Buffs4Life NIL Collective can be made to the general fund that supports all CU student-athletes or to a specific team, group of student-athletes, or an individual student-athlete. 15% of every donation goes to the Buffs4Life Foundation while the rest goes directly towards compensating student-athletes for their name, image and likeness.'").
46. *See* Albert Samaha & Emily Giambalvo, *At Colorado, Getting NIL Money Means Keeping Close to Coach Prime,* WASH. POST (Oct. 21, 2024), https://cubuffs.com/news/2024/3/26/general-cu-athletics-partners-with-new-5430-alliance-nil-collective.
47. Jonathan Adams, *Colorado QB Shedeur Sanders Is Making More NIL Money Than You Think,* ATHLON SPORTS (Nov. 16, 2024), https://athlonsports.com/college/

colorado-buffaloes/shedeur-sanders-money-contract-salary-nil-deals-how-much-make. *See also* Samaha & Giambalvo, *supra* note 46.

48. Kevin Sweeney, *Fox Sports' Joel Klatt Thinks Shedeur Sanders Could Make Eight Figures if He Stays at Colorado Next Season*, ROCHESTER FIRST (Sept. 20, 2023), https://www.rochesterfirst.com/sports/sports-illustrated/b9abc006/fox-sports-joel-klatt-thinks-shedeur-sanders-could-make-eight-figures-if-he-stays-at-colorado-next-season/.
49. *See* The Associated Press, *Prospect of Player Pay Adds Wrinkle for HBCUs, Where Big NIL Deals Are Still Taking Root*, ANDSCAPE (Aug. 21, 2024), https://andscape.com/features/prospect-of-player-pay-adds-wrinkle-for-hbcus-where-big-nil-deals-are-still-taking-root/.
50. Katherine Knott, *States Underfunded Historically Black Land Grants by $13 Billion over 3 Decades*, INSIDE HIGHER ED. (Sept. 20, 2023), https://www.insidehighered.com/news/government/2023/09/20/states-underfunded-black-land-grants-13b-over-30-years.
51. *Id.*
52. Fred Batiste, *Number of HBCU Players in NFL Hall of Fame Increases with Recent Class*, HBCU SPORTS (Jan. 15, 2025), https://hbcusports.com/2020/01/15/number-of-hbcu-players-in-nfl-hall-of-fame-increases-with-recent-class/.
53. Kourtney Brady, *Athletics Recruitment Challenges at HBCUs*, HORNET NEWSPAPER (Feb. 7, 2023), https://thehornetonline.com/2023/02/07/athletics-recruitment-challenges-at-hbcus/.
54. Shehan Jeyarajah, *Beats by Dre Signs Jackson State QB Shedeur Sanders as First Collegiate Ambassador*, CBS SPORTS (Sept. 1, 2021), https://www.cbssports.com/college-football/news/beats-by-dre-signs-jackson-state-qb-shedeur-sanders-as-first-collegiate-ambassador/.
55. Staff Reports, *Deion Sanders' Son, Jackson State's QB, Signs a NIL Deal with Tom Brady*, TALLAHASSEE DEMOCRAT (Dec. 17, 2021), https://www.tallahassee.com/story/sports/college/2021/12/17/deion-sanders-son-shedeur-sanders-jackson-state-signs-college-football-nil-deal-tom-brady/8943980002/.
56. Ryan Gaydos, *Jackson State's Shedeur Sanders Inks Historic Gatorade NIL Deal*, FOX BUS. (Jan. 27, 2022), https://www.foxbusiness.com/sports/jackson-state-shedeur-sanders-gatorade-nil.
57. *See* On3 (On3sports) X, https://x.com/On3sports/status/1828832319920345321 (last accessed Mar. 15, 2025); FRONT OFFICE SPORTS (@FOS) X, https://x.com/FOS/status/1828832106254102714 (last accessed Mar. 15, 2025); *Shedeur Sanders Pens Huge NIL Deal With Nike That Will Help Establish His Legacy*, MARCA (Aug. 28, 2024), https://www.marca.com/en/ncaa/2024/08/28/66cf6ca546163fbf198b457c.html.
58. Scott Procter & Fort Collins, *Shedeur Sanders Becomes First College Football Player to Sign NIL Deal with Nike*, YAHOO! SPORTS (Aug. 28, 2024), https://sports.yahoo.com/shedeur-sanders-becomes-first-college-165843347.html#:%7e:text=-Deion%20Sanders%20already%20has%20signature,%244.7%20million%2C%20according%20to%20On3.

59. Bryan Murphy, *How Much Does Shedeur Sanders Make? Updated 2024 NIL Earnings, Net Worth for Colorado QB*, Sporting News (Aug. 29, 2024), https://www.sportingnews.com/us/ncaa-football/news/shedeur-sanders-money-2024-nil-earnings-net-worth-colorado-qb/7bddcf592aeb4e4457d3079f; Farouk Yusuf, *Shedeur Sanders' $6.5 Million NIL Valuation Surpasses the Amount Earned by Deion Sanders from His Five-Year Rookie Contract*, sportskeeda (Dec. 27, 2024), https://www.sportskeeda.com/college-football/news-shedeur-sanders-6-5-million-nil-valuation-surpasses-amount-earned-deion-sanders-five-year-rookie-contract; Alina Tunnell, *Shedeur Sanders' Net Worth in 2024: How Worth is the Quarterback for Colorado Buffaloes?*, Wortholino (Aug. 30, 2024), https://www.wortholino.com/shedeur-sanders-net-worth/; Nate Duffett, *Shedeur Sanders' Net Worth in 2024 from NIL Deals*, Yard Barker (Aug. 29, 2024), https://www.yardbarker.com/college_football/articles/shedeur_sanders_net_worth_in_2024_from_nil_deals/s1_17125_40814652; Ariadna Pinheiro, *Shedeur Sanders' Net Worth: How Much Fortune Does the Colorado Buffaloes QB Have?*, Bolavip (Dec. 4, 2024), https://bolavip.com/en/college-football/shedeur-sanders-net-worth.
60. Jason Jones, *Deion Sanders' Staff Replacements Should Start by Promoting from Within at Colorado*, MSN (Dec. 31, 2024), https://www.msn.com/en-us/sports/other/deion-sanders-staff-replacements-should-start-by-promoting-from-within-at-colorado/ar-AA1wJYD9?apiversion=v2&noservercache=1&domshim=1&renderwebcomponents=1&wcseo=1&batchservertelemetry=1&noservertelemetry=1.
61. *Colorado's Shedeur Sanders Releases First Song, 'Perfect Timing'*, FOX Sports (May 8, 2024), https://www.foxsports.com/stories/college-football/colorados-shedeur-sanders-releases-first-song-perfect-timing.
62. Valentina Martinez, *Shedeur Sanders Buys $200,000 Luxury Car for Colorado Offensive Lineman*, Newsweek (updated Dec. 3, 2024), https://www.newsweek.com/sports/ncaa/shedeur-sanders-buys-200000-luxury-car-colorado-offensive-lineman-1994509; LW, *Did Shedeur Sanders Really Gift a Maybach to Jordan Seaton or Are They Trolling Us?*, Marca (Mar. 12, 2024), https://www.marca.com/en/ncaa/2024/12/04/674fc9e746163f1b238b456c.html.
63. *See* Farouk Yusuf, *Shedeur Sanders' $6.5 Million NIL Valuation Surpasses the Amount Earned by Deion Sanders from His Five-Year Rookie Contract*, sportskeeda (Dec. 27, 2024), https://www.sportskeeda.com/college-football/news-shedeur-sanders-6-5-million-nil-valuation-surpasses-amount-earned-deion-sanders-five-year-rookie-contract; Grant Bricker, *Shedeur Sanders Projected to Replace $9.5 Million NFL QB in Latest Mock Draft*, Athlon Sports (Dec. 28, 2024), https://athlonsports.com/college/colorado-buffaloes/shedeur-sanders-projected-replacement-tennessee-titans-quarterback-will-levis. *See also* Max Dible, *Surprise QB Could Knock Shedeur Sanders Out of No. 1 Spot in NFL Draft*, Athlon Sports (Dec. 27, 2024), https://athlonsports.com/college/colorado-buffaloes/shedeur-sanders-colorado-cade-klubnik-clemson-travis-hunter-college-football-giants-nfl-draft.
64. Bruce Feldman, *For Deion Sanders and His Sons at Colorada, Alamo Bowl Loss Provides Bittersweet Ending*, Athletic, N.Y. Times (updated Feb. 14, 2025),

https://www.nytimes.com/athletic/6024529/2024/12/29/deion-sanders-colorado-shedeur-alamo-bowl-byu/.

65. Shafiq Najib, *Tiger Woods and Son Share Hug after the Teen Hits His 1st Hole-In-One,* ABC News (Dec. 23, 2024), https://abcnews.go.com/GMA/Family/tiger-woods-son-charlie-hole-in-one/story?id=117053771.
66. Tess Demeyer, *Shedeur, Shilo and Hall of Famer Deion Are Set to Form a 'Triple Threat at Jackson State',* Dallas Morning News (Dec. 16, 2020), https://www.dallasnews.com/high-school-sports/football/2020/12/16/shedeur-shilo-and-hall-of-famer-deion-sanders-are-set-to-form-a-triple-threat-at-jackson-state/.
67. Elliot Harrison, *Top 25 Quarterbacks of All Time: Patriots' Tom Brady Leads List,* NFL (July 2, 2019), https://www.nfl.com/news/top-25-quarterbacks-of-all-time-patriots-tom-brady-leads-list-0ap3000001035041.
68. *Id.*
69. Robert Zeglinski, *Ranking the 10 Greatest NFL Quarterbacks of All Time,* For the Win (July 20, 2024), https://ftw.usatoday.com/lists/best-nfl-quarterbacks-ever-ranked.
70. LW, *How Patrick Mahomes' Style Has Become an Inspiration for Young Quarterbacks Everywhere,* Marca (Nov. 16, 2023), https://www.marca.com/en/nfl/kansas-city-chiefs/2023/11/16/65563ea4ca4741893f8b45f5.html.
71. *Id.*
72. *See* Robert Zeglinski, *Ranking the 10 Greatest NFL Quarterbacks of All Time,* For the Win (July 20, 2024), https://ftw.usatoday.com/lists/best-nfl-quarterbacks-ever-ranked.
73. *Id.*
74. Chris Cwik, *Super Bowl 2023: Patrick Mahomes, Jalen Hurts are First Black Starting Quarterbacks to Face Off in Big Game,* Yahoo! Sports (Jan. 29, 2023), https://sports.yahoo.com/super-bowl-2023-patrick-mahomes-jalen-hurts-are-first-black-starting-quarterbacks-to-face-off-in-big-game-041216328.html.
75. Andrew Lawrence, *The Black Quarterback Is Now the NFL's Leading Man. But at What Cost?,* Guardian (Oct. 4, 2024), https://www.theguardian.com/sport/2024/oct/04/the-black-quarterback-is-now-the-nfls-leading-man-but-at-what-cost.
76. *Id.*
77. LW, *Shedeur Sanders and Travis Hunter Reveal Which Legendary NFL Quarterback Is Their North Star,* Marca (Dec. 12, 2024), https://www.marca.com/en/ncaa/2024/12/13/675b6a69ca4741c9678b45bd.html.
78. *"Great Amount of Respect"—Colorado QB Shedeur Sanders Has Reportedly Caught the Eye of Legendary Passer Tom Brady,* College Football Network (Jan. 4, 2025), https://collegefootballnetwork.com/shedeur-sanders-tom-brady-respect/.
79. Zachary Y. Kerr *et al.*, *College Sports–Related Injuries—United States, 2009–10 Through 2013–14 Academic Years,* CDC (Dec. 11, 2015), https://www.cdc.gov/mmwr/preview/mmwrhtml/mm6448a2.htm.
80. Dr. Edward M. Wojtys, *The Dark Side of College Football,* SAGE Journals (October 24, 2018), https://journals.sagepub.com/doi/10.1177/1941738118805694.
81. Staff Writers, *College Athletes Often Bear the Cost of Injuries and Insurance,* Best Colleges (May 6, 2022), https://www.bestcolleges.com/news/2021-2/09/10/college-athletes-ncaa-injuries-insurance/.

82. Christine M. Baugh, Emily Kroshus, & William P. Meehan, *Accuracy of U.S. College Football Players' Estimates of their Risk of Concussion or Injury*, JAMA NETWORK (Dec. 29, 2020), https://jamanetwork.com/journals/jamanetworkopen/fullarticle/2774487.
83. Margot Putukian, *The Psychological Response to Injury in Student Athletes: A Narrative Review with a Focus on Mental Health*, NAT'L INSTITUTES OF HEALTH (Dec. 30, 2015), https://pubmed.ncbi.nlm.nih.gov/26719498/.
84. Marty Munson, *Bronny James Details the Scary Moment He Went into Cardiac Arrest*, MEN'S HEALTH (Oct. 15, 2024), https://www.menshealth.com/health/a62570243/bronny-james-cardiac-arrest-details-recovery/.
85. Nathan Kalman-Lamb & Derek Silva, *Colleges Are Abusing Injured Football Players*, CHRON. OF HIGHER EDUC. (Dec. 18, 2024), https://www.chronicle.com/article/colleges-are-abusing-injured-football-players.
86. Carl Bescoby, *From Setback to Success: Sport-Injury-Related Growth*, SPORTS INJURY BULLETIN, https://www.sportsinjurybulletin.com/diagnose-treat/from-setback-to-success-sport-injury-related-growth#:~:text=Sport%2Dinjury%2Drelated%20growth%20(,opportunity%20for%20growth%20and%20resilience (last accessed Mar. 15, 2025).
87. The Associated Press, *Colorado QB Shedeur Sanders Missed Finale with Fracture in Back*, ESPN (Nov. 27, 2023), https://www.espn.com/college-football/story/_/id/38992415/colorado-qb-shedeur-sanders-missed-finale-fracture-back; Joseph Zucker, *Shedeur Sanders Has Fractured Back Injury; QB Missed Colorado's Finale vs. Utah*, BLEACHER REPORT (Nov. 27, 2023), https://bleacherreport.com/articles/10098829-shedeur-sanders-has-fractured-back-injury-qb-missed-colorados-finale-vs-utah; Josh Tolle, *Colorado's Shedeur Sanders Reportedly Out Due to Fractured Back*, SPORTS ILLUSTRATED (Nov. 27, 2023), https://www.si.com/college/colorado/football/colorados-shedeur-sanders-reportedly-out-due-to-fractured-back.
88. *Id.*
89. *Id.*
90. *See Shedeur Sanders Player Stats*, ESPN, https://www.espn.com/college-football/player/stats/_/id/4432762/shedeur-sanders (last accessed Mar. 15, 2025).
91. Emanuel Walker, *Shedeur Sanders Expected to Be 'Grown' in Alamo Bowl Finale vs. BYU*, MSN (Dec. 28, 2024), https://www.msn.com/en-us/sports/other/shedeur-sanders-expected-to-be-grown-in-alamo-bowl-finale-vs-byu/ar-AA1wDc0R.
92. *See* Johnny Unitas Golden Arm Educational Foundation, Inc., *Shedeur Sanders Wins the 2024 Johnny Unitas Golden Arm Award® Presented by A. O. Smith*, GOLDENARMFOUNDATION.COM, https://goldenarmfoundation.com/2024/11/shedeur-sanders-wins-the-2024-johnny-unitas-golden-arm-award-presented-by-a-o-smith/ (last accessed Mar. 15, 2025).
93. Wade Perry, *Shedeur Sanders Injury Update: ESPN Broadcast Gives Latest on Colorado QB*, ON3 (Oct. 26, 2024), https://www.on3.com/college/colorado-buffaloes/news/shedeur-sanders-injury-update-espn-broadcast-gives-latest-on-colorado-qb/.

94. Luke Easterling, *How Shedeur Sanders Narrowly Avoided a Potentially Career-Altering Injury*, Athlon Sports (Nov. 23, 2024), https://athlonsports.com/college-football/shedeur-sanders-hit-knee-injury-college-football-colorado-buffaloes-nfl-draft.
95. Spencer Ostrow, *Shedeur Sanders Reveals Initial Thoughts after Kansas Cheap Shot*, Athlon Sports (Nov. 26, 2024), https://athlonsports.com/college/colorado-buffaloes/colorado-buffaloes-shedeur-sanders-reveals-initial-thoughts-after-kansas-cheap-shot.
96. Dan Lyons, *Shedeur Sanders Explains Decision to Play Alamo Bowl Rather than Opt Out*, Sports Illustrated (Dec. 27, 2024), https://www.si.com/college-football/shedeur-sanders-explains-decision-play-alamo-bowl.
97. Brent Schrontenboer, *Travis Hunter, Shedeur Sanders Have Insurance for Bowl Game. Financial Risk Still Huge*, USA Today (Dec. 27, 2024), https://www.usatoday.com/story/sports/ncaaf/big12/2024/12/27/travis-hunter-alamo-bowl-insurance-shedeur-deion-sanders/77242008007/.
98. Brent Schrontenboer, *Deion Sanders: Record Amount of Insurance Coverage Obtained to Protect Top Players in Bowl*, USA Today (Dec. 24, 2024), https://www.usatoday.com/story/sports/ncaaf/2024/12/23/deion-sanders-travis-hunter-shedeur-sanders-disability-insurance-alamo-bowl/77187627007/; Darrelle Lincoln, *Report: Shedeur Sanders & Travis Hunter Secured Historic Multi-Million Dollar Insurance Coverage Ahead of Alamo Bowl*, MSN (Dec. 28, 2024), https://www.msn.com/en-us/sports/football/report-shedeur-sanders-travis-hunter-secured-historic-multi-million-dollar-insurance-coverage-ahead-of-alamo-bowl/ar-AA1wF8xR.
99. *See* Brent Schrontenboer, *Deion Sanders: Record Amount of Insurance Coverage Obtained to Protect Top Players in Bowl*, USA Today (Dec. 24, 2024), https://www.usatoday.com/story/sports/ncaaf/2024/12/23/deion-sanders-travis-hunter-shedeur-sanders-disability-insurance-alamo-bowl/77187627007/; Darrelle Lincoln, *Report: Shedeur Sanders & Travis Hunter Secured Historic Multi-Million Dollar Insurance Coverage Ahead of Alamo Bowl*, MSN (Dec. 28, 2024), https://www.msn.com/en-us/sports/football/report-shedeur-sanders-travis-hunter-secured-historic-multi-million-dollar-insurance-coverage-ahead-of-alamo-bowl/ar-AA1wF8xR.
100. Ameek Abdullah Jamal, *Taylor Swift: Cancellations Deal Blow to Insurers*, MSN (Dec. 29, 2024), https://www.msn.com/en-us/sports/football/will-shedeur-sanders-performance-in-alamo-bowl-affect-his-draft-stock/ar-AA1wELw4.
101. Andrew Graham, *Shedeur Sanders Explains Not Opting Out of Alamo Bowl: "I Don't Do What Other People Do,"* MSN (Dec. 27, 2024), https://www.msn.com/en-us/sports/other/shedeur-sanders-explains-not-opting-out-of-alamo-bowl-i-don-t-do-what-other-people-do/ar-AA1wApvs?ocid=feedsansarticle.
102. Rebecca Schneid, *What Are "The Twisties" in Gymnastics? Simone Biles Faced the Condition at the Tokyo Olympics*, TIME (July 28, 2024), https://time.com/7004666/what-are-the-twisties-gymnastics-cause-treatments-simone-biles-condition/.

103. Scott Bregman & Jo Gunston, *Simone Biles: All Medals, and Awards—Complete List*, OLYMPICS (Aug. 1, 2024), https://olympics.com/en/news/simone-biles-all-titles-records-and-medals-complete-list-paris-2024#:~:text=The%2027%2Dyear%2Dold%20is,not%20likely%20her%20biggest%20focus.
104. *See* Brent Schrontenboer, *Travis Hunter, Shedeur Sanders Have Insurance for Bowl Game. Financial Risk Still Huge*, USA TODAY (Dec. 27, 2024), https://www.usatoday.com/story/sports/ncaaf/big12/2024/12/27/travis-hunter-alamo-bowl-insurance-shedeur-deion-sanders/77242008007/.
105. Michelle R. Martinelli & Cory Woodroof, *A Running List of College Football Players Skipping 2024–25 Bowl Games*, YAHOO! SPORTS (Dec. 17, 2024), https://sports.yahoo.com/running-list-college-football-players-214410280.html.
106. *See* Brent Schrontenboer, *Travis Hunter, Shedeur Sanders Have Insurance for Bowl Game. Financial Risk Still Huge.*, USA TODAY (Dec. 27, 2024), https://www.usatoday.com/story/sports/ncaaf/big12/2024/12/27/travis-hunter-alamo-bowl-insurance-shedeur-deion-sanders/77242008007/.
107. *Id.*
108. *Id.*
109. *Id.*
110. Taylor Herzlich, *Insurers Face Massive Hit after Taylor Swift Concerts Canceled due to Terrorist Threat*, N.Y. POST (Aug. 9, 2024), https://nypost.com/2024/08/09/business/insurers-face-massive-hit-after-taylor-swift-concerts-cancelled-due-to-terrorist-threat/; Amelia Matthewson, *Taylor Swift: Cancellations Deal Blow to Insurers*, INSURTECH (Aug. 17, 2024), https://insurtechdigital.com/insurtech/taylor-swift-cancellations-deal-blow-to-insurers.
111. *See* Taylor Herzlich, *Insurers Face Massive Hit After Taylor Swift Concerts Canceled Due to Terrorist Threat*, N.Y. POST (Aug. 9, 2024), https://nypost.com/2024/08/09/business/insurers-face-massive-hit-after-taylor-swift-concerts-cancelled-due-to-terrorist-threat/; Amelia Matthewson, *Taylor Swift: Cancellations Deal Blow to Insurers*, INSURTECH (Aug. 17, 2024), https://insurtechdigital.com/insurtech/taylor-swift-cancellations-deal-blow-to-insurers.
112. *See* Brent Schrontenboer, *Travis Hunter, Shedeur Sanders Have Insurance for Bowl Game. Financial Risk Still Huge*, USA TODAY (Dec. 27, 2024), https://www.usatoday.com/story/sports/ncaaf/big12/2024/12/27/travis-hunter-alamo-bowl-insurance-shedeur-deion-sanders/77242008007/.
113. *Id.*
114. *Id.*
115. *Id.*
116. *Id.*
117. *Id.* (Such experts mentioned are Richard Giller, a renowned sports insurance recovery attorney in Los Angeles and Josh Lens, an associate professor at Iowa who has researched insurance coverage for college athletes.).

8

Angel Reese: Persistence in Achieving One's Goals

It's cool because, one, you really don't see Black women doing a lot of deals, especially with a lot of these brands—so, just to see me being an example for a lot of young girls that look like me, and just giving them a point just to know that they can do it.

—Angel Reese[1]

OVERVIEW

Angel Reese's, aka "Bayou Barbie" and "Chi Barbie," narrative illustrates the importance of being laser-focused on one's goals, harnessing available resources, and being persistent to achieve them. On April 5, 2022, Reese entered the NCAA Transfer Portal, and, on May 6, 2022, LSU announced that she would transfer to their program for her junior year.[2] There, she led the team to its first national championship.[3] During her days at LSU, Reese signed several NIL deals and was one of just two female athletes inside the top 10 in On3's NIL valuation tracker and the top college basketball player on the list.[4] As a result, she became the first Black female NIL college millionaire. In 2024, after graduating from LSU, she signed a four-year, $324,383 contract with the WNBA Chicago Sky.[5] As of July 30, 2024, her net worth is reportedly $1.5 million.[6]

In this chapter, we focus on Reese's NIL power secret to success, which is to become self-aware of the path of least resistance[7] and to muster the creativity to achieve NIL success. This chapter will discuss how Reese (1) became self-aware of her career goals and employed the needed resources to achieve those goals, including accessing the Transfer Portal; (2) persevered through adversity, which young Black women superstars must often overcome, including mental health issues; and (3) advocated for Black women in sports and business.

PATH OF LEAST RESISTANCE

Self-Awareness

Reese's NIL success profile is nearly identical to her fellow college millionaires: She is highly talented and success-driven, overcame injury, came from an accomplished family, and received universal acclaim throughout her career. However, unlike the other NIL millionaires discussed in this book, she is unique, as she is the only one who had to overcome both sexism and racism as a Black woman. Her power secret is the importance of becoming self-aware of one's goals and seeking the path of least resistance to achieving them.

In his award-winning book, *The Path of Least Resistance*, Robert Fritz presents a revolutionary program for seeking and becoming self-aware of one's innate power to create.[8] His book takes the reader on a journey from discovering the steps of creating, the importance of creating what you truly love, and how to focus on the creative process to move from where you are to where you want to be.[9] Reese's career development and successes exemplify what Robert Fritz describes as the importance of discovering the steps to create what you truly love. From her early years, Reese had a clear vision of her life's goals, which were to become a WNBA superstar and an NIL multi-millionaire. In this chapter, you will learn both how she achieved those goals and how those lessons helped to lead other college athletes to NIL deals.

BE RESOURCEFUL: ACCESSING THE TRANSFER PORTAL

In *The Path of Least Resistance*, Robert Fritz emphasizes that after a person identifies their career goals, the next important step to success is to focus on the creative process to move from where you are to where you want to be.[10] Many people, particularly people of color who live in under-resourced communities, must learn the art of being resourceful, that is, to access the resources needed to reach their goals.

Choosing the Right College Can Make You an NIL Millionaire

Choosing the right college can be the most important decision for a college-bound athlete who wants to become an NIL millionaire. Historically, college athletes had one opportunity to get to the *right* college, which is the college that would maximize their athletic, academic, and financial aspirations. That opportunity was when they were in high school, researching and applying for admission into colleges, getting accepted by those colleges, and deciding which college to attend. With the legalization of NIL deals for college athletes, that decision-making process, particularly for highly sought-after high school superstars, has become critical to becoming a college NIL millionaire.

As was discussed previously, NIL deals can be separated into two main types: (1) those with third parties for brand endorsements, such as with Nike, and (2) those with college boosters via collectives, such as the one affiliated with the University of Michigan that contracted with Bryce Underwood in 2024. While brand endorsements can be very lucrative for a college athlete, as they are for Angel Reese and Olivia Dunne, booster-funded collectives are the source of the larger percentage of NIL deals and are responsible for making some college athletes immediate millionaires, such as the reported $10 million deal that Bryce Underwood landed. Currently, 80% of NIL money is raised by "NIL collectives," non-profit entities loosely affiliated with a school that receive donations from boosters, alumni, and fans of a particular school, then pay the funds to student athletes.[11] A college athlete may benefit from both types of NIL deals simultaneously, and neither type is usually exclusive of the other, which means that a player who signs an endorsement deal with Nike is generally not precluded from signing an NIL deal with a booster collective. As discussed in a previous chapter, collectives are frowned upon by the NCAA and criticized by less funded colleges, as the NCAA rules prohibit the use of an NIL deal to recruit an athlete to play for a particular college.[12] This rule remains controversial and is the subject of litigation. Consequently, on February 23, 2024, a federal judge in Tennessee granted a preliminary injunction that prohibits the NCAA from punishing athletes and/or boosters for negotiating NIL deals during their recruitment process or while they are in the Transfer Portal. One school, the University of Oregon, reportedly engaged in a large sum of money collective arrangements to fill its football roster.[13] Many of the top schools have active internal programs to facilitate their athletes penning NIL deals.[14] Hence, as of 2024, it appears that NIL collectives can negotiate deals with recruits without apparent fear of NCAA sanctions.[15]

Fortunately, a player, when first applying to colleges, can change their mind until they sign a formal letter of intent, as we saw in the case of Bryce Underwood's decision to choose Michigan after announcing his prior intention to play for LSU. On National Signing Day, a student will sign a National Letter of Intent and communicate that with a given college,[16] although this process has been affected by NIL-related deals.[17] With the legalization of booster collectives, the market for the top high school graduates has become intense, with an increase in the funding available to compete for a limited number of superstars. Based upon the economic maxim of supply and demand, as the supply has become more competitive, the demand has increased, which has resulted in the most sought-after superstars receiving multi-million-dollar NIL deals from collectives.[18] Many of these collective NIL deals have worked out as expected, while a few of them have floundered and resulted in lawsuits.[19]

Using the Transfer Portal as a Path to Millions of Dollars

Sometimes, after attending the college of their choice, a college athlete may have second thoughts about whether there is another college that better fits their needs and aspirations. Historically, in such a situation, a student may have found it difficult or practically impossible to transfer to another college. That changed for the betterment of a college athlete who wished to transfer colleges. In the fall of 2018, the NCAA established the "Transfer Portal,"[20] which facilitates an athlete who wishes to transfer from the college they are attending to another college.[21] The NCAA Transfer Portal is an online database that lists college athletes who are interested in changing schools.[22] In major college football, players can enter their name in the Portal during transfer windows in the winter and spring.[23] For the 2024–2025 academic year, the winter window was December 9–28, 2024, and the spring window was April 16–25, 2025.[24] For that academic year, the NCAA established a new set of rules, which include earlier Portal access, a one-time transfer exception, and stricter academic standards for players seeking to continue their college careers elsewhere.[25] Contrary to past practices, with the introduction of the Transfer Portal, a college athlete has a do-over, a second chance to attend their dream college.

To understand the value of the Transfer Portal to a player and why Angel Reese decided to transfer colleges halfway through her tenure, one needs to have a primer on the history and use of the Transfer Portal. The Transfer Portal is available to any NCAA player and is not limited to high-profile players. However, a team that will recruit a player via the Transfer Portal generally picks notable players or players they need to fill gaps in the team, primarily for college football. Some notable players who planned to access the Portal include starting quarterback Miller Moss from USC, as well as standout quarterback Jackson Arnold and wide receiver Nic Anderson from the University of Oklahoma.[26]

So, how does the Transfer Portal work, and why does a college athlete choose to utilize it? In the fall of 2024, an unprecedented number of college athletes announced their intention to access the Transfer Portal.[27] On December 9, 2024, with the end of the regular college football season, a college athlete could enter their name into the Transfer Portal through their college's compliance office which enters the player's name into a database. This process is totally confidential, although a player can make their intention to transfer public. Once a player's name appears in the Transfer Portal database, other schools are free to contact the player. Importantly, once a player enters the Portal, their college is no longer obligated to honor the athletic scholarship it gave them.[28] However, entering the Portal does not mean that a player will transfer; they can decide to stay with their existing college or transfer to another college that offers them the opportunity to do so.

Utilizing the Transfer Portal can create a win or a loss for a college athlete.[29] Notwithstanding, the Transfer Portal gives a player the power to act as a free agent, to test the market for their talents while providing coaches the opportunity to recruit that talent they value for their team's success.[30] Consequently, the Transfer Portal has increased the mobility of college athletes and gives them greater control to market themselves to coaches who might see the player's greater value playing for another team. Hence, the

Transfer Portal provides an athlete the opportunity to transfer to a higher-ranked college for more public exposure or to a lower-ranked college for greater time actually playing rather than sitting on the bench. Further, a college athlete might use the Transfer Portal to increase their chances of being recruited by a professional league. On the other hand, a college athlete might wish to transfer to another college because they simply want to play for a college that is closer to their hometown and families.

While athletes decide to transfer from one college to another for personal reasons, many of them are seeking to negotiate better NIL deals. Some expect that the move would mean getting some or more playing time, particularly becoming the number one quarterback at their new school. For example, Michigan's Alex Orji stated that he decided to enter the Transport Portal after his team's boosters reportedly spent $10–$12 million to entice Bryce Underwood to play for Michigan.[31] Others might be seeking a better fit with the team's philosophy or due to a change in the coaching staff. However, in this age of NIL deals, some are seeking some or more money they would get by going elsewhere or because of their disappointment in the money they were promised and did not receive. One highly publicized instance of the latter is that of Matt Sluka, of UNLV, whose claim of a failed NIL deal made massive headlines, as he accused the college of promising him a $100,000 NIL deal to transfer, which the college has denied, stating that such a promise would have violated NCAA rules and the law of the State of Nevada.[32] This raises the question of whether NIL deals can be used as incentives for a player to remain at a college or to enroll via transfer to another college. Some noteworthy players who entered the 2024 winter portal are Luke Kromenhoek, the quarterback for FSU; Eric Singleton, Jr., the wide receiver for Georgia Tech University; and Duce Robinson, a wide receiver for USC, perhaps hoping for better NIL deals.[33]

There are many pluses and minuses for a college athlete who accesses the Transfer Portal.[34] Most importantly, they can use a season-ending success to negotiate better financial and other benefits with the transfer schools, including a better scholarship with a better university or get more playing time on a more prestigious squad. Perhaps equally valuable, they can get out of a bad situation, such as an abusive coach or negative academic experience, or simply move closer to family. On the other hand, just like everything in life, there are some negatives to entering the Transfer Portal. These include (1) a lesser chance of scholarships, as some colleges may be less willing to give out scholarships if they believe an athlete will transfer after just a year or two and as you are in competition with other highly sought-after players; (2) more competition, as an athlete is likely competing for the same spot, so there is no guarantee a transfer will make the team or earn a scholarship; and (3) a feeling of abandonment and suspicion of disloyalty, such as having to explain the reasons why a person is seeking to leave their current college, coach, and team.

The Transfer Portal is great value to players who seek to maximize their value or find the right fit and coaches who are seeking needed talent to fit their rosters. However, critics claim that overall, the Transfer Portal causes more harm than good. They argue the Transfer Portal has created problems on all levels of college athletics: (1) it rewards selfish behavior and discourages loyalty, as it disregards relationships with a player's college, teammates, local community, and boosters; (2) it discourages fidelity and commitment, as it discourages patience and the importance of timing in career development such as waiting your turn to be the starting quarterback; and (3) it serves as an injustice to rising high school talent, as college coaches have realized that it is better to take in a new transfer player with college experience than to take in an inexperienced high school graduate, which has resulted in many talented recruits all over the country struggling to pick up athletic scholarship offers.[35]

That leaves us with the question, "How might an athlete use the Transfer Portal to maximize their NIL deals?" In other words, can the Transfer Portal enhance a player's NIL prospects? For various reasons, which are evidenced by Angel Reese's narrative, the Transfer Portal can enhance a college player's chances of landing lucrative NIL deals in several ways. In states where it is legal, a college's collective might use an NIL deal to recruit a player who has sought a transfer via the Transfer Portal, although that is technically contrary to NCAA rules. Further, by transferring from one college to another, a player might increase their performance and profile, which they hope will result in being recruited by a professional team.

How and Why Did Angel Reese Use the Transfer Portal to Enhance Her NIL Deals?

As mentioned in the introduction of this chapter, Angel Reese exemplifies a person who understands the creative process of discovering their path of least resistance. Important to that process is to first identify one's life and career goals, followed by making critical decisions that take a person from where they are to where they aspire to be. This part of Reese's narrative focuses on her journey of critical decision-making, which facilitated her goals of being a top recruit of the WNBA and being a college NIL millionaire.

Reese's path of least resistance was not easy nor was it obvious from the start. While she ended up playing for LSU, she did not begin there. Between 2020 and 2022, Angel Reese, a Baltimore native, began her college basketball career in her home state, spending her freshman and sophomore seasons playing for the University of Maryland Terrapins. There, she led the team to back-to-back Sweet 16s[36] and was recognized as a five-star recruit by 247Sports and ESPN and was the No. 2 overall in the class of 2020.[37] There, she majored in communications.

For various reasons, Reese realized that Maryland was no longer her path of least resistance. Therefore, on April 5, 2022, following her sophomore season, Reese entered the Transfer Portal, along with several of her teammates, following an eventful offseason in which Maryland lost its top two scorers.[38] About one month later, on May 6, 2022, LSU announced that Reese would be enrolling at the university's Baton Rouge campus, majoring in interdisciplinary studies.[39] At first glance, one might question the wisdom of Reese's decision to transfer. At Maryland, she was playing close to home, was the team's best player as only a sophomore, and was part of a successful Terrapins program.[40] However, Reese's decision to take a leap of faith and transfer to LSU clearly reflected her understanding that reaching one's goal often requires a change in college and a risk of failure. In explaining the reason for the move, Reese said,

> I needed a fresh start, a coach to push me to get me to the next level . . . I want to be a top draft pick, and I want to win at the highest level, so being able to come to L.S.U. and build with [women's basketball head] Coach [Kim] Mulkey and everything she has done in one year was just something that was important to me.[41]

Hence, Reese wanted to work with a coach whom she believed would position her to be a top recruit for the WNBA. Additionally, she was impressed by the school's commitment to creating a nationally recognized, winning women's basketball team.[42]

Consequently, Reese's decision to transfer to LSU has paid off by further developing her athletic and leadership skills, heightening her national visibility and profile, and leading to her being a top draft pick into the WNBA. Relative to NIL deals, her decision to transfer to LSU has meant millions of dollars in NIL deals. However, these successes have not come without Reese's ability to overcome adversity.

OVERCOMING ADVERSITY

For many Americans, negotiating the path of least resistance can be traversed relatively smoothly.[43] However, for many people, particularly for Black women, that path to achieve their goals is often obstructed by sexism and racism, including conscious, unconscious, and institutional bias.[44] Angel Reese's narrative shows how she persevered through adversity, which young Black women superstars must often overcome, including mental health issues. Consequently, she has become an advocate for sports and business development for Black women. Being familiar with championing the NIL rights for disadvantaged women, Reese could also be an effective champion for the NIL rights of all those who face personal challenges based on their background or skin color.

"Wicked": Talented Black Women as Unworthy

In the Broadway, later turned blockbuster movie, *Wicked*,[45] we see how society's racist proclivities against ultra-talented Black women severely test those women's emotional and physical wellbeing. Like *Wicked*'s heroine, Elphaba, who was mistreated because of her green skin, Reese has experienced and endured racism due to the color of her skin.[46] She faced apparent racism in sports at an early age. In January 2020, while Reese was a high school student, she was the object of an opposing coach's Instagram messages, which Reese's mother felt included racial overtones by attributing Reese's success to being genetically gifted.[47] That coach was reported to be later fired.[48]

Adding to the challenges of being a successful college athlete, during her college and her professional league career, Reese has been criticized by the media and demonized as being a "bad girl." For example, during the 2023 Women's NCAA Tournament, she flashed a "you can't see me" gesture directed against University of Iowa superstar Caitlin Clark. Reese used the taunt that was popularized by professional wrestler John Cena in pointing to her ring finger in reference to a championship ring. Some journalists and analysts criticized Reese for poor sportsmanship.[49] On the other hand, other journalists pointed out that Clark used the same gesture against Reese two games earlier.[50] In fact, Clark later defended Reese over the gesture.[51] In another racialized incident, following the championship game where LSU became the national champions, First Lady Jill Biden said that she wanted to extend an invitation to the White House to both LSU and the University of Iowa.[52] Reese initially rejected the offer but recanted after President Biden's press secretary clarified that only LSU would be invited, as the tradition was to invite only the winning team to the White House. Ultimately, President Joe Biden himself telephoned Reese individually and congratulated her on LSU's victory.[53]

In addition to challenges due to her race, Reese experienced what many college athletes of all backgrounds face, which are the pressures of athletics, academic demands, and maintaining life balance. One series of events in Reese's LSU path points specifically to the mental health challenges that are endemic to being an NIL millionaire. On November 14, 2023, during Reese's senior year at LSU, she was mysteriously benched by her coach, Kim Mulkey, in the middle of LSU's game against Kent State.[54] For undisclosed reasons, Reese did not play in her team's next four games.[55] The media speculated on why Reese was benched, including failing grades and her having a mental breakdown.[56] Under pressure to provide a reason for her decision, Mulkey later stated that it had to do with "locker room issues."[57] When Reese was asked about her absence from the game, she said, "Taking time to yourself is really important. I just felt like that was important, resetting and refocusing within the team. . . . Mental health is the most important thing before anything and I'm going to make sure I'm OK before anything because I don't want to cause harm or any cancer in the locker room."[58] As we will see, many college athletes and professional athletes must overcome mental health challenges.

Overcoming Mental Health Challenges

Angel Reese's narrative is a cautionary tale: how challenging it is to be an NIL college superstar. Think about all the demanding obligations: First, you must do all the preparation work for playing your sport, including practice and weight training, followed by the mental and physical demands of actually playing the sport, including traveling to out-of-state games. Second, you must maintain the required academic performance to be in good standing to be eligible to play. Third, you must maintain your social media profile by regularly posting interesting content and performing whatever duties are required by your NIL deal, such as making public appearances and posing for the taping of advertisements. Fourth, you have to manage your business ventures including seeking new NIL deal partners, accounting for revenue, assessing your NIL value, and ensuring compliance with NCAA, state, and university laws, rules, and regulations, including filing and paying income taxes and the like. Trying to balance all these physical, emotional, academic, and business demands results in a high level of stress. On the one hand, stress is a part of life and can be a byproduct of the excitement of sports and competition. But when there is too much stress, problems arise. Many college athletes can get stressed when they do not make the team, make a mistake, do not get the play time they want, or fall short of a metric they are working to achieve.[59]

Historically, mental health and mental illness were not on the public's conscious, which resulted in athletes at all levels and their families not being self-conscious of the negative effects of the issue and the need to address it. With several high-profile professional athletes publicly speaking about their mental health challenges, college athletes, their families, and their colleges have become more attuned to the importance of caring for the players' mental health. Highly regarded superstars including Simone Biles, Naomi Osaka, and Michael Phelps have used their platforms to advocate for mental health awareness in their respective sports.[60]

Mental health issues for top athletes are more the norm than the exception. A 2019 study found that about 35% of elite athletes have mental health concerns.[61] The top issues reported by athletes included feelings of burnout, depression, and anxiety.[62] Athletes operate under intense pressure and often face unrealistic expectations from coaches, fans, teammates, and even themselves.[63] Similarly, in a 2022 report by the NCAA, it was reported that college athletes report elevated levels of mental health concerns.[64]

Relevant to Black women in sports and high anxiety, the NCAA's report noted, "[m]ental health concerns remained highest among student-athlete demographic subgroups commonly displaying higher rates of mental distress (women, student-athletes of color, those identifying on the queer spectrum[,] and those reporting family economic hardship)."[65] "Thirty-eight percent of those in women's sports and 22% of the men's sports participants reported feeling mentally exhausted constantly or most every day, the most common concern reported."[66] In 2024, top mental health experts report that many athletes face mental health issues as they manage challenges to perform at top levels, with research showing that between 5% and 35% of elite athletes report a mental health disorder, with the numbers even higher among college athletes.[67] Consequently, mental health conditions that are common in athletes include depression, anxiety, overtraining syndrome that leads to burnout, eating disorders, traumatic stress disorder, and sleep disorder.

In a nutshell, Angel Reese has overcome the many stressful challenges of being a college NIL millionaire. It did not help when Reese read that her LSU coach, Kim Mulkey, commented that Reese was ineligible for the coveted John R. Wooden Award because Reese was one of Mulkey's players who "stay on that social media crap."[68] Notwithstanding, Reese's narrative reminds everyone that landing NIL deals is not the same as winning the lottery. Being a college NIL millionaire is very stressful and requires ongoing support and self-care.

LEADING THE WAY FOR BLACK WOMEN IN NIL DEALS

Despite the sexism, racism, and mental health challenges that Reese faced as being portrayed by the media as an "angry Black woman," her NIL deals reflect her popularity both on and off the basketball court. As a result, her success makes her a great role model for Black female college athletes. First, she is a brilliant basketball giant and an accomplished Internet social media influencer. Her talent, resilience, and resourcefulness combined to result in significant NIL deals. In 2023, during her senior year at LSU, On3 gave her a $1.8 million name, image, and likeness valuation, which put her among the top 10 highest-earning women athletes.[69] She has over 5.2 million followers across her social media platforms. In 2023, she was featured in *The Sports Illustrated Swimsuit Edition*, making history along with fellow LSU Tiger Livvy Dunne, the first two college athletes ever to be featured in the series.[70] In 2023, Reese was recognized in the TIME 100 Next list of emerging leaders from around the world.[71] In 2024, she made the *Forbes* "30 under 30" List.[72] Her captivating on-court persona and her inviting postgame pressers and social media posts have been rewarded with substantial NIL deals. These deals reportedly include Airbnb, Amazon, Beats by Dr. Dre, Bose, Coach, Discord, Good American, Intuit TurboTax, Mielle Organics, Outback Steakhouse, Pepsi Co.'s Starry, PlayStation, Reebok, Tampax, and Hershey's Reese's Pieces candy.[73] In September 2024,

Reese started a podcast called *Unapologetically Angel* on the Playmaker network, which will expand her social media network.[74]

Notwithstanding her NIL success, fortune, and athletic achievements, Reese has committed to promoting the positive image and development of young female athletes.[75] In July 2023, she launched the Angel C. Reese Foundation, which aims to empower girls through sports, education, and financial literacy.[76] She reportedly stated her goals for the Foundation were to foster equal opportunities for young women.[77] She contracted an NIL deal with the investment bank Goldman Sachs, which includes ads promoting policies aimed at combatting the pay disparity Black women face in America, stating, "Black women are still facing challenges. But I believe change is possible. I'm proud to be teaming up with Goldman Sachs One Million Black Women to make sure the voices of Black women in my community and across the country are heard."[78]

Despite Reese's fabulous successes with NIL deals, few college athletes who are Black women enjoy her success. Many women of African descent have also faced institutionalized discrimination in the form of gender norms and high testosterone "high-T" limits and bans in athletics.[79] Recent science on this issue indicates that high-T alone does not provide an athletic advantage to female, transgender, or intersex athletes. Data across Division I provided examples of racial discrimination against Black women in college sports. Despite the presence of Black players in the tournament, who make up the majority on most teams, Black women comprise just 3.8% of undergraduates at the 68 participating institutions.[80] Black women comprise 21% of the head coaches in NCAA Division I women's basketball but were outnumbered by white male coaches by five percentage points.[81]

Relative to NIL deals, college athletes who are Black women are highly represented in college basketball but generally not highly ranked in NIL valuations. Unfortunately, for these women, many of whom are leaders in their sport, historic inequalities and the lack of representation in traditional media have made it difficult to build a personal brand and profit from their accomplishments.[82] Reese is exception as is evidenced in a 2024 NIL valuation report of On3, which shows her with a very high evaluation.[83] As Reese entered the WNBA, the majority of the league's players were highly talented Black women. Hopefully, their pay and NIL deals will one day be comparable to their male counterparts who play for the NBA.

Notwithstanding, in the 2024 list of the top ten female college athletes, based on the On3 NIL valuations, only two out of the ten are African Americans.[84] They are Flau'jae Johnson, who was Reese's basketball teammate at LSU, with a $1.5 million valuation and 3.7 million social media followers, and Juju Watkins, who plays basketball for USC, with 1.1 million social media followers.[85]

Hence, Angel Reese's path of least resistance provides a roadmap for other women, particularly those who are African American, to emulate to become NIL college millionaires. Hers is a unique narrative of parlaying outstanding athlete achievements combined with savvy marketing to be at the top of the NIL game. It is inspirational to see how Reese is reaching back to encourage young women to find their creative selves. In summary, in addition to having to master her skills as a female college basketball superstar and NIL millionaire, Reese navigated through instances of racism, mental health, and sexism. She has been an advocate for opportunities for all women particularly Black women in NIL deals and for mental health awareness.

NIL POWER SECRET #8: EMULATE ANGEL REESE'S PATH OF LEAST RESISTANCE

Angel Reese has explored a unique power secret to become a college NIL millionaire. From an early age, she discovered her creative self and the path of least resistance. In doing so, she plotted out the most effective path from where she started as a college athlete to achieve her career goals of being a star player for the WNBA and an NIL multi-millionaire while still in college. With this power secret, Reese employed the Transfer Portal to lead LSU to a national championship. Most importantly, by envisioning her goals, she overcame the obstacles that highly talented female athletes and particularly those of color face in college athletics. Becoming a highly successful NIL millionaire and now a leading WNBA player, Reese proves the power of self-realization and goal-setting is one of the most powerful secrets that every college athlete should emulate, particularly Black women. Doing so could means millions of dollars in brand endorsements, as well as a leadership role for female athletes and particularly Black women and girls.

Further Reading

Kyra Alessandrini, Angel Reese Says WNBA Players Could Go on Strike over Salary, Benefits, Blavity (Mar. 13, 2025), https://blavity.com/angel-reese-says-wnba-players-could-go-on-strike.

Liz Robbins, *Fifty Years Ago, Billie Jean King Won Equal Pay—But She's Not Done Yet*, NY Times (update July 24, 2023), https://www.nytimes.com/2023/07/15/sports/tennis/billie-jean-king-us-open-equal-pay.html.

Max Escarpio, *Angel Reese Sends Warning to WNBA over Salary Concerns*, Athlon Sports (Mar. 7, 2025), https://athlonsports.com/wnba/angel-reese-sends-warning-wnba-over-salary-concerns.

Michelle Steele, *Sky Forward Angel Reese: "The WNBA Don't Pay My Bills,"* ESPN (Oct. 7, 2024), https://www.espn.com/wnba/story/_/id/41858086/sky-angel-reese-wnba-pay-my-bills.

Endnotes

1. Natasha Dye, *Angel Reese Says She's 'Done a Lot of Shopping Lately' after Major NIL Deals*, People (Aug. 8, 2023), https://people.com/angel-reese-done-a-lot-of-shopping-lately-after-nil-deals-7571387.
2. Alexa Philippou, *Maryland Terrapins' Angel Reese, Ashley Owusu Entering Women's Basketball Transfer Portal*, ESPN (Apr. 5, 2022), https://www.espn.com/womens-college-basketball/story/_/id/33675450/maryland-junior-guard-ashley-owusu-announces-entering-transfer-portal.
3. CBS Baltimore Staff, *Baltimore Native Angel Reese Leads LSU to First National Championship with Win over Iowa*, CBS News (Apr. 2, 2023), https://www.cbsnews.com/baltimore/news/baltimore-native-angel-reese-leads-lsu-to-first-national-championship-beats-iowa-102-85/.
4. Weston Blasi, *These 10 College Athletes Are Making over $1 Million a Year from NIL*, Market Watch (Oct. 13, 2023), https://www.marketwatch.com/story/these-10-college-athletes-are-making-over-1-million-a-year-from-nil-2199fe5a#.
5. Max Escarpio, *Angel Reese Sends Warning to WNBA over Salary Concerns*, Athlon Sports (Mar. 7, 2025), https://athlonsports.com/wnba/angel-reese-sends-warning-wnba-over-salary-concerns.
6. *Angel Reese Net Worth*, Celebrity Net Worth, https://www.celebritynetworth.com/richest-athletes/nba/angel-reese-net-worth/ (last accessed Mar. 14, 2024).
7. *See* Robert Fritz, The Path of Least Resistance: Learning to Become the Creative Force in Your Own Life (1989). I am especially thankful to my long-time best friend and fellow Yalie, attorney Steven Cousins, who introduced me to Robert Fritz's groundbreaking work.
8. *Id.*
9. *Id.*
10. *Id.*
11. *See* Serena Morones & Paul Heidt, *Following the Money in College Sports*, Morones Analytics (last accessed Mar. 11, 2025), https://moronesanalytics.com/following-the-money-in-college-sports/#_ftnref6.citing; Dan Whateley & Ashley Rodriquez, *How NIL Deals and Brand Sponsorships Are Helping College Athletes Make Money*, Insider (Sept. 19, 2023), https://www.businessinsider.com/how-college-athletes-are-getting-paid-from-nil-endorsement-deals.

12. Josh Moody, *The Current State of NIL*, Inside Higher Ed (June 7, 2023), https://www.insidehighered.com/news/students/athletics/2023/06/07/two-years-nil-fueling-chaos-college-athletics.
13. *See* Arden Cravalho, *How Much Money Built Oregon Ducks Current Roster*, MSN (Aug. 27, 2024), https://www.msn.com/en-us/sports/other/how-much-nil-money-built-oregon-ducks-current-football-roster/ar-AA1pwwF7?ocid=socialshare&pc=DCTS&cvid=b12c0ae7ca014b06906a30d70a11d971&ei=15.
14. *See Ranked: Which American College Has the Most NIL Athletes?*, EssentiallySports (Sept. 20, 2024), https://www.msn.com/en-us/sports/other/ranked-which-american-college-has-the-most-nil-athletes/vi-AA1qUjPC?ocid=socialshare&pc=DCTS&cvid=b14eb3a93a29407db7e0c3fc7e837377&ei=31.
15. *See* Stewart Mandel, *NCAA Recruiting Pay-For-Play Is Here, and the Only Surprise is How Fast it Happened*, Athletic, NY Times (Feb. 23, 2024), https://www.nytimes.com/athletic/5296175/2024/02/23/ncaa-nil-paying-recruits-tennessee-injunction/.
16. *National Letter of Intent*, nationalletter.org, http://www.nationalletter.org/ (last accessed Mar. 14, 2025).
17. Claire Boyer, *National Letter of Intent Edged Out of College Signing Day by NIL, Revenue Sharing*, MSN (Dec. 5, 2024), https://www.msn.com/en-us/sports/other/national-letter-of-intent-edged-out-of-college-signing-day-by-nil-revenue-sharing/ar-AA1vkskY?ocid=BingNewsSerp.
18. Nate Cunningham, *Highest Paid College Athletes via NIL Deals*, Sports Illustrated (Mar. 7, 2025), https://www.si.com/college-basketball/highest-paid-college-athletes-via-nil-deals.
19. *Caught in a Raging Storm: 5 Steps Your School Should Take as NIL Disputes Continue to Cause Problems for Universities*, Fisher Phillips (Feb. 5, 2025), https://www.fisherphillips.com/en/news-insights/nil-disputes-continue-to-cause-problems-for-universities.html#:~:text=The%20players%20allegedly%20never%20received,the%20payments%2C%20or%20lack%20thereof.
20. *See* Greg Johnson, *What the NCAA Transfer Portal Is... and What It Isn't*, NCAA.com (10/8/2019), https://www.ncaa.org/news/2023/2/8/media-center-what-the-ncaa-transfer-portal-is-and-what-it-isn-t; Alyssa, *Understanding the NCAA Transfer Portal and Recent Rule Changes*, Sports Recruiting Blog (Apr. 30, 2024), https://blog.sports recruits.com/2024/04/30/understanding-the-ncaa-transfer-portal-and-recent-rule-changes/.
21. Tom VanHaaren, *College Football's New Transfer Portal Windows, Explained*, ESPN (Nov 9, 2022), https://www.espn.com/college-football/story/_/id/34967085/college-football-new-transfer-portal-windows-explained.
22. Max Olson, *What Is the College Football Transfer Portal? When Is it?*, ESPN (Nov. 15, 2024), https://www.espn.com/college-football/story/_/id/42394369/what-college-football-transfer-portal-works-dates-explained.
23. *Id.*
24. *Id.*

25. Elizabeth Flores, *What Are the Changes to the NCAA College Football Transfer Portal?*, USA TODAY (Dec. 8, 2024), https://www.usatoday.com/story/sports/ncaaf/2024/12/08/ncaa-winter-transfer-portal-new-changes-explained/76839227007/.
26. *Id.*
27. James Parks, *College Football Transfer Portal Tracker: Live Updates in 2025 Cycle*, MSN (Dec. 13, 2024), https://www.msn.com/en-us/sports/other/college-football-transfer-portal-tracker-live-updates-in-2025-cycle/ar-AA1vdxqc?ocid=BingNewsSerp.
28. *Id.*
29. Mark Long & Eddie Pells, *More Playing Time? A Fresh Start? Extra Cash? The Transfer Portal Produces Winners and Losers*, AP (Dec. 13, 2024), https://apnews.com/article/transfer-portal-gabriel-etienne-16beb9f80d4b613e53003148a8317c49.
30. David Robinson, *The Transfer Portal: The Good, the Bad, and the Ugly*, SCHOLAR CHAMPION ATHLETE (Dec. 2023), https://www.scarecruiting.com/sports-recruiting-blog/the-transfer-portal-the-good-the-bad-and-the-ugly.
31. Morgan Moriarity, *Transfer Portal QB Tracker 2024: Latest News on Miller Moss, Thomas Castellanos and Others on the Move*, MSN (Dec. 29, 2024), https://www.msn.com/en-us/sports/other/transfer-portal-qb-tracker-2024-latest-news-on-miller-moss-thomas-castellanos-and-others-on-the-move/ar-AA1v8x0H?ocid=BingNewsSerp.
32. Mark Anderson, *Matthew Sluka, Who Left UNLV over NIL Dispute, Enters Transfer Portal*, AP (Oct. 31, 2024), https://apnews.com/article/sluka-unlv-nil-transfer-portal-50e2e14ac39f2cd5a980023bb9f531b3.
33. Morgan Moriarty, *Transfer Portal Rankings 2025: Updated List of Best College Football Players by Position*, SPORTING NEWS (Jan. 9, 2024), https://www.sportingnews.com/us/ncaa-football/news/college-football-transfer-portal-rankings-2025-best-players/243d2de559c8fce680b4ff68.
34. Sportse Media, *Transfer Portal Pros and Cons | the Wild West of College Sports*, SPORTSEPRENEUR (Dec. 14, 2024), https://sportsepreneur.com/transfer-portal-pros-and-cons-college-sports/; Luke Schlumpberger, *Angel Reese Transfer Portal: Top 5 Landing Spots if Star Forward Decides to Leave LSU*, SPORTSKEEDA (Mar. 21, 2024), https://www.sportskeeda.com/college-basketball/angel-reese-transfer-portal-top-5-landing-spots-star-forward-decides-leave-lsu; Spencer Davis, *NCAA Announces Immediate Change to Football Transfer Portal Windows*, SATURDAY DOWN SOUTH (Oct. 8, 2024), https://www.saturdaydownsouth.com/sec-football/ncaa-announces-immediate-change-to-football-transfer-portal-windows/.
35. Dylan DeBiccari, *Why the Transfer Portal Is Ruining College Football*, SHAKER BISON, STUDENT NEWS SITE OF SHAKER HIGH SCHOOL (Apr. 7, 2023), https://theshakerbison.com/2500/sports/why-the-transfer-portal-is-ruining-college-football/.
36. Univ. of Md. Terps, *2021–22 Women's Basketball Roster: Angel Reese*, UMTERPS.COM, https://umterps.com/sports/womens-basketball/roster/angel-reese/9591 (last accessed Mar. 15, 2024).

37. *Id.*
38. *See* Alexa Philippou, *Maryland Terrapins' Angel Reese, Ashley Owusu Entering Women's Basketball Transfer Portal*, ESPN (Apr. 5, 2022), https://www.espn.com/womens-college-basketball/story/_/id/33675450/maryland-junior-guard-ashley-owusu-announces-entering-transfer-portal.
39. Alexa Philippou, *LSU Lands Women's Basketball Transfer Angel Reese*, ESPN (May 6, 2022), https://www.theadvertiser.com/story/sports/college/lsu/2024/03/22/why-angel-reese-transferred-lsu-womens-basketball-maryland-kim-mulkey-portal/73004310007/.
40. *Id.*
41. Cabral Opiyo, *Why Did Angel Reese Transfer? LSU*, SPORTSKEEDA (Feb. 27, 2024), https://www.sportskeeda.com/college-football/news-why-angel-reese-transfer-lsu-wbb-star-s-transfer-timeline-revisited.
42. *See* Alexa Philippou, *LSU Lands Women's Basketball Transfer Angel Reese*, ESPN (May 6, 2022}, https://www.espn.com/womens-college-basketball/story/_/id/33866293/lsu-lands-women-basketball-transfer-angel-reese.
43. *See* Cheryl I. Harris, *Whiteness as Property*, 106 HARV. L. REV. 1707 (1993).
44. *See generally*, Mitchell F. Crusto, *Blackness as Property: Sex, Race, Status, and Wealth*, 1 STAN. J.C.R. & C.L. 51 (2005) (focusing on Black women's struggle for property rights).
45. Jon M. Chu, *Wicked* (2024), https://www.imdb.com/video/vi3628910361/?listId=ls053181649.
46. Charles Hallman, *Stereotypes Influence Black Women Athletes' NIL Deals*, MINN. SPOKESMAN-RECORDER (July 5, 2023), https://spokesman-recorder.com/2023/07/05/stereotypes-influence-black-women-athletes-nil-deals/.
47. Jerry Bembry, *Top Prospect Angel Reese the Target of Offensive Messages from Opposing Coach*, ANDSCAPE (Jan. 17, 2020), https://andscape.com/features/top-prospect-angel-reese-the-target-of-offensive-messages-from-opposing-coach/.
48. *Id.*
49. Rachel Treisman, *How a Hand Gesture Dominated a NCAA Title Game and Revealed a Double Standard*, NPR (Apr. 3, 2023), https://www.npr.org/2023/04/03/1167704651/angel-reese-caitlin-clark-you-cant-see-me-gesture.
50. Randi Richardson, *LSU Coach Reacts to Social Media Attacks on Angel Reese after Viral Hand Gesture*, TODAY (Apr. 3, 2023), https://www.today.com/news/sports/lsu-coach-kim-mulkey-angel-reese-you-cant-see-me-gesture-rcna77902.
51. Ben Morse, *Caitlin Clark Defends Angel Reese, Says She Shouldn't Be "Criticized" for Gesture Directed Toward Her*, CNN SPORTS (Apr. 5, 2023), https://www.cnn.com/2023/04/05/sport/caitlin-clark-defend-angel-reese-gesture-spt-intl/index.html.
52. Jonathan Franklin, *After Outcry, Jill Biden's Office Says White House Invitation Is for LSU Women's Team*, NPR (Apr. 4, 2023), https://www.npr.org/2023/04/04/1167965013/iowa-lsu-jill-biden-ncaa-basketball-championship.
53. Zoe Richardson, *President Biden Calls Angel Reese to Congratulate Her on LSU's Championship*, NBC NEWS (Apr. 7, 2023), https://www.nbcnews.com/politics/white-house/biden-calls-angel-reese-congratulate-lsus-championship-rcna78760.

54. Emma Hruby, *Why LSU Coach Kim Mulkey Did Not Play Angel Reese in Second Half*, JUST WOMEN'S SPORTS (Nov. 15, 2023), https://justwomenssports.com/reads/lsu-womens-basketball-kim-mulkey-angel-reese-kent-state-2023/.
55. Katie Barnes, *LSU Survives Virginia to Stay Unbeaten Without Angel Reese*, ESPN (Nov. 25, 2023), https://www.espn.com/womens-college-basketball/story/_/id/38980381/lsu-survives-virginia-stay-unbeaten-angel-reese.
56. *Id.*
57. Brett Martel, *LSU's Angel Reese Returns, Says She Wants People to Realize She Is Not Just an Athlete*, AP (Dec. 1, 2023), https://apnews.com/article/lsu-angel-reese-c4e8a3e350389903526b682328fc2a66.
58. *Id.*
59. Amelia Gulliver, Kathleen M. Griffiths, & Helen Christensen, *Barriers and Facilitators to Mental Health Help-Seeking for Young Elite Athletes: A Qualitative Study*, BMC PSYCHIATRY (Sept. 26, 2012), https://doi.org/10.1186/1471-244X-12-157.
60. Andrea Wurzburger & Paris C., *16 Times Athletes Opened Up About Their Mental Health: From Simone Biles to Michael Phelps*, PEOPLE (Aug. 14, 2014), https://people.com/athletes-discussing-mental-health-8695196.
61. *Barriers and Facilitators to Mental Health Help-Seeking for Young Elite Athletes: A Qualitative Study*, MASS GENERAL BRIGHAM, MCLEAN HOSPITAL, https://www.mcleanhospital.org/essential/athlete-mh#:~:text=A%202019%20study%20found%20that,%2C%20teammates%2C%20and%20even%20themselves (last accessed Mar. 15, 2025).
62. *Id.*
63. *Id.*
64. Greg Johnson, *Mental Health Issues Remain on Minds of Student-Athletes*, NCAA (May 2–2022), https://www.ncaa.org/news/2022/5/24/media-center-mental-health-issues-remain-on-minds-of-student-athletes.aspx.
65. *Id.*
66. *Id.*
67. *Mental Health in Athletes: Breaking the Stigma*, CLEVELAND CLINIC (July 22, 2024), https://health.clevelandclinic.org/mental-health-in-athletes.
68. Kent Babb, *The Kim Mulkey Way*, WASH POST. (Mar. 30, 2024), https://www.washingtonpost.com/sports/2024/03/30/kim-mulkey-lsu-griner-reese/.
69. Shivam Pratap Singh, *$1.7 Million NIL-Valued Angel Reese Goes Ballistic as Instagram Faces a Major Glitch—"What's Going On???,"* SPORTSKEEDA (Mar. 5, 2024), https://www.sportskeeda.com/college-basketball/news-1-7-million-nil-valued-angel-reese-goes-ballistic-instagram-faces-major-glitch-what-s-going-on.
70. Griffin Adams, *Boardroom NIL Report Card: LSU's Angel Reese*, BOARDROOM (July 2, 2023), https://boardroom.tv/angel-reese-nil-deals-valuation-lsu/#:~:text=The%20Sports%20Illustrated.
71. Candace Parker, *Time100 Next: Angel Reese*, TIME (Sept. 13, 2023), https://time.com/collection/time100-next-2023/6308506/angel-reese/.
72. *30 Under 30*, FORBES, https://www.forbes.com/30-under-30/2024/sports (last accessed Mar. 15, 2025).

73. Michelle Steele, *Sky Forward Angel Reese: "The WNBA Don't Pay My Bills,"* ABC News (Oct. 17, 2024), https://abcnews.go.com/Sports/sky-forward-angel-reese-wnba-pay-bills/story?id=114916200#:~:text=Make%20no%20mistake%2C%20Reese%20is,10%20highest%2Dearning%20women%20athletes; Stephanie Apstein, *LSU Stars Angel Reese and Olivia Dunne Are Rolling in NIL Deals,* Sports Illustrated (Sept. 13, 2023), https://www.si.com/college/2023/09/13/lsu-leader-nil-deals-women-athletes-angel-reese-livvy-dunne; Elizabeth Flores, *Angel Reese Becomes First Major NIL Signing for Shaq in New Role with Reebok,* USA Today (Oct. 17, 2023), https://www.usatoday.com/story/sports/2023/10/17/angel-reese-signs-nil-deal-with-shaq-reebok/71215220007/.
74. Liam McKeone, *Angel Reese Reveals New Weekly Podcast Titled "Unapologetically Angel,"* Sports Illustrated (Aug. 27, 2024), https://www.si.com/media/angel-reese-reveals-new-weekly-podcast-unapologetically-angel.
75. Alejandro Danois, *Angel Reese's Next Goal: Breaking the Stereotypes of Girls Sports and Giving Hope to Young Athletes,* Baltimore Banner (July 21, 2023), https://www.thebaltimorebanner.com/sports/angel-reese-girls-sports-stereotypes-B5LSD6GQ7FCONGMLY7IVCTQLKQ/.
76. Charna Flam, *Angel Reese to Launch Foundation Dedicated to Female Empowerment,* Variety (July 13, 2023), https://variety.com/2023/sports/athletes/angel-reese-announces-foundation-female-empowerment-1235667355/.
77. *Id.*
78. Jeroslyn JoVonn, *Angel Reese Joins Goldman Sachs "One Million Black Women" to Combat Pay Disparity,* Black Enterprise (Apr. 2, 2024), https://www.blackenterprise.com/angel-reese-goldman-sachs-one-million-black-women/; Jasmine Browley, *Angel Reese Is Racking Up NIL Deals and We're Here for It,* Essence (Apr. 24, 2023), https://www.essence.com/news/money-career/angel-reese-nil-lsu-ncaa-march-madness/.
79. Donald Earl Collins, *Misogynoir in Sports: How Black Women Athletes Are Devalued,* Aljazeera (Sept. 28, 2022), https://www.aljazeera.com/opinions/2022/9/28/black-women-athletes-are-undervalued-and-undermined#:~:text=Many%20Black%20and%20African%20women,%2C%20transgender%2C%20or%20intersex%20athletes.
80. Lois Elfman, *Report: Black Female Student-Athletes Face Lack of Diverse Support,* Diverse Education (Apr. 3, 2024), https://www.diverseeducation.com/sports/article/15667891/report-shows-that-black-female-studentathletes-face-lack-of-diverse-support.
81. *Id.*
82. Charles E. Campbell, *Empowering Black College Athletes with NIL Deals,* Medium (Jan. 29, 2024), https://medium.com/@wbsbpd88/empowering-black-college-athletes-with-nil-deals-d911fdeaf1d1.
83. *On3 Women's NIL Valuations,* On3 (updated Mar. 12, 2025), https://www.on3.com/nil/rankings/player/womens-nil-100/.
84. *Id.*
85. *Id.*

9

Dr. Myron Rolle: Pursuit of One's Education

"These institutions have a machinery to move you where you need to be. If you stick in a bubble of just football or basketball, you miss out on it."

—Dr. Myron Rolle[1]

OVERVIEW

Dr. Myron Rolle is not your average football star. He is a Rhodes Scholar and was a former All-American player at Florida State University ("FSU"), at a time when NIL deals were not permitted. He enjoyed a promising career as a professional football player, but he was not swayed by the glamour and money that come from playing for the NFL. Instead, he capitalized on his athletic and academic scholarships to pursue his ultimate dream. Along the way, he was an outstanding college football player and was drafted into the NFL as a safety for the Tennessee Titans in 2010. While others were chasing fame and fortune in football and NIL deals, Rolle became enriched through education. Consequently, he gave up a lucrative deal as an NFL player to become a pediatric neurosurgeon at Johns Hopkins All Children's Hospital in Baltimore, Maryland.

Dr. Rolle's NIL power secret is not to be enchanted by NIL money and an apparent charmed life as a professional football player but to embrace a different dream: to become a medical professional, with greater longevity and less risk of physical injury than professional football. In sharing the wisdom of his journey, he has become a motivational speaker. His inspirational story and lessons learned are captured in his book, *The 2% Way: How a Philosophy of Small Improvements Took Me to Oxford, the NFL, and Neurosurgery*. In 2025, Rolle launched a "Health Is Wealth" show on Players TV, the first television network owned by professional athletes.

After college, Rolle had a promising career with the NFL. In 2010, he signed a four-year contract with the Tennessee Titans. About two years later, he reportedly signed a three-year contract with the Pittsburgh Steelers, averaging $480,000 a year. In 2022, he reportedly made $259,300 in annual total annual compensation as a Independent Director at Abiomed Inc. Today, as a pediatric neurosurgeon, his estimated annual salary is about $400,000 a year. Rolle's net worth is reportedly between $1 million and $5.[2]

AN OUTSTANDING SCHOLAR-ATHLETE

Myron Rolle is the son of Whitney and Beverley Rolle, who are Bahamian Americans who instilled in him hard work and the value of education.[3] He grew up in New Jersey and, while in high school, played saxophone in the school band, sang in a school play, and was the sports editor of the school newspaper. Most importantly, he also played football, basketball, and ran track. In high school, he was a talented athlete and, in 2005, was the No. 1 rated college-bound recruit in America.[4] He was an equally outstanding, dedicated student who, throughout high school, maintained a 4.0 grade point average. In 2006, after a nationwide search, Rolle won the prestigious Franklin D. Watkins Memorial Trophy for the top African American male scholar-athlete.[5]

As the No. 1 football college-bound recruit in 2005, with an outstanding academic record, Rolle was determined to enroll in a college that would facilitate three separate, conflicting goals: (1) He wanted to be a top recruit to the NFL, following the example of his two cousins, Antrel and Samari. (2) He wanted to be awarded the prestigious Cecil J. Rhodes Scholarship ("Rhodes Scholarship"), following the inspiration of Bill Bradley, who was a Rhodes Scholar before playing for the NFL and eventually becoming a U.S. Senator representing the state of New Jersey. And (3) he wanted to enroll in a strong pre-med program, which would facilitate his dream to attend medical school and become a neurosurgeon. He found support for all his dreams at FSU, which had both an outstanding football program and an equally outstanding pre-med program. Further, he later reported on a transformative lesson that he learned from defensive coordinator Mickey Andrews.[6] That lesson was to "Get 2 percent better" each day.[7]

By 2008, Rolle had laid the foundation for all his diverse goals. That year, he graduated magna cum laude from FSU with a Bachelor of Science in Exercise Science in just two and a half years. Additionally, while playing for FSU, he had earned all the athlete accolades to qualify him as a recruit for the NFL. As three-year starter as a safety, he was awarded Associated Press All-American, All-ACC, and College Sports Information Directors of America Academic All-America honors. As if these achievements were not enough, in 2008, Rolle was awarded a prestigious Rhodes Scholarship, which would allow him to study at the University of Oxford in England. There, in 2009, he earned an MSc degree in medical anthropology. Not forgetting his humble beginnings and the role that God played in his successes, in 2009, he founded the Myron L. Rolle Foundation, which is dedicated to the support of health, wellness, educational, and other charitable initiatives that benefit children and families in need.[8]

In 2010, Rolle realized another of his dreams, one to which many college athletes aspire. Returning from Oxford, he was drafted in the sixth round by the Tennessee Titans. On June 14, 2010, he signed a four-year contract and was a Titan for two seasons.[9] He later played for the Pittsburgh Steelers until 2012.[10] Rolle left the NFL with a unique distinction: he was only the third person to have received a Rhodes Scholarship and a contract with an NFL team.

Having achieved two of the major milestones in his dream journey, Rolle had one more goal to check off his wish list: to become a neurosurgeon. In 2013, to reach that goal, he announced his intent to leave the NFL to attend medical school. While being a star athlete at FSU, Rolle had completed the necessary pre-med requirements to enroll in medical school. Consequently, he enrolled at the FSU College of Medicine and graduated in May 2017. He later completed his medical residency in neurosurgery at Massachusetts General Hospital and Harvard Medical School and was a Global Neurosurgery Fellow at Harvard Medical School. In 2024, he was reportedly appointed as a pediatric neurosurgery fellow at Johns Hopkins All Children's Hospital.[11]

Rolle has several additional accomplishments. On February 17, 2021, Abiomed, a member of the S&P 500, elected Rolle to join its board of directors. He serves on the Knight Commission on Athletics and the Clinton

Global Initiative. He is also the co-creator of the Emerging Scholars Project for underrepresented college students applying for a Rhodes Scholarship.

In achieving his medical career goal, Rolle is not the only former NFL athlete who has become a doctor. In addition to Rolle, several NFL players have gone on to pursue careers in medicine and become doctors. Some notable examples include Laurent Duvernay-Tardif, who played as an offensive lineman for the Kansas City Chiefs before becoming a doctor; John Frank, who played as a tight end for the San Francisco 49ers before becoming a successful orthopedic surgeon in California; and Ken Mok, who played as a linebacker for the New Orleans Saints before becoming an anesthesiologist in California. These individuals have shown that it is possible to excel in both professional sports and medicine, demonstrating the importance of pursuing one's passions and goals outside of the athletic arena.

Of course, becoming a doctor is one of many professions that former and would-be NFL and professional athletes have opted for. In addition to Rolle, another outstanding Rhodes Scholar, who left the NFL for another profession, became both a lawyer and a famous U.S. Supreme Court justice. His name is Byron Raymond "Whizzer" White, who established himself as a judicial giant, having sat on the Court from 1962 to 1993.[12]

Dr. Rolle's narrative illustrates how important it is for college athletes to take advantage of educational opportunities while they play sports. However, that is not an easy task, as many athletes would not be enrolled in many of their colleges but for an athletic scholarship. Further, athletics is not a side hustle; it is a full-time commitment, with practices, weight training, and games both at home and on the road. In too many instances, players come from disadvantaged communities with under-resourced educational programs. All too often, they are directed to remedial programs to ensure they remain academically eligible to play their sport. Further, managing their NIL business and creating social media can be very stressful. Consequently, when it comes to balancing education with NIL opportunities, a college athlete can learn a lot from the experiences of Dr. Rolle.

COLLEGE ATHLETES WHO FORGO NIL DEALS FOR THE NFL

Rolle was a college athlete during a time when players were not legally allowed to capitalize on their NIL or to receive compensation of any kind. In fact, when he interviewed for the Rhodes Scholarship, the

NCAA permitted him to take a chartered plane from his interview in Birmingham, Alabama, to College Park, Maryland, where his team was playing a game that same day.[13] As a result, it is unknown whether he would have taken advantage of NIL deals if they were available to him. However, it seems clear that he would not have deviated from his career goal of becoming a doctor to take potentially short-term money. Later, after NIL deals became legal for college athletes, when asked what advice he would give to college athletes considering NIL deals, he sees opportunity for the players. Notwithstanding, he noted that more important than the money is the opportunity to challenge an athlete's college to deliver on an athlete's overall career goals. "These [educational] institutions have a machinery to move you where you need to be. If you stick in a bubble of just football or basketball, you miss out on it.[14] "You have an opportunity to change your life and change your family's life."[15]

However, contrary to Rolle's advice, today many players are rushing to maximize how much money they can make as soon as possible. Some of these are deciding to seek out and sign off on NIL deals. In addition, there are players who are deciding to cut short their college education to enter the professional league early. Some college athletes, such as the narrative of Bronny James, reportedly seek to leave college early to enter the draft. Fortunately, the NBA no longer allows its teams to draft star players right out of high school. Because of this regulation, some high school basketball stars are traveling overseas for a year or two to play in Canada or Europe. They then return to the U.S. when they qualify for the NBA draft. Consequently, NBA's rosters have been filled with 19-year-old kids who head for the NBA draft after just one season of playing in college.[16]

Consistent with Rolle's advice to focus on the long-game, many college athletes are choosing to forgo NIL deals, despite the potential financial and endorsement opportunities those deals offer. As noted in a previous chapter, many are deciding to pass on NIL deals for several distinct reasons. Some players find NIL deals too risky and may choose to avoid potential violations of NCAA rules or eligibility issues that could jeopardize their athletic careers. Perhaps those reluctant players recognize that NIL is highly regulated, that NIL laws vary from state to state, and that federal legislation and litigation may change the nature of NIL deals. Further, the NCAA has specific rules and regulations governing NIL activities for college athletes. Or perhaps those players have weighed the cost to benefit and believe that for most college athletes, particularly those who are not star football, basketball, or baseball players, pursuing NIL deals is too costly in time and money. In fact, most NIL deals are not the multi-million-dollar deals we read about. Most of them are under $10,000 a year. Or perhaps those players, particularly those who play high-profile sports like football, know that the odds of them being recruited into the NFL are very slim, as the NFL only hires 300 athletes each year out of thousands of college players.

Needless to say, in addition to participating in intercollegiate sports, most college students attend college for reasons other than making money while they are in college and so might not be interested in pursuing NIL deals. Not all college athletes may be interested in or comfortable with leveraging their NIL for endorsement deals or sponsorships. Further, some athletes may simply prefer to maintain a low profile and avoid the spotlight that comes with NIL opportunities. Then there is the challenge of time management. Balancing the demands of being a college athlete with academic coursework, training sessions, and competitions can be challenging. Some athletes likely feel that they do not have the time or resources to actively pursue and manage NIL deals on top of their existing commitments.

Furthermore, many college students, including athletes, have long-term goals and do not want to be sidelined by the lure of an NIL deal. They prioritize their athletic performance and commitments, focusing on training, competitions, and academics. They may feel that pursuing NIL deals could be a distraction from their sports career or academic responsibilities. Additionally, some college athletes may have personal values or beliefs that lead them to prioritize other aspects of their college experience over financial opportunities. They may prefer to focus on academics, team camaraderie, or personal growth rather than pursuing NIL deals. Reflecting on the fact that not every NIL is a good deal, some players might figure that taking some quick money early might mean that they are selling their talent short. Perhaps it is better to wait for the deal that truly reflects their maximum value or to pass on NIL altogether.

In summary, the decision to forgo NIL deals is a personal one and can be influenced by a variety of factors, including athletic priorities, NCAA regulations, personal values, lack of interest, time constraints, and uncertainty about the future. Each college athlete may have their own reasons for choosing whether or not to pursue NIL opportunities, and pursuing their education should be a major priority.

WHY FOCUS ON EDUCATION

The Value of an Education Is Often Missed

When Rolle decided to leave the NFL for medical school, some NFL draft experts estimated that this decision cost him an estimated $8 million.[17] Yet, Rolle noted in an interview that some statistics show that 78% of NFL players face financial duress just two years after their retirement.[18] Does "get rich quick" mean "lose rich quick" too?

Dr. Rolle's inspirational narrative of educational success raises a dark side of college athletics. Unfortunately, he is a rare exception compared to many college athletes. Rolle received an excellent high school education, graduating from a top-flight high school with a 4.0 grade point average. By comparison, many college athletes, particularly those from disadvantaged backgrounds, who enroll in college with athletic scholarships come from substandard elementary and high schools. Compare this to Rolle's stellar high school academic achievements that included completing Advanced Placement credits, which means that he entered college with less coursework needed to graduate. With his commitment to education and athletics, Rolle completed college in two and a half years. Further, with the award as a Rhodes Scholar, FSU permitted him to credit his time at Oxford toward his college degree.

By comparison, many college athletes are required to enroll in remedial classes, which means it would take them more years, not less time, to graduate. Further, many college athletes never complete their education, leaving without earning a degree. In fact, according to NCAA data, about 30% of college athletes do not earn a degree within six years of enrolling in college. However, the graduation rate varies among different demographics, including race. For example, historically, Black college athletes have had lower graduation rates compared to their white counterparts. While the specific percentage of Black college athletes who do not earn a degree may vary, studies have shown that there is a significant disparity in graduation rates based on race in college athletics. Furthermore, most college athletes will never become professional athletes. The reality is that there are more than a million high school football players, but very few of them ever make the NFL—only about 300 athletes join the League each year. In summary, Rolle's hard work, intelligence, academic preparation, and athleticism meant that he earned the option to play for the NFL or to become a doctor. He ultimately chose the latter to become an M.D.

With the goal of better preparing college athletes for life's success beyond professional sports, the Knight Commission on Intercollegiate Athletics ("Commission") was established in October 1989.[19] It was formed by the John S. and James L. Knight Foundation[20] in response to highly visible scandals in college sports. The Commission's goal is to promote a reform agenda that emphasizes academic values in a climate in which the commercialization of college sports often overshadows the underlying goals of higher education. Their work is invaluable considering all the media hype over NIL deals.

To provide greater financial transparency on colleges' athletic spending, the Commission's Athletic and Academic Spending Database provides financial data for more than 220 public institutions. To create a stronger focus on the educational mission of college sports, the Commission has recommended several initiatives that will strengthen the educational focus, including providing four-year athletic scholarships and guaranteeing financial assistance for former scholarship athletes to complete degree requirements. Other recommendations include reducing the athletics time demands on athletes; revising revenue distribution for the College Football Playoff and the NCAA Men's Basketball Championship to reduce the emphasis on winning and increase the emphasis on educational values; and requiring Division I institutions to make NCAA financial reports public to provide needed transparency for how the money in college sports is used to strengthen the educational mission. In 2014, the Commission welcomed Dr. Rolle as one of its members.[21] He is a living testimony to the value of a college and professional education. In response to these concerns, over the years, the NCAA has adopted several of the Commission's recommendations, including the rule that requires teams to be on track to graduate more than 50% of their players to be eligible for postseason competition.

Inherent Risks in Playing for the NFL

With so many college athletes who aspire to play for the NFL or other professional leagues, some might question Rolle's decision to seek a career in medicine in lieu of playing professional football. The truth is that professional sports, particularly the NFL, are not always a dream come true, a pathway to wealth, health, and longevity. In fact, for many NFL players, a career with the NFL leads to financial ruin, poor health, and a shorter lifespan.

Of course, not all college athletes have either the skills or the aspiration to play professional sports. The typical college athlete varies widely by sport and division. However, NCAA data suggest that the majority of college athletes are white (around 60% overall), with significant representation from middle-class families.[22] Female athletes often outnumber male athletes in sports like volleyball, soccer, and softball due to Title IX. The demographic trends also depend on whether it is a revenue-generating sport, like football or basketball, which tends to have more racial diversity, particularly a higher percentage of Black athletes.

These demographics of college athletes leads a discussion of how colleges use athletic scholarships to their advantage.[23] Only about 2% of high school athletes receive athletic scholarships to play at the college level, and within the NCAA, less than 60% of athletes are awarded any scholarship funds.[24] Many scholarships are partial, with full scholarships typically reserved for revenue-generating sports such as football and basketball. Athletic scholarships are often awarded on a year-to-year basis, not for the full duration of a college career. Whether or not a player will have their athletic scholarship renewed depends on athletic and academic performance as well as the coach's discretion. Consequently, multi-year scholarships do exist but are less common. An athletic scholarship typically covers tuition, fees, room, board, and books, but often do not cover additional living expenses, travel costs, or certain educational materials like computers. As a result, cost of attendance and stipends have become more common to help bridge these gaps.

As one might suspect, scholarships are contingent on the athlete remaining eligible and playing for the team. If a student fails to meet performance or conduct standards or leaves the team, the scholarship can be revoked. Further, a scholarship is contingent on good academic standing, which means an athlete must meet the NCAA minimum grade point average requirement of 2.3 for Division I and 2.2 for Division II, though individual schools and teams may have higher standards. A student's academic progress is also monitored through the NCAA's Progress Toward Degree requirements. Hence, athlete scholarships are not a guarantee throughout a player's college tenure, nor are they guaranteed if a player choose not to or cannot play, perhaps due to injury.

The scholarship picture changes when it comes to the high revenue sport of mens' football. There, NCAA Division I football teams often have over 50% Black players, particularly in revenue-generating positions. Many of these athletes come from lower-income backgrounds, with fewer resources and opportunities compared to their white counterparts. High expectations, sometimes low academic qualifications, the demands of the sport, and financial pressures create a very stressful environment for these players. Facing these financial realities, relative to a college athlete from an impoverished background, both NIL and professional sports money are prized opportunities. The average salary of an NFL player is about $2 million per year, but median salaries are lower. The average career length is 3.3 years, reflecting the physical toll of the sport. The average NBA salary is approximately $9.6 million annually, making it the highest among major leagues. The average career length is around 4.5 years. Additionally, the average MLB salary is roughly $4.9 million annually, with career lengths averaging about 5.6 years. Minor league players, however, earn significantly less. While the money is good when it is flowing, when the well runs dry, a professional athlete needs a plan to make it financially when their sports career ends. For example, the data suggest that 60% of former NBA players face financial hardships within five years of retirement due to poor financial planning, extravagant spending, and lack of support.[25] The problem is common across professional sports, although programs now exist to educate athletes on financial literacy.[26]

In addition to financial risks, college athletes face significant potential injuries that can also result in a loss of scholarship. For example, studies indicate that up to 50% of college football players experience injuries each season, ranging from minor to severe concussions, ligament tears, and stress fractures, which are among the most common injuries. Long-term effects like chronic traumatic encephalopathy ("CTE") from repeated head trauma are significant concerns in contact sports like football. These health risks are greatly increased for those college athletes when they play professional sports.

Hence, Rolle likely made a calculated risk: playing for the NFL meant some quick big bucks, potential concussion, possible bankruptcy, and a shortened lifespan. Or he could choose to become a neurosurgeon, with a large, steady source of income, a healthy lifestyle, and financial security. It is clear that he made a wise choice.

CALL TO COMPENSATE COLLEGE ATHLETES AS EMPLOYEES

Reflecting on Dr. Rolle's success story and its exceptionalism as well as the dangers of risks inherit to playing a college sport, it has been suggested that colleges should treat and compensate their athletes as employees through some sort of revenue-sharing arrangement. As previously noted, currently college athletes are not paid any money, other than scholarships and expenses, for their play. There are persuasive arguments on both sides. Those in favor of treating players as employees of their schools argue that (1) as many college athletes generate significant revenue for their schools and the NCAA through their performances, treating athletes as employees would allow them to receive fair compensation for their contribution; (2) as employees, athletes would have more legal protections and rights regarding issues such as healthcare, working conditions, and fair treatment, particularly against sexual harassment; (3) college athletes often dedicate a significant amount of time to their sports, which can impact their ability to focus on academics and other aspects of college; treating them as employees could recognize and compensate them for this time commitment; and (4) while the law permits college athletes to benefit from the use of their NIL by third parties, colleges can use their players' NIL for free.

Then there are arguments against treating players as employees. Some of these arguments include: (1) it would have a negative impact on amateurism, which has been a fundamental principle in college athletics, and paying athletes could undermine this concept; (2) some players contribute more to the media and other sports-related revenue of their college, so treating some as employees and not all raises equity and fairness issues and can lead to potential disparities in compensation and benefits; and (3) as men's college sports bring in more revenue than women's sports, treating college athletes as employees could raise concerns about gender equity and compliance with Title IX regulations.

Overall, the debate over whether college athletes should be treated as employees is complex and involves considerations of fairness, equity, and the fundamental principles of collegiate athletics. Notwithstanding, past and present college students continue to press their demand for compensation and other benefits that inure to college employees in the court of law. In the past, some courts have decided that college athletes are not employees. However, in September 2021, the National Labor Relations Board issued a memorandum stating that certain college athletes can be considered employees under the National Labor Relations Act and, therefore, are workers eligible to unionize. This would allow college athletes to earn salaries, qualify for worker's compensation benefits, and access all the benefits of employees under U.S. labor law, including the right to form a union. However, this is at odds with NCAA rules, which prohibit athletes from being institutional employees.[27]

The issue of compensation for play continues to be litigated in the courts. Following the Supreme Court's decision in *Alston v. NCAA*, the tide seems to be turning in favor of the players. That case effectively threw out limits the NCAA had set on compensating college athletes. In the meantime, there is a movement to unionize college athletes. For example, in March 2024, Dartmouth College men's basketball players voted to join a union, becoming the first U.S. college athletes to do so.[28] A regional director with the labor board determined that the players were Dartmouth's employees because the basketball program generates publicity, alumni engagement, and financial donations, and the school has significant control over them.[29] Previously, in 2014, football players at Northwestern University in Evanston, Illinois, became the first college athletes to vote in a union election, but the ballots were impounded due to a legal challenge by the school.[30] Hence, at this time, college athletes are generally not being compensated for their athletic roles and are not unionized, but there is continued pressure for colleges to pay athletes to play.

Players' being compensated for their contribution to their school's athletic revenue raises an issue of fairness. College athletic programs generate an estimated $8.5 billion in revenue for top schools each year, while less than 7% of that money is passed on to athletes in the form of scholarships and stipends, according to a 2020 report by the National Bureau for Economic Research.[31] In July 2024, in *Johnson v. NCAA*, a U.S. appeals court created a test for courts to determine when college athletes are the employees of their schools and the NCAA, making them eligible for the minimum wage.[32] That test states that athletes may be regarded as employees under federal wage laws if they primarily perform services for their schools' benefit "in return for express or implied compensation or in-kind benefits."[33] The court stated:

> The issue raised by this interlocutory appeal is not whether the athletes before us are actually owed the protections of the Fair Labor Standards Act (FLSA), but rather, whether college athletes, by nature of their so-called amateur status, are precluded from ever bringing an FLSA claim. Our answer to this question is no.[34]

This case opens the matter of employee status for athletes to further litigation by both past and present athletes. Related to this matter, in June 2025, in *House v. NCAA*, a federal court approved a landmark $2.8 billion settlement by the NCAA, which seeks to resolve class-action lawsuits claiming it had violated antitrust law by restricting the compensation and benefits to students for their athletic service.[35] One aspect of the settlement is a revenue-sharing prevision by which the NCAA and its member colleges will compensate past, present, and future college athletes, within a given cap. However, the settlement contains many contentious provisions. For example, it would bar college athletes from unionizing.

Hence, Dr. Rolle's experience and decisions raise many concerns for college athletes: the high risk of injury, the lack of adequate compensation for college athletes, and the importance of providing college athletes a quality educational experience.

NIL POWER SECRET #9: ADOPT DR. MYRON ROLLE'S PURSUIT OF EDUCATION AND NON-ATHLETIC PROFESSIONS

In summary, Dr. Myron Rolle's decision to prioritize education and his passion for medicine over a potentially lucrative football career is a testament to his dedication, intelligence, and perseverance. He is a role model for college athletes everywhere, showing that it is possible to pursue multiple passions and achieve success in different fields. Despite the pressure to focus solely on his football career, Rolle made the difficult decision to defer his NFL aspirations to focus on engaging educational opportunities to achieve the medical profession. He is now a distinguished neurosurgeon and an inspirational writer and speaker.

When faced with the opportunity to ink an NIL deal, a college athlete might choose to opt out of NIL deals, and instead to focus on their education. Consequently, every college athlete should take advantage of their educational opportunity during their college to prepare for non-athletic careers. To facilitate pursuit of non-athletic careers, colleges and the NCAA should strive to ensure that their players are benefiting from their rich learning environment.

In a world where NIL deals tempt young athletes, Rolle's story serves as a reminder of the power of education. While some players chase quick money, others, like Rolle, prioritize their long-term goals and personal growth. The decision to forgo NIL deals is a personal one, influenced by factors like NCAA regulations, career aspirations, and personal values. Dr. Myron's journey emphasizes the importance of balancing athletics with education, a message that resonates with the Knight Commission on Intercollegiate Athletics. By promoting academic values in college sports, colleges should ensure that college athletes benefit both on and off the field.

In a world of uncertainties and temptations, Dr. Myron Rolle's pursuit of becoming a neurosurgeon stands as a beacon of inspiration. His story challenges us to dream big, work hard, and never compromise on our true aspirations. As we navigate the complex landscape of NIL deals and college sports, let us remember the wisdom of Dr. Myron Rolle: education is the key to unlocking one's true potential. In summary, Rolle's NIL power secret is to consider NIL deals within the context of one's non-athletic, professional career goal and the realities of the relatively short duration and financial shortcomings of playing on a professional sports team.

Further Reading

Jeffri Chadiha, *Life After NFL a Challenge for Many*, ESPN (May 31, 2012), https://www.espn.com/nfl/story/_/id/7983790/life-nfl-struggle-many-former-playrs.

Johnson v. NCAA, No. 22–1223 (3d Cir. 2024), https://www2.ca3.uscourts.gov/opinarch/221223p.pdf.

Myron L. Rolle, The 2% Way: How a Philosophy of Small Improvements Took Me to Oxford, the NFL, and Neurosurgery (2022).

Nicolas Vega, *Hall of Famer Dwyane Wade Wants to 'Maximize Each Day' of His Post-NBA Career*, CNBC (May 18, 2024), https://www.cnbc.com/2024/05/18/nba-star-dwyane-wade-wants-to-maximize-each-day-of-his-retirement.html.

Endnotes

1. Dan Wetzel, *What Does Myron Rolle See When He Looks at the Current College Sports Landscape? Opportunity*, Yahoo! Sports (July 8, 2022), https://sports.yahoo.com/what-does-myron-rolle-see-when-he-looks-at-the-current-college-football-landscape-opportunity-140731895.html.
2. *Myron Rolle*, Networth Mirror (updated June 3, 2024), https://networthmirror.com/myron-rolle/.

3. *See* Poch de la Rosa, *The Life and Career of Myron Rolle (Story)*, PRO FOOTBALL HISTORY (July 19, 2022), https://www.profootballhistory.com/myron-rolle/.
4. ESPN News Services, *Colorado Two-Way Star Travis Hunter Wins Heisman Trophy*, ESPN (Dec. 14, 2024), https://www.espn.com/college-football/story/_/id/42973895/colorado-two-way-star-travis-hunter-wins-heisman-trophy; *See* Wetzel, *supra* note 1.
5. *Myron Rolle Picks Academics over Millions*, ESSENCE (Oct. 29, 2020), https://www.essence.com/news/myron-rolle-picks-academics-over-millions/.
6. Myron L. Rolle, THE 2% WAY: HOW A PHILOSOPHY OF SMALL IMPROVEMENTS TOOK ME TO OXFORD, THE NFL, AND NEUROSURGERY (2022).
7. *Id.*
8. The Myron L. Rolle Foundation, ROLLEFOUNDATION.ORG, https://www.rollefoundation.org/ (last accessed Mar. 14, 2025).
9. Michael Tunison, *Myron Rolle Signs Rookie Deal with Titans*, SBNATION (June 14, 2010), https://www.sbnation.com/2010/6/14/2316455/myron-rolle-signs-rookie-deal-with-titans.
10. *See* Elena Bergeron, *It's Never Too Late to Pivot from N.F.L. Safety to Neurosurgeon*, N.Y. TIMES (updated Dec. 5, 2022), https://www.nytimes.com/2022/10/11/sports/football/myron-rolle-career-pivot-football-neurosurgeon.html.
11. J.C. Barrott, *FSU and NFL Player-Turned Neurosurgeon to Speak in Tampa*, TAMPA BAY BUS. & WEALTH (July 16, 2024), https://tbbwmag.com/2024/07/16/fsu-and-nfl-player-turned-neurosurgeon-to-speak-in-tampa/.
12. *See generally*, DENNIS J. HUTCHINSON, THE MAN WHO ONCE WAS WHIZZER WHITE: A PORTRAIT OF JUSTICE BYRON WHITE (1998).
13. Pete Thamel, *For Florida State Player and Scholar, Game Day Is Different*, N.Y. TIMES (Nov. 20, 2008), https://www.nytimes.com/2008/11/20/sports/ncaafootball/20rolle.html.
14. *See* Dan Wetzel, *What Does Myron Rolle See When He Looks at the Current College Sports Landscape? Opportunity*, YAHOO! SPORTS (July 8, 2022), https://sports.yahoo.com/what-does-myron-rolle-see-when-he-looks-at-the-current-college-football-landscape-opportunity-140731895.html.
15. *Id.*
16. *Myron Rolle's Decision: Long-Term Education over a Short-Term Fortune*, BLEACHER REPORT (June 5, 2018), https://bleacherreport.com/articles/342841-education-versus-dollars.
17. *Id.*
18. *Id.*
19. *Knight Commission on Intercollegiate Athletics*, KNIGHTCOMMISSION.ORG, www.knightcommission.org (last accessed Mar. 14, 2025).
20. The Knight Commission supports transformational ideas that promote quality journalism, advance media innovation, engage communities, and foster the arts. *See Knight Commission on Intercollegiate Athletics*, KNIGHTCOMMISSION.ORG, www.knightcommission.org (last accessed Mar. 14, 2025).
21. Knight Commission on Intercollegiate Athletics, *Knight Commission Welcomes New Member, Rhodes Scholar and Former All-American Football Player Myron Rolle*, KNIGHT-

COMMISSION.ORG (Sept. 8, 2014), https://www.knightcommission.org/2014/09/knight-commission-welcomes-new-member-rhodes-scholar-and-former-all-american-football-player-myron-rolle/.

22. Scott White, *Well-To-Do, White Legacies a Focus after SCOTUS Ruling. Athletes: "Hold My Glass,"* FORBES (Oct. 6, 2023), https://www.forbes.com/sites/scottwhite/2023/10/06/college-athletes-get-way-more-than-a-slice-of-the-admissions-pie/#.
23. *See* Serena Morones & Paul Heidt, *Following the Money in College Sports,* MORONES ANALYTICS (lastaccessedMar. 11, 2025), https://moronesanalytics.com/following-the-money-in-college-sports/#_ftnref6.citing.
24. *NCAA Recruiting Facts,* NCAA.ORG, https://ncaaorg.s3.amazonaws.com/compliance/recruiting/NCAA_RecruitingFactSheet.pdf (last accessed Mar. 14, 2025).
25. David Skilling, *ESPN "Broke"—What's Changed?,* CULTURE OF SPORT (Dec. 24, 2024), https://cultureofsport.substack.com/p/espn-broke-whats-changed.
26. *Id.*
27. Mark P. Henriques & Mike Ingersoll, *NLRB, Labor Laws and the Impact on NCAA Athletes,* NAT'L LAW REV. (Oct. 28, 2021), https://natlawreview.com/article/nlrb-labor-laws-and-impact-ncaa-athletes.
28. Daniel Wiessner, *Dartmouth Basketball Team Votes to Form First Union in U.S. College Sports,* REUTERS (Mar. 5, 2024), https://www.reuters.com/sports/basketball/dartmouth-basketball-team-votes-form-first-union-us-college-sports-2024-03-05/.
29. *Id.*
30. *Id.*
31. Craig Garthwaite, Jordan Keener, Matthew J. Notowidigdo, & Nicole F. Ozminkowski, *Who Profits from Amateurism? Rent-Sharing in Modern College Sports,* NAT'L BUREAU OF ECON. RESEARCH (updated Nov. 2020), https://www.nber.org/papers/w27734.
32. *Johnson v. NCAA,* https://law.justia.com/cases/federal/appellate-courts/ca3/22-1223/22-1223-2024-07-11.html, https://www2.ca3.uscourts.gov/opinarch/221223p.pdf.
33. *Id.*
34. *Id.*
35. *House v. NCAA,* https://www.nacua.org/docs/default-source/new-cases-and-developments/2023/20231103_house-v-ncaa.pdf?sfvrsn=1eab4ebe_1/. As discussed above, this case has been settled with the NCAA agreeing to pay nearly $2.8 billion to past, present, and future college athletes.

10

Caitlin Clark: Wealth Creator for Women Athletes

Obviously, it should have been a thing for a really long time. . . . It's like the NIL part of it—like the true like endorsements, like you're doing a commercial for you know the local coffee shop or like whatever it is—like it's something so easy and so simple. And I think, you know, like a normal student can do that, but like, why couldn't an athlete? . . . It's just like such a simple thing that should have been a thing for a long time, but also it was challenging to navigate, and it still is.

—Caitlin Clark[1]

OVERVIEW

Caitlin Clark's narrative is both personal and epic. It shows how a woman's personal journey to success and wealth can have a positive, profound, and transformative impact on society as a wealth creator. She is one of the greatest college athletes of all time. Most notably, on March 3, 2023, she became the NCAA All-Time Leading Scorer when she smashed the 54-year-old all-time scoring record formerly held by the legendary Peter "Pistol Pete" Maravich.[2] In 2023, she decided to forgo her final year of college basketball and was the No. 1 pick in the 2024 WNBA Draft.[3] In the 2024 season, she continued to break records and win awards playing as a point guard for the Indiana Fever (the "Fever").[4]

Clark is a NIL multi-millionaire. She became a NIL millionaire while playing for the University of Iowa ("Iowa") and continues to amass millions in NIL deals as a professional athlete.[5] In 2024, she signed a four-year contract with the Indiana Fever for the paltry sum of $338,000, or $76,535 in her first year and ending with $97,582 in the final year.[6] Notwithstanding, in 2024, her net worth was reportedly $5 million.[7] On April 18, 2024, Nike announced an NIL deal with Clark for an estimated $28 million over eight years, or $3.5 million a year.[8] Further, she is projected to earn a net worth of approximately $416.34 million by the end of a 20-year period.[9]

Clark's NIL power secret is being a wealth creator. This chapter describes how her breakout moments, which distinguished her as the best in her sport, resulted in her becoming a NIL college millionaire. It explains how she generated wealth for herself, her teammates, her school, and the economy: the "Caitlin Clark Effect," which describes Clark's positive impact on the popularity of women's basketball, as measured by increased ticket prices, attendance at games, and television viewership.[10] Further, it shows how she is a champion for "girl power" and gender inclusion. Overall, she is considered one of the most impactful athletes of our time, as *Time Magazine* recognized by naming her its 2024 Athlete of the Year.[11]

CLARK'S JOURNEY TO NIL MILLIONS

Leveling the Playing Field

For many reasons, Clark is a unique success story for college NIL millionaires compared to other NIL college millionaires. For Livvy Dunne, the NIL deals reflected her athleticism along with her outstanding work establishing her brand as a leading social media influencer. For Bronny James, his NIL deals were influenced by his father's name and position as one of the greats. For Arch Manning, he was able to forgo NIL deals as he planned on benefitting from the Manning family dynasty. For Bryce Underwood, his NIL millions come from a deal with a booster collective, where top-ranked male football and basketball high school students agree to play for the boosters' college.

However, Clark did not share some of the advantages of some of those and other NIL college millionaires. While she is the subject of many social media influencers, she did not rise to fame by being a social media influencer like Livvy Dunne. She was not born into a sports legacy family like Bronny James, Arch Manning, and Shedeur Sanders. Further, she did not receive a million-dollar booster-sponsored NIL deal to play her sport in college like Bryce Underwood did. Additionally, she has a rare genetic quality that is unlike almost all the college NIL millionaires: she is a female athlete. With all of these disadvantages, Clark had only one goal: to prove herself solely for her athletic abilities.

In proving herself as worthy of becoming a college NIL millionaire, Clark discovered a highly effective power secret. It is a power secret that other college athlete superstars, such as Steph Curry, LeBron James, and Michael Jordan, have employed over the years, which led to their financial success. However, it is not a power secret that one can simply turn on like a light switch. On the contrary, it is a power secret that an athlete needs to visualize sometime in the future and do all that is necessary to prepare for that moment, including practicing, weight training, working with coaches, and developing relationships with one's teammates. It is a power secret that, when employed, goes off like a flash of lightning in a summer storm. It is a power secret that, once it is exercised, will completely transform the trajectory of a person's career. It is a power secret that makes a person an instant celebrity and a legend in their own time. Such a moment can be a turning point, a defining moment, a leap forward, a big break, or sudden success in an athlete's career. It is a power secret that can change the way society views a sport and, in the case of Clark, accelerates gender equality for women's professional basketball. It is a power secret that results in notoriety, for which brands will pay millions for the right to hire that person to endorse their products or services.

What is the name of this NIL power secret? It is called the breakout moment. It is the time or event in a person's career that transforms an athlete from a notable player to a legendary superstar. Notoriety, for Caitlin Clark, has resulted in fame and fortune. Becoming a highly successful NIL millionaire and now a leading WNBA player, Clark proves the power of the breakout moment is one of the most powerful secrets that every college athlete should seek to emulate, particularly female athletes. Doing so means millions of dollars in brand endorsements, as well as a leadership role for female athletes. Most importantly, the breakout moment led to what is called the "Caitlin Clark Effect," the unique phenomenon where an athlete's personal achievements can create wealth beyond that of the player, transforming our society relative to the equitable treatment of women and to valuing their substantial contribution to the U.S. economy. To become a wealth creator and relative to becoming a NIL college millionaire, Clark's power secret reflects a lesson learned from some of the greatest college athletes of all time.

Breakout Moments

The road to NIL millions has an important signpost, which indicates a person is headed in the right direction. That signpost is what is referred to as a "breakout moment." Many sports legends, including LeBron James and Steph Curry, have experienced a breakout moment.[12] A breakout moment refers to a sudden, significant event or achievement that marks a major leap forward in someone's personal or professional development to a new level of success or recognition. Relative to legendary college athletes, a breakout moment is when an athlete achieves a personal best record in a competition, signifying a new level of performance. Most often, a breakout moment is when an athlete breaks a previously held monumental record, such as at the Beijing 2008 Summer Olympics, when American swimmer Michael Phelps won an unprecedented eight gold medals, which broke fellow American swimmer Mark Spitz's 1972 record-breaking seven gold medals.[13] Of course, in most cases, a breakout moment is followed by a continuous performance at the highest level, such as Phelps becoming one of the most decorated Olympic swimmers in Team USA history with 28 total medals, including 23 gold.[14] Clark's performance mimics that of the GOATs, both while she attending Iowa and while playing for the Fever.

The Breakout Process

While each athlete's breakout moment is uniquely personal to that player, every breakout moment has some common elements, including that they (1) require gradual progress and are not sudden or unexpected; (2) sometimes come after facing challenges or setbacks; and (3) lead to substantial professional growth, increased visibility, or notable accomplishments. Looking at Clark's college achievements, it is difficult to imagine that she needed to or did prepare for her breakout moments. Notwithstanding, often glory follows pain and preparation, and this is true when it comes to Clark. Her successes were preceded by years of preparation and hard work, along with overcoming challenges and obstacles, both physical and emotional. These all helped her grow and become more visible, famous, and fortunate.

Preparation and Hard Work

NIL college millionaires, even the ones with legacy names like Bronny James, are not born with greatness; they must earn it. This certainly applies to Caitlin Clark, who was raised by hard-working middle-class Catholic parents in Des Moines, Iowa.[15] She reportedly competed in a boys' basketball league at the age of five because there were no basketball league for girls.[16] At the end of an illustrious high school career, ESPN rated her a five-star recruit and the fourth-best player in her class.[17] On November 12, 2019, she committed to play for Iowa due to their up-tempo style of offense and proven track record.[18] During her four years at Iowa, her workout and practice routines were grueling, to say the least.[19] NBA legend Kevin Garnett, known for his intense training and work ethic, highlighted Clark's workout video, pointing out that unlike many basketball players who take breaks or go on vacations during the summer, Clark is dedicated to rigorous training sessions, focused on improving her shooting skills and overall fitness.[20]

Overcoming Challenges and Setbacks

To become an NIL college millionaire via a breakout moment, one must prepare for it, such as Clark did through her years of hard work. But that is not enough. A quintessential quality of a NIL college millionaire is their ability to overcome setbacks. Those setbacks come in many forms, including physical injury, mental fatigue, and emotional challenges. Success does not mean you have won the lottery and can retire. To the contrary, success means more hard work, more need to focus, and more distractions. What's more, the truly successful superstars like Clark refuse to allow obstacles or failures to shape their identity. Instead, an essential aspect of their legacy is demonstrating resilience and determination in the face of adversity.

Clark is no exception to experiencing the physical and psychological pressures of NCAA Division I intercollegiate athletics, particularly in national tournaments. For Clark, one set of emotional challenges comes from several criticisms that have been levied against her.[21] For example, when she was named *Time Magazine*'s 2024 Athlete of the Year,[22] it was suggested, by Washington Mystics owner Sheila Johnson that Clark did not deserve such an honor that better belonged to the entire WNBA, many of whose players are African American.[23] Throughout that and other such criticisms, Clark has exhibited poise and sensitivity to the unique challenges that Black women basketball players experience.[24] Following her being named *Time Magazine*'s 2004 Athlete of the year, she responded to racial inequities in NIL deals:

> I want to say I've earned every single thing, but as a white person, there is privilege. . . . A lot of those players in the league that have been really good have been Black players. This league has kind of been built on them. The more we can appreciate that, highlight that, talk about that, and then continue to have brands and companies invest in those players that have made this league incredible, I think it's very important. I have to continue to try to change that.

You can see from that comment that Clark is aware of her white privilege and hopes that her fellow Black colleagues can enjoy some of those privileges as well.[25]

Clark's Breakout Moments

Clark, as with many superstar athletes, had more than one breakout moment while at Iowa.[26] Out of the many memorable moments, Clark celebrated several that stand out as breakout moments.[27] In her second year at Iowa, she was the first women's player to lead Division I in points and assists per game in a single season, as well as total points, free throws, and triple-doubles.[28] On April 2, 2023, during the 2023 NCAA tournament in her junior year, she garnered national attention when she set tournament records with eight three-pointers, the most by a men's or women's player in the title game.[29] USA TODAY reporter Lindsay Schnell reported that due to this moment, "Caitlin Clark" became a "household name."[30] In her senior year, Clark broke multiple Division I records at Iowa, including, to name a few, Iowa's all-time women's leading scorer, the Big Ten's all-time women's leader in assists and points, and the NCAA's Division I women's career scoring leader.[31] However, her most significant breakout moment was on March 3, 2024, when she became the NCAA all-time men's and women's scoring leader in points scored in Division I history, shattering Peter "Pistol Pete" Maravich's

54-year-old record.[32] In her usual humble self, Clark said that team objectives have been foremost in her mind, so she has not given all her records a lot of thought.[33] As if breaking Pete's longstanding record was not enough, on March 8, 2024, Clark shattered the record of another, more contemporary and more famous GOAT: She broke Steph Curry's NCAA Division I record for 3-pointers in a season by a man or woman.[34]

Fame Leads to Fortune: NIL Deals

One common element of a breakout moment is that it leads to fame followed by great fortune. In 2024, Caitlin Clark enjoyed the greatest name recognition of any college basketball player, female or male, in the U.S. by a 2-to-1 margin, with 44% of the public correctly recognizing her name and 69% of college sports fans.[35] In February 2024, FOX Sports began devoting a camera, called the "Caitlin Cam," to record Clark during its broadcasts of Iowa games and to stream on TikTok.[36]

Such incredible name recognition and media coverage lead to NIL opportunities. As mentioned in previous chapters, there are two main types of college athlete NIL deals: (1) brand endorsement and (2) booster-collective. Generally, multi-million-dollar booster-collective NIL deals, such as the one that Bryce Underwood agreed to in 2024, are only available, so far, to highly sought-after male athletes who play large revenue-generating sports, namely football and basketball. Unfortunately, to date, as female basketball is just beginning to take off in terms of generating media and ticket revenues for colleges, generally speaking, female athletes have not seen multi-million-dollar NIL deals from collectives. That leaves college women athletes to seek out NIL deals for endorsement of products or services based on their notoriety or social media influence, such as that of Livvy Dunne. Fortunately, Clark has established a significant social media following; as of June 2024, she reportedly had about 3 million social media followers combined across X (formerly Twitter), Instagram, and TikTok.[37] However, as noted, it is notoriety as a breakout athlete that is her source of fame and NIL fortune.

Consequential to her breakout moments, Clark has become an NIL phenomenon. While in college, she signed millions of dollars in NIL deals, from brand endorsements that female college athletes seldom get.[38] Her first publicized NIL venture came in August 2021, partnering with The Vinyl Shop, a Des Moines-based and female-owned company, to produce a limited supply of custom T-shirts.[39] Another Clark NIL endorsement deal is with Hy-Vee, a supermarket chain with more than

280 locations across the Midwest and the South.[40] Under the Hy-Vee brand, Clark has appeared in its seasonal magazine and several regional ads and commercials.[41] Further, on March 1, 2022, Clark announced a partnership with H&R Block, a national tax preparation company, as part of its new "A Fair Shot" campaign, designed to help female athletes earn fair compensation in the NIL space compared to male athletes. Clark has appeared in several national ads through the company's campaign.

Clark has signed an inevitable variety of NIL deals. She has reportedly signed NIL deals with Gatorade, Bose, Buick, Goldman Sachs, Shoot-A-Way, and Topps.[42] In 2023, she became the first college athlete to be a spokesperson for State Farm, appearing in national television commercials for the company.[43] In 2024, Hy-Vee released a limited-edition cereal called "Caitlin's Crunch Time" in select stores in Iowa to benefit youth in Iowa.[44] Upon graduating from college, Clark continued sponsorship deals with Gatorade and Hy-Vee.

After graduating from Iowa in May 2024, Clark, the first overall pick of the 2024 WNBA draft, signed a four-year contract with the Indiana Fever, valued at $338,000, which is a paltry payroll compared to her NBA counterparts.[45] In the WNBA, rookies drafted with the top four overall picks in 2024 received a base salary of $76,535 during their first pro season.[46] However, with her celebrity, Clark was projected to sign more and bigger NIL deals while maintaining many of her sponsorship deals as she moves into the WNBA.[47]

That projection was right. Just prior to her turning professional and shortly thereafter, Clark signed several new endorsement deals. In February 2024, she became the top-selling college athlete on the online sports merchandise retailer Fanatics, surpassing Shedeur Sanders.[48] In March 2024, she became the first female athlete to have an exclusive partnership with Panini America, Inc., signing a multi-year contract with the trading card company.[49] In 2024, an autographed trading card featuring Clark sold for $78,000, the most ever for a women's basketball card.[50] The record was broken later that year after her card sold for $84,000, the second-most expensive card of a female athlete, behind tennis player Serena Williams.[51] In March 2024, she signed a multi-year sponsorship with Gainbridge, an Indianapolis-based financial platform, joining Billie Jean King and Annika Sörenstam as brand ambassadors.[52] In May 2024, she signed a multi-year deal with Wilson Sporting Goods, becoming the first athlete since Michael Jordan to release a signature Wilson basketball collection.[53] The Wilson website has released the first Clark collection, which is a limited edition of gold-colored basketballs featuring a drawing of Clark with her signature for $49.95.[54]

Clark's most notable NIL deal is a multi-million-dollar deal with Nike, which was announced on April 18, 2024.[55] It reportedly includes a signature shoe deal and is the largest sponsorship deal ever for a female basketball player.[56] It is reportedly worth an estimated $28 million over eight years.[57] That is an annual payment of $3.5 million or $9,600 per day. So, every 7.8 days, Clark earns more money than her entire WNBA rookie salary.[58] Clark's 2024 Nike deal was a renegotiated extension of an NIL contract that Clark signed in October 2022. After leaving college, she essentially became a free agent in the shoe market and courted a deal with Under Armour, who reportedly brought in Steph Curry to close the deal. Unfortunately, Clark turned down a deal from Under Armour, as their offer was only $16 million over four years.[59] In addition to NIL deals to endorse products, Clark is also seeking great investment opportunities. For example, in November 2024, it was announced that she had joined an ownership group to bring an expansion National Women's Soccer League team to Cincinnati in 2026.[60]

Consequently, notwithstanding her stellar, yet underpaid, performance on the court, Clark's athletic accomplishments and notoriety are paying off with multi-million-dollar NIL deals. However, while she has excelled at highly lucrative third-party NIL deals, she and other women have not received substantial NIL deals from booster cooperatives, which have generally focused on the most-sought-after men's football or men's basketball superstars.

Furthermore, Clark's narrative show how women are grossly unpaid in the sports arena. She is outstanding and unique among NIL college millionaires. For Caitlin Clark, her NIL deals show how record-breaking sports performance, plus a popular public image, pays big bucks. However, even the best of WNBA players are poorly compensated compared to top men who play for the NBA. While Clark's on court performance has been compared to Steph Curry's, to date, her NIL deals have yet to compare to his, which are phenomenal. Along with being a leader in her athletic performance, Clark is making her mark in raising the profile of women in professional sports and the opportunity for reaching gender equity. Hence, Caitlin Clark's power secret is her record-breaking athletic performance, beyond compare, in a world where money follows notoriety. Notwithstanding, when it came to making the decision to leave Iowa for the WNBA, Clark needed to assess the impact that decision would have on her NIL deals.

NIL Deals and Deciding to Become a Professional

As mentioned in the previous section, female college athletes have few options to play for a professional league after graduating from college, with the WNBA as one notable exception. As a result, one issue that female college athletes must face relative to NIL deals involves the question of whether to stay in college for a fifth year, such as Livvy Dunne did, or leave college early, after one year, as Bronny James did. What considerations did each face, and what does gender have to do with it? A related question is "Do college athletes lose their NIL deals if they decide to leave college, possibly by playing for the WNBA, as did Clark?" Clark addressed that second question with a resounding no.[61] But not so fast, Caitlin. The answer to that question is much more nuanced; that is, it depends on the type of NIL deal and what happens to your platform if you decide to leave college.

Let me explain. Clark is correct when she says that if you have an NIL endorsement deal(s), you do not automatically lose that deal by getting employed by the WNBA. In fact, as was the case for Clark, she was able to renegotiate some of her endorsement deals for more money than before. A savvy NIL college millionaire may want to limit the term of their college NIL deal so that it can be renegotiated if a player moves on to play for a professional team. Fortunately, Clark played a sport in college for which there is a professional league. However, there are many college athletes who do not have a professional league to play for after graduation. In addition, considering how little salary the WNBA is paying Clark, there was an argument for her to stay in college for another year. Unfortunately, there are gender equity issues when compared to what the NBA pays. For example, Victor Wembanyama, the NBA's No. 1 pick in the 2023 draft, can make 120% of the rookie scale salary, so he earned around $12 million this year. But the WNBA is still a relatively new league and does not have the financial backing the NBA has.[62] Further, NBA athletes get 50% of the league's revenue share, while WNBA athletes only get 10%.[63]

So, how is Clark's remark about the wisdom of leaving college after four years incorrect? That would be when an NIL college millionaire has a booster-sponsored collective deal, which usually will only compensate a college athlete if and only if they are playing for a particular school. Such a deal is like the one that Bryce Underwood signed to play for Michigan, although that contract is not public and is being used for hypothetical illustration only. One could assume that that deal would not continue to pay Underwood if he decided to leave Michigan after playing for three years to play for an NFL team. There is also another possibility, which is illustrated by Livvy Dunne's decision to stay a fifth year at LSU. In a case like hers, there may be good reasons to remain in college. For one reason, there is no professional league for women gymnasts. Another reason is that Dunne's NIL deals are for brand endorsements. Perhaps, in a case like hers, her social media influence might be more valuable were she to remain in college.

Highly talented male college athletes, particularly those whose talent is highly sought-after by professional leagues such as the NFL, the NBA, and the MLB rarely decide to remain in college after four years. Some, like Bronny James, only attend college for one year, as the NBA rules provide for a limited number of years in college before players can be recruited to "go pro." Those male college superstars have insanely large salaries and benefits awaiting them for leaving college to play for a professional league, including post-college NIL endorsement deals. Unfortunately, the same opportunities do not exist for female college superstars. That is because currently there is the WNBA, which is for female basketball players, but there is nothing comparable to the NFL or the MLB for women.

Hence, Clark, following hard work and overcoming adversity, reached NIL millionaire status following breakout moments. It is the time or event in a person's career that transfers an athlete from a notable player to a legendary superstar. Notoriety, for Caitlin Clark, has resulted in fame and fortune. Becoming a highly successful NIL millionaire and now a leading WNBA player, Clark proves the power of the breakout moment is one of the most powerful secrets that every college athlete should seek to emulate, particularly female athletes. Doing so means millions of dollars in brand endorsements, as well as a leadership role for female athletes. Most importantly, the breakout moment led to what is called the "Caitlin Clark Effect," the unique phenomenon where an athlete's personal achievements can create wealth beyond that of the player's to substantially increase the wealth of her team, the Fever, the WNBA, and local economies.

BEING A WEALTH CREATOR: THE CAITLIN CLARK EFFECT

Caitlin Clark is more than an athletic phenom, a sports icon, and an NIL multi-millionaire. In a nutshell, Clark is a wealth creator. A wealth creator is a superstar, such as Taylor Swift, whose notoriety transcends their specific talent such that they generate wealth not only for themselves but for others as well as for local and national economies. Clark's profound ability to create wealth for herself, her teammates, her college, her professional league, and local and national economies has a positive impact on society, which has been labeled the "Caitlin Clark Effect."[64]

An Economics Lesson from Taylor Swift

Taylor Swift's The Eras Tour was a cultural and economic phenomenon, a concert tour that began on March 17, 2023, and ended on December 8, 2024, with 149 shows across five continents.[65] The tour grossed reported box office sales of over $2 billion.[66] The tour enriched both Swift and the economy in general and the economies of the communities where she appeared. Swift was personally enriched by the concert tour; on December 9, 2024, her net worth was reportedly $1.6 billion which was triple what it was when she started Eras, from multiple sources of income.[67] More relevant to Caitlin Clark, Swift's tour has an unprecedented economic impact on local economies. For example, the tour's weekend in Los Angeles reportedly generated $20 million in sales and local taxes and $9 million in hotel taxes, with a total positive economic impact on Los Angeles County of $320 million.[68] Swift's economic impact illustrates that female superstars have the power to move the needle to encourage investors to bet on female talent. That applies to the most popular female entertainers, such as Swift, Rihanna, and Beyoncé. The question is can female athletes have such an economic impact?

Proof of Concept

On the popular reality television show *Shark Tank*, multi-millionaire and sports mogul Mark Cuban and other "sharks" judge the business proposals of entrepreneurs who are seeking capital from these would-be investors. One lesson that comes out of the program is the importance of "proof of concept" as a means of enticing the shark investors to invest their money in the developing businesses. "Proof of concept" in business and investing is evidence that demonstrates the financial feasibility of a product idea or a business plan. For example, showing a year of profitable sales of a new skin product in a test market, such as the Los Angeles market, might compel an investor to lend or invest their money to scale up production and marketing of the product to sell it nationally with the expectation of earning a significant profit from their investment. Why is proof of concept relevant to Clark and college NIL?

The answer is that investors need evidence of the potential success of a product or service before investing in that product or service. When applied to professional sports, one wonders why male college athletes make more on NIL than their female counterparts. The simple answer is that men's professional leagues and collegiate sports, such as football, basketball, baseball, and soccer, produce substantially more revenue, particularly from television revenue, than female sports. For example, as reported on October 7, 2024, the NBA generated $10.58 billion in annual revenue compared to the WNBA's $200 million.[69] Consequently, when it comes to compensation, the average salary for an NBA player was $11.9 million compared to $119,590 for a WNBA player. The result of this substantial difference in revenue is a substantial difference in players' salaries: Steph Curry being the highest-paid NBA player at $55.8 million per year compared to Jackie Young whose annual salary is $252,450.[70] Where does this revenue come from? Is it simply based on average attendance in arenas? When the NBA's average attendance is only double that of the WNBA's: 18,324 versus 9,195, why is the NBA so much richer than the WNBA? The answer is in the average media viewership: in 2023, the NBA's regular season numbers were 1.6 million versus 505,000 for the WNBA, and for playoffs, the NBA had 5.47 million and 11.64 million for the finals.[71] In the same year, the WNBA has a paltry 400,000 viewers for their playoffs and only 728,000 for their finals.[72] Why does television viewership matter? It is because viewership numbers or ratings drive marketing/advertising income, which is advertising revenue. For example, in 2023, the NBA generated $842 million in postseason revenue, which was third to the NFL and the NCAA.[73] Whereas, the WNBA only generated about $60 million in postseason revenue.[74] Notwithstanding these poor ratings for the WNBA, viewership is changing for the WNBA exponentially. Viewership of WNBA games is on the rise. The 2023 WNBA Finals were the most watched in 20 years, with a 36.0% increase in viewership from 2022, to 728,000 viewers.[75] As a result of these numbers, it was projected that the WNBA would see its next deal quadruple in value from $60 million to $240 million.[76]

Why present these numbers? The numbers help to understand why a men's sport league, the NBA, is more lucrative for its investors and more generous to its players than the WNBA is for women athletes. Notwithstanding, it also shows how the WNBA is providing the "proof of concept" to investors that there is a growing market for women's professional basketball. Further, it introduces why the Caitlin Clark Effect is a thing: Since Clark joined the league, the 2024 WNBA Finals was reportedly the most watched in 25 years, up 115% over 2023, with its regular session viewership across ESPN platforms up 170%.[77] The June 23, 2024, regular season game between Clark's Indiana Fever and Angel Reese's Chicago Sky was the most-watched WNBA game, with an average of 2.3 million viewers.[78] In addition, in 2024, engagement with WNBA-focused posts across ESPN's social media accounts for the regular and postseason play was up 413% versus 2023, with video views increasing by 642%, year over year.[79] What did the phenomenal increase in viewership mean for the value of the WNBA? The answer is much more money. On July 24, 2024, the WNBA announced that more than 125 WNBA regular season games will be broadcast each season through an 11-year media rights deal with Disney, Amazon Prime, and NBC for about $200 million a year, or a total of $2.2 billion. That number is more than tripling the league's current media contract of $60 million a year.[80]

What is the reason for the meteoric rise in the viewership of WNBA games in 2024 and the league's new found increase in media revenue? One major contributor is what has been labeled the "Caitlin Clark Effect."

The Caitlin Clark Effect

What is the "Caitlin Clark Effect?" It is the label for Clark's profound ability to create wealth for herself, her teammates, the University of Iowa, the Indiana Fever, the WNBA, and particularly for local and national economies. It reflects Clark's impact on increasing the value of women's basketball and its positive impact on the wealth of players, teams, and communities, because of increased attendance at games, higher ticket prices, and television viewership.

Game Attendance and Higher Ticket Prices

As to increased game attendance, Clark's popularity, combined with that of many of her opponents, including Angel Reese, drove increased home-game attendance in Iowa and at away games.[81] Entering her senior season, her Iowa team sold out all its home games for the first time, after previously selling out only three regular season games in program history.[82] Further, on October 15, 2023, before the 2023–2024 season, Iowa broke the women's basketball all-time attendance record for a single game at 55,646 attendees against DePaul University in Kinnick Stadium, home to Iowa's football team.[83] Consequently, in the 2023 season, Iowa set the Big Ten single-season average attendance record (14,998), surpassing its own mark from the previous season (11,143).[84] Additionally, the 2024 Big Ten tournament, where Clark led her team to the title, sold out for the first time in event history.[85]

Clark's positive impact on game attendance continued when she joined the WNBA. During her first month in the WNBA, she helped the Fever set attendance records for their home games against the Los Angeles Sparks (19,103), New York Liberty (17,735), and Seattle Storm (18,343).[86] Due to Clark's popularity, her opponents also had an increase in attendance when playing the Fever; many of which reportedly moved home games against the Fever to larger arenas.[87] For example, her game against the Mystics on June 7, 2024, which was moved to the Capital One Arena, had an attendance of 20,333, the most for a WNBA game since the 2007 WNBA Finals and the fifth-most for a regular season game.[88] The two teams met again at Capital One Arena on September 19, 2024, for the regular season finale and drew the WNBA's highest-ever attendance for a regular season game, at 20,711.[89]

In addition to increased game attendance, ticket prices for her games increased. For example, her regular-season finale against Ohio State was reportedly the most expensive women's college basketball game of all time, with an average ticket price of $408.[90] Hence, one can see how the Caitlin Clark Effect had, and continues to have, a positive impact on game attendance and ticket prices. She rocks the house!

Television Viewership

While attendance and ticket prices matter, the most important aspect of the Caitlin Clark Effect is its positive impact on media viewership, particularly increasing television audiences. As such, a quintessential feature of the Caitlin Clark Effect is one that results in many financial benefits for herself, her teammates, her team, her league, and her communities where she plays. As was previously pointed out, her record-breaking performance, charisma, and American heartland background are credited as the leading factors in substantially increasing television viewership.[91] As previously highlighted, increased television viewership has resulted in increased media revenue for the WNBA. In effect, Clark's college career is the "proof of concept" that she moved markets. She drove historic levels of television viewership during her final two seasons at Iowa, which led the *Wall Street Journal* to proclaim her the "GOAT of TV Ratings," noting that her impact on television viewership exceeded any other modern athlete.[92]

During college playoffs, Clark contributed to increased viewership. For example, during the 2023 Final Four Championship Game, Iowa's game against LSU was the second-highest-viewed women's college basketball game ever, with nearly 10 million viewers, which compares favorably to the 11.4 million who watched the Texas Rangers clinch their first World Series championship.[93] Furthermore, during the 2024 NCAA tournament, her final three games each broke the women's college basketball viewership record. The tournament culminated with 18.9 million for the final game against the University of South Carolina, which was the most-viewed basketball game at any level since 2019 and the first women's NCAA tournament final to draw more viewers than the men's final.[94] Consequently, the Common Sense Institute Iowa, an economic research organization, estimated in March 2024 that the Caitlin Clark Effect increased Iowa's gross domestic product by between $14.4 million and $52.3 million while generating about $82.5 million in consumer spending.[95]

In addition to how she increased viewership of college basketball, Clark continued to move the needle of viewership as a professional player for the Indiana Fever. Before Clark's first season with the Indiana Fever, a study led by Michael J. Hicks of Ball State University estimated that Clark would bring over $2.4 million to central Indiana and draw 26,000 more fans to Fever games.[96] In 2024, in her first WNBA season, she continued to drive historic attendance and viewership, setting a franchise single-season attendance record, and with their regular season finale, setting the league attendance record (20,711).[97]

Clark continued to set viewership records upon entering the WNBA.[98] The 2024 WNBA draft, where the Indiana Fever selected Clark with the first overall pick, averaged 2.45 million viewers, the most in WNBA draft history and the most-watched WNBA telecast since 2000.[99] When it came to her impact on increased viewership, Clark's regular season debut against the Connecticut Sun on May 14, 2024, was the most-watched WNBA game since 2002 and the most-watched ever on ESPN2 or any cable network.[100] On May 18, 2024, her game against the New York Liberty set the league's ABC viewership record with 1.71 million viewers.[101] In the following week, Clark's games set WNBA viewership marks on ESPN, Ion, and NBA TV.[102] The June 23, 2024, regular session game between Clark's Indiana Fever and Angel Reese's Chicago Sky was the most-watched WNBA game, with an average of 2.3 million viewers.[103] Additionally, since Clark joined the WNBA, the 2024 WNBA Finals was reportedly the most watched in 25 years, up 115% over 2023, with its regular session viewership across ESPN platforms up 170%.[104] This phenomenal increase in viewership substantially increased the value of the WNBA. Consequently, as in July 2024, the league signed an 11-year media rights deal with Disney, Amazon Prime, and NBC for a total payout of $2.2 billion, as previously noted.[105]

In summary, Clark has a unique effect, which is to generate wealth for herself, her teammates, her school, and the economy: the "Caitlin Clark Effect." While many college NIL millionaires earn money for themselves, few of them have a multiplier effect, where their success benefits so many others. She joins Taylor Swift and other such superstars whose stardom has a profoundly positive impact on economies. Further, she provides the proof of concept that women's sports are a very promising investment. Furthermore, Clark's positive impact on the marketplace illustrates the importance of women in society and the need for their greater inclusion in local, national, and world economics.

"GIRL POWER" AND INCLUSION ECONOMICS

Beyond her outstanding, positive impact on college and professional sports, Clark is playing a distinct role in our society: she is a champion for "girl power" and inclusion economics. When it comes to women in sports, she is a force of nature who is changing markets and creating wealth for herself, for other women, and for society in general. Moreover, Clark is self-aware of her unique mission as a change agent. She described her influence on women's sports as "historic," stating, "I've been able to captivate so many people that have never watched women's sports, let alone women's basketball, and turn them into fans."[106] Not surprisingly, knows firsthand the challenges that female athletes face in college, in professional sports, and in the NIL marketplace. Intentionally or not, she is leading the worldwide movement to include women in the economic order, which is predicted to add substantial value to the U.S. and world economy. Consequently, her monumental, positive impact on women's sports raises some important, broader questions: Is there a market for women's sports? Are female athletes benefitting from college NIL deals? How important is racial diversity in women's sports? What role is Clark playing in promoting women's sports? What can be done to grow women's opportunities for sports? And, most importantly, what impact does and will Clark have on the importance of including women in the world economic order? One approach to answering these questions involves an understanding of the concept of inclusion economics.

Inclusion Economics

Relative to Clark's potential impact on world economics, inclusion economics seeks to grow the world economy by intentionally including historically discriminated-against people, particularly women. "Inclusion economics" refers to the economic benefits to the greater U.S. economy that result from three factors: (1) the removal of segregating and discriminatory barriers to markets; (2) the provision of substantial access to resources needed for economic development, particularly capital, information, infrastructure, and skills; and (3) the creation of an inclusive economy. The goal of inclusion economics is to create an inclusive economy, which is defined as "an economic system that includes everyone, regardless of age, gender, race/ethnicity, educational attainment, personal background, disability status, or other traits, and respects their individual roles as workers, dependents, students, family members, entrepreneurs, and business owners."[107] According to a major consulting firm, McKinsey & Company, economic inclusion seeks to achieve economic empowerment, beyond basic subsistence, to acquire and pass on intergenerational wealth, which minimizes the risk of slipping back into poverty.[108] Relative to historically disenfranchised groups, inclusion economics seeks to close the wealth gap between men and women, as well as the racial wealth gap between white and Black Americans, as well as other such groups. Historically, one giant step toward achieving inclusion economics in the United States, relative to equal opportunity and the role of law, is that when President Lyndon B. Johnson signed into law the Civil Rights Act of 1964,[109] he unleashed a powerful, positive economic transformation in America.[110] In addition to protecting the rights of marginalized racial, religious, and foreign-born minorities, he made it illegal to discriminate against a person based on their gender, thus setting the stage for an explosion in women's contribution to the U.S. economy.[111]

Applying the concept of inclusion economics to the world economy, in a 2021 Report, the World Bank noted that many countries recognize the financial value of including women in their economies. They reported a rise of economic inclusion programs in 75 countries around the world, reaching approximately 20 million households and benefitting nearly 92 million individuals, and with nearly 90% of programs surveyed in the report having a gender focus.[112] Consequently, inclusion economics means growing the economy, not redistributing wealth. Pertaining to this strategy, lessons can be learned from the struggle to address racial inequity in the United States: "[c]losing the revenue gap between Black and white businesses would generate an *additional* $290 billion for the U.S. economy."[113] Relative to racial inclusion, on a micro level, the Kellogg Foundation and the Urban League reported on their study, which concluded that by merely lessening and ultimately eliminating disparities and opportunity differentials that limit the human potential and economic contributions of people of color in the Greater New Orleans Region, "[b]y 2050, Metro New Orleans stands to realize a $43 billion gain in economic output by closing the racial equity gap."[114] If one refutes how these studies of the positive impact on the economy relative to race might apply to the positive impact of the inclusion of women, one recent economic phenomenon, the earlier discussion of the the earlier discussion of the Taylor Swift's The Eras Tour, provides invaluable evidence of the untapped, underappreciated value of women to the U.S. and world economy. It is irrefutable based on the economic effect of Taylor Swift's Eras Tour that promoting female entertainment, and arguably sports, will pay off big for the performers and athletes as well as the national and local economies.

Women in Sports

Returning to Clark and the world of sports, the discussion of inclusion economics leads to the question: Is there a market for women's sports? We start with the recognition that women, young and old, have a profound place in sports at all levels. Despite the proven economic impact of women superstars in non-athletic endeavors, it is obvious that women in sports are grossly underappreciated by the gatekeepers of the marketplace. One notable example of such gender inequity is evidenced in the salary disparity for women who play basketball for the

WNBA versus men who play for the NBA.[115] As previously noted, when it comes to compensation, the average salary for an NBA player was $11.9 million compared to $119,590 for a WNBA player, with Steph Curry being the highest-paid NBA player at $55.8 million per year compared to Jackie Young, whose annual salary is $252,450.[116] In 2024, Clark signed a four-year contract with the Indiana Fever for the paltry sum of $338,000, or $76,535 in her first year and ending with $97,582 in the final year.[117] One wonders how or why Caitlin Clark, a renowned, generational sports phenom and economic engine can be paid so little money to play as a rookie in the WNBA. Notwithstanding, in January 2025, Clark reportedly rejected an offer of over $1 million to play in the inaugural season of the Unrivaled League.[118]

One might argue that the reason for the wealth disparity has more to do with the media and ticket sales value of the NBA over that of the WNBA. However, there is proof that when the bias of middlemen who control the "normal" media markets is removed, women and racial minorities soar in market value and wealth. Evidence is the makeup of the top social media influencers, who arguably provide unfiltered, direct-to-consumer content. According to one source, women make up 11 of the top 20 most popular social media influencers in the world in 2024, including #2 Selena Gomez, #5 Kylie Jenner, #7 Ariana Grande, #8 Kim Kardashian, #10 Taylor Swift, #11 Katy Perry, #13 Charli D'Amelio, #14 Addison Rae, #16 Huda Kattan, #17 Nikkie de Jager, and #20 Lilly Singh.[119]

Notwithstanding the challenges that female athletes face at all levels, the marketplace has slowly but steadily recognized the economic value of female athletes and is moving, albeit somewhat slowly, to greater parity in compensation.[120] One report provides numerous examples of how women in sports should be equitably compensated because brands, media, and broadcasts should recognize their value in the marketplace.[121] For example, they point out that:

> The USWNT knows how to bring in views, and its World Cup games are some of the most-watched sporting events in U.S. television history, consistently outpacing expectations (and the U.S. men's team), often racking up more views than other popular sports competitions—like the NBA Finals and Stanley Cup—and shattering records. What the numbers make clear is that people care about and want to watch women's soccer.[122]

In addition to salary inequality, a woman who plays a college sport faces other challenges, including discrimination and sexual exploitation. There was so much historical discrimination that it took and continues to take federal legislation, specifically Title IX, to level the unlevel sports environment to ensure that women are provided equal access to college sports.[123] However, some speculate that the Trump Administration's anti-DEI (diversity, equity, and inclusion) policies and Executive Orders will seek to eviscerate Title IX guarantees to women's participation in college sports and ensure the continuation of gender inequality.[124] In addition to a lack of equal access to college sports for women, women in sports are all to often sexually abused. Time and again the news is filled with accounts of sexual abuse of women athletes, making life on college campuses most precarious for female athletes.[125] One survey showed that "[m]ore than 1 in 4 current or former student athletes surveyed reported being sexually assaulted or harassed by someone in a position of power on campus, compared with 1 in 10 of those in the general population."[126] Another real threat to the health of female athletes is the physical, emotional, and mental stress they endure, both at the hands of coaches as well as self-inflicted. Many coaches often prioritize players' performance over their well-being. As a result, coaches drive college athletes to play through injuries and discourage them from showing vulnerability, including mental health issues. These pressures are added to the exhaustion of balancing academics and sports practice.[127]

The law requires gender equality in college sports; however, male sports, particularly football, basketball, and baseball, continue to capture the lion's share of money and resources on college campuses and in the NCAA. Despite these inequities, women's college basketball stands out as a growing area of national interest. To that point, Clark is demonstrating that there is a clear, certain demand for high-quality women's sports and that the media is taking notice. The question remains whether the "Caitlin Clark Effect" has changed the opportunity for female athletes to benefit from college NIL deals. Before we address that question, we need to briefly discuss some other obstacles that female collect athletes face on college campuses relative to NIL deals.

Gender Inequity in College NIL?

Are female athletes benefitting from college NIL deals? The unfortunate reality is that female athletes are not benefitting from college NIL, with the rare exception of Livvy Dunne, Angel Reese, Flau'jae Johnson and Caitlin Clark.[128] There is some basis for that assumption when one looks at the On3 list of top valuations of college athletes, which, in January 2025, had only two women listed in the top 45, with Olivia Dunne at #7 and Flau'jae Johnson at #45, both of whom compete for LSU.[129] The On3 valuations, which On3 have revealed, are based on their a proprietary algorithm with Roster Value as the primary factor influencing most athletes' NIL valuation.[130] Roster Value is "determined mainly by collected deal data within the college marketplace and represents the compensation athletes receive from schools and collectives for competing, similar to contracts and salaries for professional athletes."[131] That means that the On3 valuations weigh heavily in favor of college collective NIL deals for top athletes who play high-revenue-producing sports at the college and professional levels, which are men's football and basketball. Olivia Dunne at #7 made the list due to her immense social media followings of over $5 million![132]

The problem with trying to assess whether NIL is benefitting female college athletes is that NIL deals are generally private, and we lack data to make an analysis. However, on October 21, 2024, the *Washington Post* reported on its investigation of college NIL deals, providing some invaluable information about the state of college NIL deals, particularly as it related to female athletes.[133] It raises the question, "Yes, college athletes are getting paid. But how? And how much? A [Washington] Post analysis of $125 million in payments reveals the patterns and disparities of a murky NIL market."[134] Overall, the report concluded that there are clearly gender-based inequities in how colleges handle their NIL deals.[135] However, the report points out that some female college athletes are, in fact, benefitting from NIL deals. Two examples stand out: UCLA star gymnast Jordan Chiles reportedly has brand NIL deals that are worth $1.3 million.[136] The women's basketball team at LSU disclosed NIL payments, perhaps from brand endorsements, totaling $5.5 million over the past three years, compared to the $8.7 million of the football program and more than tripling the income of the men's basketball team.[137] Notwithstanding, female athletes have received very little money from collectives; it has been estimated that in 2023, 95% of collective money goes to male athletes.[138] Remember, as previously discussed in earlier chapters, collective-based NIL deals account for the largest percentage of such college NIL deals.

Consistent with belief that female college athletes are paid less, particularly when it comes to collective deals, some of those athletes are filing lawsuit to redress the inequities. For example, in December 2023, in *Schroeder et al. v. University of Oregon,*[139] members of the university's women's beach volleyball and club rowing teams alleged that Oregon is violating Title IX through the university's "vastly superior treatment" of football players in comparison to female student athletes in practice facilities, academic support, meals and snacks, scholarships, and NIL opportunities.[140] Relative to NIL, the lawsuit alleges the university provides its male athletes "much greater" NIL opportunities through the collectives that support the university's athletic programs, including Division Street, its NIL collective, and Opendorse, the Oregon Ducks NIL Marketplace.[141] This lawsuit, including gender inequity in college NIL programs, unequal compensation in professional leagues, and the failure of brands and media NIL deals, evidences that Caitlin Clark's NIL is exceptional and is not indicative of broad-based success for female college athletes. Unfortunately, these gender inequalities have other effects on how female athletes approach career decisions.

Another gender equity issue is whether a female athlete should continue to play in college as long as possible, such as Dunne's decision to remain for another year at LSU. One facing such a decision should weigh the financial issues and assess what post-graduation opportunities exist. In 2023, Caitlin Clark and Angel Reese went viral after the NCAA Women's Championship Game had 9.9 million viewers. With this newfound fame, would they have been financially better off to stay in their colleges if they were eligible to do so? That might depend on whether their colleges had booster-sponsored collectives with enough money to entice them to do so. Perhaps, whether via litigation or market forces, there will be more collective-based NIL deals for the next generation of college female superstars, including Flau'jae Johnson of LSU basketball and Paige Bueckers of UConn basketball.[142]

Gender equity in NIL deals reflects a greater issue in sports and in society overall. Female college athletes, particularly those of color, are not only paid less for the same or better work, but they are also denied equal economic resources and facilities, do not receive fair marketing and coverage, and suffer stereotyping, sexualization, and discrimination. Despite the passage of Title IX in 1972, female athletes—at the club, high school, collegiate, and professional levels—face substantial roadblocks to true equality. While some colleges do a good job supporting their student athletes who are women, the institution of sport overall is still skewed to support men who play high-visibility, high-revenue sports, and their success.[143] The unequal treatment of women in college sports is exasperated when sexual discrimination merges with racial discrimination.

Racial Diversity in Women's Sports

How important is racial diversity in women's sports? Another issue related to gender equity is the intersection of race and gender, that is, how are college athletes of color treated in college sports and particularly in NIL deals. One knowledgeable source, Forbes, stated that racial diversity is adding value to the NIL market, which is approaching $1.14 billion.[144] Opendorse estimated the top 100 college athletes in the U.S. could collectively earn up to $1 billion per year from NIL deals, with the great majority of those athletes being young men who are African Americans.[145] That is a good thing when that money comes from a legitimate source, such as the one that Bryce Underwood is receiving to play for Michigan. It is not a good thing when the funds that were promised do not materialize or when they are in consideration of a player agreeing to trade away their future earnings at a deep discount, such as what is alleged in several lawsuits like Jaden Rashada's lawsuit against the UF.[146] But, let's be clear, those NIL deals involve Black men who play for wealthy colleges in high-revenue sports, particularly football. The reality is that college athletes of color, particular Black women, are not receiving their equal share of NIL deals. Furthermore, when compared to their white female counterparts, the few Black female college athletes, such as Angel Reese, while well compensated, are not paid as well as their white colleagues, such as Caitlin Clark. Hopefully, in the near future we will see the gender and racial gender NIL deal vanish and see more NIL deals for all female athletes. Moreover, as previously discussed, NIL deals with female college athletes, regardless of their racial background, should be protected from sexual or economic exploitation.[147]

Clark as Advocate for Gender Equity

This leads to the question, "What role is Clark playing in promoting women's sports?" The answer is plenty for a good start. For example, on March 1, 2022, Clark announced a partnership with H&R Block, a national tax preparation company, as part of its new "A Fair Shot" campaign, designed to help female athletes earn fair compensation in the NIL space compared to male athletes. Clark has appeared in several national ads through the company's campaign.[148] Further, in October 2023, she established the Caitlin Clark Foundation with the stated goal "to uplift and improve the lives of youth and their communities through education, nutrition, and sport."[149] Many of her sponsorship and endorsement deals reportedly include pledges of support or monetary donations to the Caitlin Clark Foundation.[150] For example, as part of Clark's multi-year deal with Gatorade, the company donated $22,000 to the Caitlin Clark Foundation, a nod to her jersey number and birthday, in late 2023.[151] Furthermore, in January 2024, State Farm announced it intended to donate $22,000 to the Caitlin Clark Foundation in honor of Clark's 22nd birthday.[152] Similarly, in November 2024, Gainbridge Group presented Clark with a $22,000 grant to the Caitlin Clark Foundation.[153]

Hopefully, as a champion for "girl power" and gender equity, Clark can alleviate the unlevel playing field for women in sports, particularly at the college level, and especially relative to NIL deals. She stands on the cusp of history, where the arch of positive, overwhelming inclusion of women in sports and in the economy will be realized. Her rise on the national stage as an icon of gender inclusion will be hailed as the dawn of the Renaissance of women's equality in sports. She will be remembered as having led the worldwide movement to include women in the economic order, which is predicted to add substantial value to the U.S. and world economy.

How to Achieve Gender Equity in NIL Deals?

The last question is "What can be done to grow NIL opportunities for females in college sports?" Based upon the research in this book, there are several recommendations to do so. Colleges, the NCAA, and society should (1) eradicate barriers to success, including protecting female athletes from sexual harassment, and embrace inclusion economics; (2) seek out partnerships with high-ranking female and male social media influencers to promote NIL deals for college women; (3) create, increase, and finance booster-sponsored collectives to entice college females to play college sports; (4) build more female professional leagues and other means for female college athletes to obtain salaries equal to male athletes after college; and (5) increase financial literacy training for female athletes so they can make knowledgeable career decisions and land lucrative NIL deals.[154]

Hence, Clark's journey to NIL millions is nearly identical to her fellow college millionaires: She is highly talented, success-driven, overcame injury, came from an athletically accomplished family, and received universal acclaim throughout her career. She is already changing the face of branding and of gender equity. Gender equity is economic equity and produces positive benefits for the U.S. economy. It is irrefutable based on the economic effect of Taylor Swift's The Eras Tour that promoting female entertainment, and arguably sports, will pay off big for the performers and athletes as well as the national and local economies.

NIL POWER SECRET #10: EMULATE CAITLIN CLARK AS A WEALTH CREATOR AND CHAMPION FOR GENDER EQUITY

Caitlin Clark is a study of a social phenomenon. She is more than a record-breaking college athlete turned professional, with tremendous name recognition and millions of dollars in NIL deals. The "Caitlin Clark Effect" creates wealth for herself, her teammates, and the economy. Further, she is an icon for "girl power" and gender equality in NIL deals.

What is Clark's NIL power secret? It is her ability to be a wealth creator. The lesson is to be the best, even in a gender-challenged, restricted opportunity, and watch the market reward your excellence. Caitlin Clark is a living legend whose fame and fortune are just beginning to rise; her name is already mentioned among the GOATS, who are mega-millionaire professional athletes.

Further Reading

Howard Megdal, BECOMING CAITLIN CLARK: THE UNKNOWN ORIGIN STORY OF A MODERN BASKETBALL SUPERSTAR (2025).

Joseph Galizia, *A'Ja Wilson Net Worth: The Three-Time MVP Has Earned Big Bucks over the Years*, SPORTS ILLUSTRATED (Mar. 6, 2025), https://www.si.com/onsi/athlete-lifestyle/news/a-ja-wilson-net-worth-three-time-mvp-earned-big-bucks.

Sanjesh Singh, *Here Are the Highest-Paid WNBA Players for 2024*, NBCDFW (Apr. 16, 2024), https://www.nbcdfw.com/news/sports/highest-paid-wnba-players-2024-season/3516944/.

Endnotes

1. New Heights, *Caitlin Clark on "Life Changing" Rookie Year, Chiefs Fandom, NBA Ratings Debate and More | Ep 117*, YouTube (Jan. 2, 2025), https://www.youtube.com/watch?v=vvqdiXCrMZA.
2. Courtney Hill, *Caitlin Clark Surpasses Pete Maravich to Set New NCAA All-Time Scoring Record*, Olympics.com (Mar. 4, 2024), https://olympics.com/en/news/caitlin-clark-surpasses-pete-maravich-to-set-new-ncaa-all-time-scoring-record.
3. *Id.*
4. *Indiana Fever's Caitlin Clark Wins 2024 Kia WNBA Rookie of the Year Award*, WNBA (Oct. 3, 2024), https://www.wnba.com/webview/news/2024-kia-rookie-of-the-year.
5. Dan Treacy, *Caitlin Clark's NIL Deals, Explained: How Much Money Iowa Star Makes from Nike, Other Sponsors in 2024*, Sporting News (Mar. 30, 2024), https://www.sportingnews.com/us/ncaa-basketball/news/caitlin-clark-nil-deals-money-iowa-nike-sponsors-2024/e58534cadc3b2960663a36cb.
6. Elizabeth Flores, *Caitlin Clark's Exploding Value: List of Fever Star's Endorsements and Contract Details*, USA Today (updated May 21, 2024), https://www.usatoday.com/story/sports/wnba/2024/04/19/caitlin-clark-contract-details-endorsement-lists/73375721007/.
7. *Caitlin Clark Net Worth*, Celebrity Net Worth, https://www.celebritynetworth.com/richest-athletes/nba/caitlin-clark-net-worth/ (last accessed Mar. 14, 2024).
8. *Id.*
9. Reed Berglund, *What Will Be Caitlin Clark's Net Worth after a 20-Year Career?*, LinkedIn (Apr. 21, 2024), https://www.linkedin.com/pulse/what-caitlin-clarks-net-worth-after-20-year-career-reed-berglund-pz4ne/.
10. King Jemison, *Buying Season Tickets to Go to One Game? That's the Caitlin Clark Effect*, USA Today (Jan. 31, 2024), https://www.usatoday.com/story/sports/ncaaw/2024/01/31/caitlin-clark-iowa-womens-basketball-team-fill-up-big-ten-arenas-sellout-crowds-season-tickets/724219740077; Corbin McGuire, *The Caitlin Clark Effect: How Caitlin Clark Has Captivated the Country and Rewritten the NCAA Record Books One Bucket at a Time*, NCAA (Feb. 15, 2024), https://www.ncaa.org/news/2024/2/15/media-center-the-caitlin-clark-effect.aspx?os=firetvykofehsy&ref=app.
11. Sean Gregory, *2024 Athlete of the Year: Caitlin Clark*, TIME (Dec. 10, 2024), https://time.com/7200904/athlete-of-the-year-2024-caitlin-clark/.
12. Bleacher Report Staff, *Ranking the 25 Most Incredible Sports Moments from the Last Quarter Century*, Bleacher Report (Jan. 1, 2025), https://bleacherreport.com/articles/10147784-ranking-the-25-most-incredible-sports-moments-from-the-last-quarter-century.
13. *Michael Phelps*, Team USA, https://www.teamusa.com/profiles/michael-phelps#:~:text=Biographical%20Information,record%20for%20his%20age%20group (last accessed Mar. 14, 2025).
14. *Id.*

15. *Caitlin Clark,* USA Basketball, https://www.usab.com/players/caitlin-clark (last accessed Mar. 14, 2025).
16. *Id.*
17. *Caitlin Clark,* ESPN, https://www.espn.com/high-school/girls-basketball/recruiting/player/_/id/225153 (last accessed Mar. 14, 2025).
18. Matt Eisenberg, *Point Guard Caitlin Clark Commits to Iowa Hawkeyes,* ESPN (Nov. 12, 2019), https://www.espn.com/womens-college-basketball/story/_/id/28066539/point-guard-caitlin-clark-commits-iowa-hawkeyes.
19. Abhishek Sharma, *"No Days Off": Despite Summer Break, 21 YO NCAA Star's Intense Workout Amazes Former NBA MVP,* Essentially Sports (June 7, 2023), https://www.essentiallysports.com/nba-ncaa-basketball-news-no-days-off-despite-summer-break-yo-ncaa-stars-intense-workout-amazes-former-nba-mvp-caitlin-clark/.
20. *Id.*
21. Kyle Hightower, *Caitlin Clark, Much like Larry Bird, the Focus of Talks about Race and Double Standards in Sports,* AP (May 12, 2024), https://apnews.com/article/caitlin-clark-race-women-college-basketball-b277e81e47c8d9ecc6554720b1a35065.
22. *See* Sean Gregory, *2024 Athlete of the Year: Caitlin Clark,* TIME (Dec. 10, 2024), https://time.com/7200904/athlete-of-the-year-2024-caitlin-clark/.
23. Johannes Sasay-Wada & Amanda Davies, *Caitlin Clark Should Not Have Been Singled Out by Time, Says Washington Mystics Owner Sheila Johnson,* CNN Sports (Dec. 13, 2024), https://www.cnn.com/2024/12/13/sport/sheila-johnson-caitlin-clark-time-magazine-spt-intl/index.html.
24. Damian Rancez, *WNBA Superstar Caitlin Clark Breaks Barriers and Sparks Debate on White Privilege,* MSN (Jan. 6, 2025), https://www.msn.com/en-us/society-culture-and-history/race-and-racial-identity/caitlyn-clark-white-privilege-and-me/ar-AA1w1KFT.
25. *Id.*; Kevin McCormick, *As a White Person, There Is Privilege"—Caitlin Clark Takes Strong Stand on Racial Status as Time's 2024 Athlete of the Year,* sportskeeda (Dec. 11, 2024), https://www.sportskeeda.com/us/wnba/news-as-white-person-privilege-caitlin-clark-takes-strong-stand-racial-status-time-s-2024-athlete-year.
26. Louisa Franklin, *What Records Does Caitlin Clark Hold? Iowa and NCAA Honors to Know,* ESPN (Feb. 2, 2025), https://www.espn.com/womens-college-basketball/story/_/id/39626372/what-records-does-caitlin-clark-hold-iowa-ncaa-honors-know.
27. *Caitlin Clark,* Iowa, https://hawkeyesports.com/sports/wbball/roster/season/2023-24/player/caitlin-clark (last accessed Mar. 14, 2025); https://apnews.com/article/caitlin-clark-iowa-ncaa-1d88d50c2db783b6e5b075e7243dcc85.
28. *Id.*
29. Tim Reynolds, *Caitlin Clark's College Career Is over but Her Impact on the Game Is Not. The Numbers Back That Up,* AP (Apr. 8, 2024), https://www.cbssports.com/womens-college-basketball/news/caitlin-clarks-historic-ncaa-tournament-by-the-numbers-iowa-star-sets-numerous-records-on-title-game-run/; Liam McKeone, *Caitlin Clark Can't Stop Breaking Records,* Sports Illustrated (Mar. 27, 2024), https://www.si.com/college/2024/03/27/caitlin-clark-iowa-record-ratings-ncaa-tournament.

30. Lindsay Schnell, *Caitlin Clark's Impact in Iowa and Women's Game Is Monumental—And She's Just Getting Started*, USA Today (Apr. 2, 2023), https://www.usatoday.com/story/sports/ncaaw/2023/04/02/caitlin-clark-impact-tournament-means-everybody-knows-her-name/11590444002/#.
31. *Id.*
32. Laken Litman, *Caitlin Clark Breaks All-Time NCAA Scoring Record, Passing Pete Maravich*, FOX Sports (Mar. 3, 2024), https://www.foxsports.com/stories/womens-college-basketball/caitlin-clark-breaks-all-time-ncaa-scoring-record-passing-pete-maravich; Michael Voepel, *Iowa's Caitlin Clark Passes Pete Maravich for Scoring Record*, ESPN (Mar. 3, 2024), https://www.espn.com/womens-college-basketball/story/_/id/39646481/iowa-caitlin-clark-passes-pete-maravich-div-1-scoring-mark.
33. *See* Michael Voepel, *Iowa's Caitlin Clark Passes Pete Maravich for Scoring Record*, ESPN (Mar. 3, 2024), https://www.espn.com/womens-college-basketball/story/_/id/39646481/iowa-caitlin-clark-passes-pete-maravich-div-1-scoring-mark.
34. *Caitlin Clark Breaks Steph Curry's NCAA Record for 3s in a Season as Iowa Beats Penn State in Big Ten Tourney*, FOX Sports (Mar. 8, 2024), https://www.foxsports.com/stories/college-basketball/caitlin-clark-breaks-steph-currys-ncaa-record-for-3s-in-a-season-as-iowa-beats-penn-state-in-big-ten-tourney.
35. Michael Ricciardelli, *Poll on Caitlin Clark in USA Today, Forbes, Chronical, More*, Seton Hall Univ. (Mar. 27, 2024), https://www.shu.edu/business/news/poll-on-caitlin-clark-in-usa-today-forbes-chronical-more.html.
36. Nick Schultz, *"Caitlin Clark Cam" to Return for Iowa vs. Nebraska*, On3 (Feb. 8, 2024), https://www.on3.com/college/iowa-hawkeyes/news/caitlin-clark-cam-return-iowa-vs-nebraska-fox-sports-tiktok/.
37. David Suggs, *Why Is Caitlin Clark Famous? Inside WNBA Rookie's Star Power, Nike Endorsement Deal and More*, Sporting News (June 1, 2024), https://www.sportingnews.com/us/wnba/news/caitlin-clark-popularity-endorsements-nike-gatorade-followers/29d4eb84fea6e6f0b66981bc.
38. *See* Dan Treacy, *Caitlin Clark's NIL Deals, Explained: How Much Money Iowa Star Makes from Nike, Other Sponsors in 2024*, Sporting News (Mar. 30, 2024), https://www.sportingnews.com/us/ncaa-basketball/news/caitlin-clark-nil-deals-money-iowa-nike-sponsors-2024/e58534cadc3b2960663a36cb.
39. *Iowa's Caitlin Clark Has Impressive List of NIL Deals. From Bose to Nike, Here's a Look*, Hawk Central (Mar. 27, 2023), https://www.hawkcentral.com/story/sports/college/iowa/basketball-women/2023/03/27/iowa-womens-basketball-caitlin-clark-list-nil-deals-nike-bose-hyvee/70053195007/.
40. *Id.*
41. *Id.*
42. *Id.*
43. Elizabeth Flores, *Caitlin Clark Has Become the First College Athlete to Secure an NIL Deal with State Farm*, USA Today (Oct. 10, 2024), https://www.usatoday.com/story/sports/ncaaw/2023/10/10/caitlin-clark-sign-nil-deal-with-state-farm/71131146007/.

44. KCRG Staff, *Hy-Vee, Caitlin Clark Partner on Launch of Exclusive Cereal to Benefit Iowa Youth*, ABC 9 (Jan. 11, 2024), https://www.kcrg.com/2024/01/11/hy-vee-caitlin-clark-partner-launch-exclusive-cereal-benefit-iowa-youth/.
45. *See* Elizabeth Flores, *Caitlin Clark's Exploding Value: List of Fever Star's Endorsements and Contract Details*, USA TODAY (updated May 21, 2024), https://www.usatoday.com/story/sports/wnba/2024/04/19/caitlin-clark-contract-details-endorsement-lists/73375721007/.
46. *Id.*
47. *See* Dan Treacy, *Caitlin Clark's NIL Deals, Explained: How Much Money Iowa Star Makes from Nike, Other Sponsors in 2024*, SPORTING NEWS (Mar. 30, 2024), https://www.sportingnews.com/us/ncaa-basketball/news/caitlin-clark-nil-deals-money-iowa-nike-sponsors-2024/e58534cadc3b2960663a36cb.
48. Jack Baer, *Caitlin Clark Becomes Fanatics' Top-Selling College Athlete in NIL Era, by a Chasmic Margin*, YAHOO! SPORTS (Feb. 20, 2024), https://sports.yahoo.com/caitlin-clark-becomes-fanatics-top-selling-college-athlete-in-nil-era-by-a-chasmic-margin-232357588.html?guccounter=1&guce_referrer=aHR0cHM6Ly9lbi53aWtpcGVkaWEub3JnLw&guce_referrer_sig=AQAAAGUl64MDoU1d0-wrr6LGAQmREhxmg2lc8tCJRnzWS675HrkbVxgY5ri1Vx92XZEh6dFw_-unBRxDkOPwNxP7CLCtmqA6oNce1J0US_jfi9aMwh1Nldj6d7BRKWfWQE9AQQhSRkOXeXVKiUCJ698x9g2QT7DJn16cVuvxT0VRxJKG.
49. Jeff Zillgitt, *Iowa's Caitlin Clark Becomes First Female Athlete to Have Exclusive Deal with Panini*, USA TODAY (Mar. 6, 2024), https://www.usatoday.com/story/sports/ncaaw/bigten/2024/03/06/caitlin-clark-reaches-endorsement-deal-panini-iowa/72865492007/.
50. Dargan Southhard, *Caitlin Clark 1-of-a-Kind Rookie Trading Card Sells for $78,000 in Online Auction*, HAWK CENTRAL (Jan. 26, 2024), https://www.hawkcentral.com/story/sports/college/iowa/basketball-women/2024/01/26/caitlin-clark-trading-card-sells-for-record-78000-on-online-auction-iowa-womens-basketball-hawkeyes/72364911007/.
51. Brooks Pecks, *Caitlin Clark Autograph Card Sells for $84,000, Setting New Women's Basketball Card Record*, ATHLETIC (Sept. 26, 2024), https://www.nytimes.com/athletic/5782026/2024/09/20/caitlin-clark-card-record-sale/.
52. *Gainbridge® Signs College Basketball Star Caitlin Clark as Brand Ambassador*, GROUP1001 (Mar. 5, 2024), https://www.group1001.com/news/caitlin-clark-brand-ambassador.
53. Tyler Conway, *Caitlin Clark Lands Wilson Contract; 1st Athlete Since Michael Jordan with Collection*, BLEACHER REPORT (May 21, 2024), https://bleacherreport.com/articles/10121863-caitlin-clark-lands-wilson-contract-1st-athlete-since-michael-jordan-with-collection.
54. *See* Elizabeth Flores, *Caitlin Clark's Exploding Value: List of Fever Star's Endorsements and Contract Details*, USA TODAY (updated May 21, 2024), https://www.usatoday.com/story/sports/wnba/2024/04/19/caitlin-clark-contract-details-endorsement-lists/73375721007/.
55. *Caitlin Clark Net Worth*, CELEBRITY NET WORTH, https://www.celebritynetworth.com/richest-athletes/nba/caitlin-clark-net-worth/ (last accessed Mar. 14, 2024).

56. *Id.*
57. *Id.*
58. Joey Held, *Caitlin Clark Will Make Her Entire WNBA Rookie Salary Every 8 Days from the Nike Deal She Just Signed*, Celebrity Net Worth (Apr. 18, 2024), https://www.celebritynetworth.com/articles/sports-news/caitlin-clark-nike-deal/.
59. *Id.*
60. Melanie Anzidei, *Caitlin Clark Joins Ownership Group Looking to Bring NWSL Team to Cincinnati*, Athletic (Nov. 21, 2024), https://www.nytimes.com/athletic/5939553/2024/11/21/caitlin-clark-nwsl-cincinnati-team-ownership/.
61. Meghan L. Hall, *8 Times We Told You Caitlin Clark Wasn't Going to Lose Money by Joining the WNBA*, USA Today Sports (Apr. 15, 2024), https://ftw.usatoday.com/lists/caitlin-clark-iowa-ncaa-tournament-2024-wnba-nil-deals.
62. *See* Joey Held, *Caitlin Clark Will Make Her Entire WNBA Rookie Salary Every 8 Days from the Nike Deal She Just Signed*, Celebrity Net Worth (Apr. 18, 2024), https://www.celebritynetworth.com/articles/sports-news/caitlin-clark-nike-deal/.
63. *Id.*
64. *See* King Jemison, *Buying Season Tickets to Go to One Game? That's the Caitlin Clark Effect*, USA Today (Jan. 31, 2024), https://www.usatoday.com/story/sports/ncaaw/2024/01/31/caitlin-clark-iowa-womens-basketball-team-fill-up-big-ten-arenas-sellout-crowds-season-tickets/724219740077; Corbin McGuire, *The Caitlin Clark Effect: How Caitlin Clark Has Captivated the Country and Rewritten the NCAA Record Books One Bucket at a Time*, NCAA (Feb. 15, 2024), https://www.ncaa.org/news/2024/2/15/media-center-the-caitlin-clark-effect.aspx?os=firetvykofehsy&ref=app.
65. *Taylor Swift: The Eras Tour*, taylorswift.com, https://tstheerastour.taylorswift.com/ (last accessed Mar. 14, 2025).
66. Mary Whitfill Roeloffs, *Taylor Swift Eras Tour Grossed $2 Billion Double Any Other Tour in History, Report Says*, Forbes (Dec. 9, 2024), https://www.forbes.com/sites/maryroeloffs/2024/12/09/taylor-swifts-eras-tour-grossed-2-billion-double-any-other-tour-in-history-report-says/.
67. Shannon Power, *Taylor Swift's Net Worth: How Much Has the Singer Made from the Eras Tour?*, Newsweek (Dec. 9, 2024), https://www.newsweek.com/taylor-swift-eras-tour-album-net-worth-billion-earnings-1997516.
68. Ellie Usdin, *The Economic Impact of Taylor Swift's Eras Tour*, Fieldston News (Feb. 14, 2024), https://fieldstonnews.com/home/2024/02/the-economic-impact-of-taylor-swifts-eras-tour/.
69. *NBA vs WNBA: Revenue, Salaries, Viewership, Attendance and Ratings*, WSN (Oct. 7, 2024), https://www.wsn.com/nba/nba-vs-wnba/.
70. *Id.*
71. *Id.*
72. *Id.*
73. *Id.*
74. *Id.*
75. *Id.*
76. *Id.*

77. *WNBA Secures Landmark Media Rights Deals with the Walt Disney Company, Amazon Prime Video and NBCUniversal*, WNBA (July 24, 2024), https://www.wnba.com/news/media-rights-deal-disney-prime-nbc; Santa Brito, *The 2024 WNBA Season Delivers Record Viewership Across ESPN Platforms*, ESPN Press Room (Oct. 25, 2024), https://espnpressroom.com/us/press-releases/2024/10/the-2024-wnba-season-delivers-record-viewership-across-espn-platforms/.
78. *Id.*
79. *Id.*
80. *Id.*
81. *See* King Jemison, *Buying Season Tickets to Go to One Game? That's the Caitlin Clark Effect*, USA Today (Jan. 31, 2024), https://www.usatoday.com/story/sports/ncaaw/2024/01/31/caitlin-clark-iowa-womens-basketball-team-fill-up-big-ten-arenas-sellout-crowds-season-tickets/724219740077; Corbin McGuire, *The Caitlin Clark Effect: How Caitlin Clark Has Captivated the Country and Rewritten the NCAA Record Books One Bucket at a Time*, NCAA (Feb. 15, 2024), https://www.ncaa.org/news/2024/2/15/media-center-the-caitlin-clark-effect.aspx?os=firetvykofehsy&ref=app.
82. *Id.*
83. Maya Ellison, *History from Kinnick! Iowa's Sets Women's Basketball Attendance Record at 55,646*, NCAA (Oct. 16, 2023), https://www.ncaa.com/news/basketball-women/article/2023-10-12/history-kinnick-iowas-sets-womens-basketball-attendance-record-55646.
84. *See* King Jemison, *Buying Season Tickets to Go to One Game? That's the Caitlin Clark Effect*, USA Today (Jan. 31, 2024), https://www.usatoday.com/story/sports/ncaaw/2024/01/31/caitlin-clark-iowa-womens-basketball-team-fill-up-big-ten-arenas-sellout-crowds-season-tickets/724219740077; Corbin McGuire, *The Caitlin Clark Effect: How Caitlin Clark Has Captivated the Country and Rewritten the NCAA Record Books One Bucket at a Time*, NCAA (Feb. 15, 2024), https://www.ncaa.org/news/2024/2/15/media-center-the-caitlin-clark-effect.aspx?os=firetvykofehsy&ref=app.
85. *Id.*
86. *Id.*
87. *Id.*
88. *Id.*
89. *Id.*
90. Barry Svrluga, *$243 for a Ticket? Pay Up. Caitlin Clark Might Be Worth it*, Wash Post (Feb. 2, 2024), https://www.washingtonpost.com/sports/2024/02/02/caitlin-clark-crowds-attendance-sell-out/.
91. Alex Leeds Matthews, *How Women's NCAA Basketball and Caitlin Clark Broke Viewership Records, in Three Charts*, CNN (Apr. 10, 2024), https://www.cnn.com/2024/04/10/us/ncaa-womens-basketball-ratings-dg/index.html; Jack Baer, *Here's Every Way Caitlin Clark Made Ratings History This Year*, Yahoo! Sports (Sept. 20, 2024), https://sports.yahoo.com/heres-every-way-caitlin-clark-made-ratings-history-this-year-181048197.html.
92. Rachel Bahman, *Caitlin Clark Is Already the GOAT of TV Ratings*, WSJ (May 12, 2024), https://www.wsj.com/sports/basketball/caitlin-clark-tv-audiences-b15d193e.

93. *See* Liam McKeone, *Caitlin Clark Can't Stop Breaking Records*, SPORTS ILLUSTRATED (Mar. 27, 2024), https://www.si.com/college/2024/03/27/caitlin-clark-iowa-record-ratings-ncaa-tournament.
94. Richard Deitsch, *South Carolina's Win Over Iowa Draws Record 18.9 Million Viewers, Most Watched Basketball Game Since 2019*, ATHLETIC, N.Y. TIMES (Apr. 8, 2024), https://www.nytimes.com/athletic/5400210/2024/04/08/south-carolina-iowa-caitlin-clark-viewership-record/.
95. Kate Kealey, *How Much Money Does the "Caitlin Clark Effect" Generate for Iowa?*, HAWK CENTRAL (Mar. 25, 2024), https://www.hawkcentral.com/story/sports/college/iowa/basketball-women/2024/03/25/caitlin-clark-effect-iowa-econony-hawkeye-womens-basketball-common-sense-institute/73066881007/.
96. *Ball State, Game Day Studies: "Caitlin Clark Effect" Means Millions of Dollars, Media Exposure for Central Indiana*, BALL STATE UNIV. (Apr. 11, 2024), https://www.bsu.edu/news/press-center/archives/2024/04/caitlin-clark-effect-means-millions-of-dollars-for-central-indiana#:~:text="This%20will%20bring%20a%20net,for%20Business%20and%20Economic%20Research.
97. *See* Jack Baer, *Here's Every Way Caitlin Clark Made Ratings History This Year*, YAHOO! SPORTS (Sept. 20, 2024), https://sports.yahoo.com/heres-every-way-caitlin-clark-made-ratings-history-this-year-181048197.html; *So Far This Season, Fans Are Engaging with the Indiana Fever in Record Numbers*, INDIANA FEVER (Aug. 14, 2024), https://fever.wnba.com/news/so-far-this-season-fans-are-engaging-with-the-indiana-fever-in-record-numbers; *WNBA-Record Crowd Sees Clark, Fever Drop Season Finale to Mystics*, ESPN (Sept. 19, 2024), https://www.espn.com/wnba/story/_/id/41335428/wnba-record-crowd-sees-clark-fever-drop-finale-mystics.
98. *Caitlin Clark Helps WNBA Shatter Draft Viewership Record*, ESPN (Apr. 16, 2024), https://www.espn.com/wnba/story/_/id/39957802/caitlin-clark-helps-wnba-shatter-draft-viewership-record; *10 Things to Know About Caitlin Clark*, INDIANA FEVER (Apr. 15, 2024), https://fever.wnba.com/news/10-things-to-know-about-caitlin-clark.
99. Jon Lewis, *Caitlin Clark Debut Is Most-Watched WNBA Game Since 2001*, SPORTS MEDIA WATCH (May 14, 2024), https://www.sportsmediawatch.com/2024/05/caitlin-clark-debut-ratings-largest-wnba-audience-23-years/.
100. *Id.*
101. Nick Schultz, *Indiana Fever vs. New York Liberty Draws 1.71 Million Viewers, Sets New ABC Record for WNBA Game*, ON3 (May 21, 2024), https://www.on3.com/her/news/indiana-fever-vs-new-york-liberty-1-71-million-viewers-new-abc-record-wnba-game-caitlin-clark/.
102. David Rumsey, *Nearly Every WNBA Broadcaster Has Set a Ratings Record This Season*, FRONT OFF. SPORTS (May 29, 2024), https://frontofficesports.com/nearly-every-wnba-broadcaster-has-set-a-ratings-record-this-season/.
103. *See WNBA Secures Landmark Media Rights Deals with the Walt Disney Company, Amazon Prime Video and NBCUniversal*, WNBA (July 24, 2024), https://www.wnba.com/news/media-rights-deal-disney-prime-nbc; Santa Brito, *The 2024 WNBA Season Delivers Record Viewership Across ESPN Platforms*, ESPN PRESS ROOM (Oct. 25, 2024), https://espnpressroom.com/us/press-releases/2024/10/the-2024-wnba-season-delivers-record-viewership-across-espn-platforms/.

104. *Id. See* Santa Brito, *The 2024 WNBA Season Delivers Record Viewership Across ESPN Platforms*, ESPN PRESS ROOM (Oct. 25, 2024), https://espnpressroom.com/us/press-releases/2024/10/the-2024-wnba-season-delivers-record-viewership-across-espn-platforms/.
105. *Id.*
106. *See* Sean Gregory, *2024 Athlete of the Year: Caitlin Clark*, TIME (Dec. 10, 2024), https://time.com/7200904/athlete-of-the-year-2024-caitlin-clark/.
107. *How Do You Define an Inclusive Economy?*, ASPEN INST. (May 23, 2023), https://www.aspeninstitute.org/blog-posts/how-do-you-define-an-inclusive-economy/#:~:text=While%20questions%20of%20global%20supply,is%20dynamic%20and%20ever%2Dchanging.
108. *What Is Economic Inclusion?*, McKinsey & Co. (Mar. 14, 2024), https://www.mckinsey.com/featured-insights/mckinsey-explainers/what-is-economic-inclusion.
109. Pub. L. 88–352, 78 Stat. 241, enacted July 2, 1964.
110. Gavin Wright, SHARING THE PRIZE: THE ECONOMICS OF THE CIVIL RIGHTS REVOLUTION IN THE AMERICAN SOUTH (2013).
111. Sophie Gardner, *What Women Have Gained from Affirmative Action*, POLITICO (June 16, 2023), https://www.politico.com/newsletters/women-rule/2023/06/16/what-women-have-gained-from-affirmative-action-00102397.
112. Open Knowledge Repository, *The State of Economic Inclusion Report 2021: The Potential to Scale*, WORLD BANK GROUP, https://openknowledge.worldbank.org/entities/publication/b12f8624-c03d-5f1d-a7e3-8bb857e733b7 (last accessed Mar. 12, 2025).
113. National Association for the Advancement of Colored People, *Inclusive Economy*, NAACP, https://naacp.org/issues/inclusive-economy#:~:text=Economic%20equity%20is%20crucial%20to,access%20to%20resources%20and%20opportunity (last accessed Mar. 12, 2025).
114. *New Studies by W.K. Kellogg Foundation and Altarum Make the Business Case for Racial Equity in New Orleans and Mississippi*, WKKF (June 19, 2018), https://www.wkkf.org/news-and-media/article/2018/06/new-studies-by-w-k-kellogg-foundation-and-altarum-make-the-business-case-for-racial-equity-in-new-orleans-and-mississippi/.
115. *NBA vs WNBA: Revenue, Salaries, Viewership, Attendance and Ratings*, WSN (Oct. 7, 2024), https://www.wsn.com/nba/nba-vs-wnba/.
116. *Id.*
117. *See* Elizabeth Flores, *Caitlin Clark's Exploding Value: List of Fever Star's Endorsements and Contract Details*, USA TODAY (updated May 21, 2024), https://www.usatoday.com/story/sports/wnba/2024/04/19/caitlin-clark-contract-details-endorsement-lists/73375721007/.
118. George Gordillo, *Caitlin Clark's Refusal to Take a $1 Million Offer Proves Her Worth Even Though the WNBA Star Earns Much Less with the Fever*, MARCA (Jan. 1, 2025), https://www.marca.com/en/basketball/wnba/indiana-fever/2025/01/08/677db13ae2704eb5338b45a1.html.
119. Fourthwall Blog, *Top 20 Social Media Influencers to Watch in 2025*, FOURTHWALL (Nov. 28, 2024), https://fourthwall.com/blog/top-20-social-media-influencers.

120. Liz Elting, *Going for Gold: Women's Sports Are Profitable—When Brands, Media and BroadcastBuyIn,* FORBES (July12,2023), https://www.forbes.com/sites/lizelting/2023/07/12/going-for-gold-womens-sports-are-profitable-when-brands-media-and-broadcast-buy-in/.
121. *Id.*
122. *Id.*
123. International Platform on Sport and Development, *How Title IX Changed the Landscape of Sports,* SPORTANDDEV.ORG (July 29, 2022), https://www.sportanddev.org/latest/news/how-title-ix-changed-landscape-sports.
124. Asia Alexander, *Colleges Comply with Anti-DEI Mandates with Firings . . . and Finesse,* FORBES (Aug. 19, 2024), https://www.forbes.com/sites/asiaalexander/2024/08/19/colleges-comply-with-anti-dei-mandates-with-firingsand-finesse/.
125. N'dea Yancey-Bragg, *1 in 4 College Athletes Say They Experienced Sexual Abuse from an Authority Figure, Survey Finds,* USA TODAY (updated Aug. 26, 2021), https://www.usatoday.com/story/news/nation/2021/08/26/college-athlete-report-sexual-assault-common-survey/8253766002/.
126. *Id.*
127. Adi Guajardo, *Female Athletes Face More Pressure When Opening Up about Mental Health,* SCRIPPS NEWS (Aug. 4, 2023), https://www.scrippsnews.com/sports/female-athletes-face-more-pressure-when-opening-up-about-mental-health.
128. *See* Vanesha McGee, *NIL Deals Lack Equity for Women College Athletes,* BEST COLLEGES (Feb. 20, 2023), https://www.bestcolleges.com/news/analysis/nil-deals-lack-equity-for-women-college-athletes/#.
129. *See On3 NIL Valuation,* ON3, https://www.on3.com/nil/rankings/player/nil-valuations/ (last accessed Dec. 30, 2024).
130. *See* Vanesha McGee, *NIL Deals Lack Equity for Women College Athletes,* BEST COLLEGES (Feb. 20, 2023), https://www.bestcolleges.com/news/analysis/nil-deals-lack-equity-for-women-college-athletes/#.
131. *Id.*
132. *Id.*
133. Albert Samaha *et al.*, *How NIL Money Is Paid to College Athletes,* WASH. POST (Oct. 21, 2024), https://www.washingtonpost.com/sports/interactive/2024/nil-money-deals-college-sports-athlete-pay/.
134. *Id.*
135. *Id.*
136. *Id.*
137. *Id.*
138. Carly Wetzel, *What NIL Collectives Mean for Women's Sports,* VOICE IN SPORT (Jan. 31, 2024), https://www.voiceinsport.com/post/advocacy/what-nil-collectives-mean-for-womens-sports.
139. *Schroder et al. v. University of Oregon,* https://www.classaction.org/media/schroeder-et-al-v-university-of-oregon.pdf.
140. *Id.*
141. *Id.*

142. *Women Collegiate Athletes and NIL: Why They Should Finish Eligibility Instead of Going Pro*, VILL. SPORTS L. BLOG (Dec. 26, 2023), https://www.novasportslaw.com/post/women-collegiate-athletes-and-nil-why-they-should-finish-eligibility-instead-of-going-pro.
143. Magdalena Mihaylova, *How Women Student Athletes Navigate College Life*, MICH. DAILY (Apr. 13, 2021), https://www.michigandaily.com/statement/how-women-student-athletes-navigate-college-life/.
144. Kori Hale, *How NIL Diversity Is Driving the Market up to $1.1 Billion*, FORBES (Mar. 10, 2023), https://www.forbes.com/sites/korihale/2023/03/10/how-nil-diversity-is-driving-the-market-up-to-11-billion/.
145. *Id.*
146. *Jaden Rashada-Florida NIL Lawsuit: What to Know, What Comes Next*, ESPN (May 21, 2024), https://www.espn.com/college-football/story/_/id/40190447/jaden-rashada-florida-gators-nil-lawsuit-next.
147. Nicole Sadek & Ronnie Greene, *College Athletes Lured by NIL Deals, Exploited by Fine Print*, BLOOMBERG LAW (July 18, 2023), https://news.bloomberglaw.com/antitrust/college-athletes-lured-by-nil-deals-exploited-by-fine-print.
148. *See Iowa's Caitlin Clark Has Impressive List of NIL Deals. From Bose to Nike, Here's a Look*, HAWK CENTRAL (Mar. 27, 2023), https://www.hawkcentral.com/story/sports/college/iowa/basketball-women/2023/03/27/iowa-womens-basketball-caitlin-clark-list-nil-deals-nike-bose-hyvee/70053195007/.
149. Caitlin Clark Foundation, https://caitlinclarkfoundation.org/ (last accessed Mar. 11, 2025).
150. Mike Hlas, *I'd Bet $11 That Big 12 Doesn't Remain 10*, GAZETTE (Jan. 30, 2013), https://www.thegazette.com/iowa-basketball/caitlin-clark-works-to-use-her-platform-for-a-lot-of-good-with-her-own-nonprofit/Id.
151. Michael Ehrlich, *Iowa's Caitlin Clark Adds Gatorade to Growing Nil Portfolio*, NIL DAILY (Dec. 12, 2023), https://www.si.com/fannation/name-image-likeness/news/iowas-caitlin-clark-adds-gatorade-to-growing-nil-portfolio-michael9.
152. Kenna Roering, *State Farm Donates $22,000 to Caitlin Clark Foundation for the Basketball Star's 22nd Birthday*, DAILY IOWAN (Jan. 22, 2024), https://dailyiowan.com/2024/01/22/state-farm-donates-22000-to-caitlin-clark-foundation-for-the-basketball-stars-22nd-birthday/.
153. *No. 22 Caitlin Clark Surprised with 22nd Parity Week by Gainbridge® Grant to the Caitlin Clark Foundation*, GROUP1001 (Nov. 18, 2024), https://www.group1001.com/news/caitlin-clark-foundation.
154. DJ Sixsmith, *NIL-Era College Athletes Navigate New Realm of Financial Literacy*, CNBC SPORT (Apr. 12, 2024), https://www.cnbc.com/2024/04/12/nil-era-college-athletes-navigate-new-realm-of-financial-literacy.html.

Conclusion

HOW LAW CAN CREATE WEALTH OPPORTUNITIES AND NIL POWER SECRETS

A Time To Celebrate

The rule of law creates winners and losers. The change in NIL law is a case study for how the law can create wealth opportunities particularly for young people. For many years, the NCAA's amateurism rules effectively denied college athletes the right to benefit from their notoriety and to be compensated for their athletic performance. This practice changed following a seminal Supreme Court decision and state legislation, which resulted in the law's recognition of college athletes' equal rights to benefit financially from the use of their name, image, and likeness. The result of this change in the law is the creation of wealth opportunities for college and high school athletes. Consequently, many college and high school athletes are cashing in on NIL deals; some of them have become NIL millionaires. This has greatly transformed college sports and the change continues.

This book provides a case study of how a change in the law has granted college athletes the right to benefit from their NIL. It provides secret lessons from the superstars who have become millionaires due to a change in NIL law. This case study supports the thesis that the law has the power to create wealth opportunities by redressing past injustice relative to marginalized groups of people, that is, young college athletes, many from disadvantaged backgrounds. It is the author's hope to assist the many college and high school athletes, their families, their schools, their coaches. their supporters, the NCAA, legal and financial advisors and agents, and advertisers and promoters, who want and need to understand NIL deals and related social justice issues facing college athletes.

Ten NIL Power Secrets

In addition to showing how the law can redress past injustice, relative to players' benefitting from their NIL, this book provides invaluable power secrets of the most successful college millionaires relative to NIL deals. To summarize these NIL power secrets from outstanding present and former NIL college millionaires, they are as follows:

1. Follow Chase Young and Reggie Bush's Power Play to Fly Past Adversity
2. Adopt O'Bannon's, Alston's, and House's Passion of Justice
3. Mimic Olivia Dunne's Mastery of Social Media Influence
4. Aspire to Bronny James's Focus on the Prize
5. Scramble with Bryce Underwood through the NIL Pitfalls
6. Play Arch Manning's Long Game to Mega-Millions
7. Savor Shedeur Sanders's Savvy in Maximizing One's Value
8. Emulate Angel Reese's Path of Least Resistance
9. Adopt Dr. Myron Rolle's Pursuit of Education & Non-Athletic Professions
10. Copy Caitlin Clark's Role as Wealth Creator for Women Athletes

College sports is big business, and NIL deals are transforming the business. That business is driven by media revenue, particularly coverage of men's football and basketball, although other sports, including men's soccer, women's gymnastics, and women's basketball, are capturing increased media attention. In addition to the billions in media revenue, college sports are driving collateral revenue in the marketing of products and services, sports memorabilia, blogs and podcasts, gaming, virtual/fantasy sports, legal as well as illegal betting, and non-fungible tokens plus other digital assets. Further, sports in general provides invaluable insight into our culture and values.[1] NIL is an important means to begin to address the inequitable distribution of media and other revenue that many NCAA colleges derive from men's college football and basketball. Consequently, college athletes have become American heroes!

Change Brings New Challenges

The change in the NIL law is a cause for celebration. However, some current developments may rob college athletes of their NIL rights, as NIL, along with other changes in college sports, is controversial. As evidence of the continuing transformation, on June 6, 2025, in *House v. NCAA*,[2] a federal judge approved a settlement of a class action lawsuit for nearly $2.8 billion.[3] There the NCAA agreed to a revenue-sharing model that allows member colleges to distribute funds up to $20 million to Division I athletes who have played since 2016 and a removal of caps on athletic scholarships.[4] For the first time in the history of college sports, the NCAA and its member colleges will be legally permitted to pay their athletes to play their sports. What appears to be another victory for college athletes has been criticized as a victory for the NCAA's efforts to limit its exposure to costly litigation. Nevertheless, the House settlement comes with a hefty price tag for college budgets. This will result in the need to find nonathletic revenue sources to support these increases in athletic expenses. Consequently, the House settlement is predicted to be a financial strain on the budgets of colleges' non-athletic programs, many of which are already subsidizing their athletic programs.[5] The negative financial impact that the House settlement, along with the realignment of the conferences and the Transfer Portal, was described in a 2024 critique by two distinguished university presidents. They stated that "[t]wo years ago, a Southeastern Conference NIL collective paid $150,000 to keep a defensive end from transferring. To retain him this season, it had to pay $1.5 million—and that's just for one player."[6] They observed that in addition to the realignment of the conferences . . . "[t]he introduction of name, image, and likeness (NIL) rights, increased use of the transfer portal, and lack of salary caps are exacerbating the divide and have the potential to bankrupt the entire system."[7] Consequently, they called on college presidents to consider a "radical" change to the conference model.[8]

Further, the House settlement contains some provisions that could negatively impact the growth of NIL for college athletes.[9] Of particular concern is the cap that the settlement places on payouts, which is set for now at 22% of the average revenue earned annually by Power 5 schools. That figure is much lower than the portion of revenue paid out in professional sports like the NFL and NBA, where players take home about half of the revenue. In addition, one knowledgeable observer has listed some major critiques of the settlement: (1) the damages amount in the proposed settlement is too low, (2) the revenue-sharing cap is unlawful and unsupported (including that it violates applicable federal antitrust law), (3) it includes an unfair restriction on NIL collectives, (4) it is being used as a "stalking horse" for federal legislation to grant the

NCAA antitrust immunity, and (5) it is being improperly used to promote legislation that would deny employee status to college athletes.[10] Along similar lines, the National College Players Association claims that the settlement gives the NCAA authority to immediately end NIL payments paid by collectives to athletes; allows individual conferences and the NCAA to limit or ban colleges from directly paying college athletes; permits colleges and conferences to cut as many sports as they would like; and would shortchange former college athletes on damages payouts.[11] Hence, those who support NIL deals for college athletes without undue restrictions should be leery of the House settlement's negative impact on the open market for NIL deals.

Renewed Call for Federal Legislation

The changes in the NIL law benefitting college athletes have come from federal court decisions at all levels and state legislation from throughout the country. For many and varied reasons, many have called for federal legislation to enact a uniform NIL statute, to curtail litigation, and to protect players from abusive NIL contracts. Over the last several years, several bills related to NIL have been proposed at the federal level.[12] The stated concern of the proposed legislation is to add uniformity to the NIL laws which vary state by state. Four bills that were introduced in 2023 include the College Athlete Economic Freedom Act,[13] The Protecting Athletes, Schools, and Sports Act of 2023, the Student Athlete Level Playing Field Act,[14] and the College Athletes Protection and Compensation Act of 2023.[15] The NCAA is the driving force behind the federalization of NIL law. One commentator notes that the NCAA is seeking to achieve three goals: (1) a uniform national NIL standard to preempt the patchwork of state NIL laws; (2) limited antitrust protection to minimize legal challenges; and (3) designation that student-athletes are not employees of their schools, conferences, or the NCAA.[16] A college athlete, who is a party to a NIL deal or is expecting to benefit from an NIL deal, needs to be diligent, as NIL law is fluid, with an interplay between state law, court decisions, and federal legislative proposals.[17]

In conclusion, *Game Changers* provides invaluable insight into the NIL revolution relative to college athletes' right to share in the wealth of college sports. However, while understanding NIL is an invaluable aspect of college sports, its significance is universal, that is, beyond college sports. That is because how the law treats college athletes' NIL will determine the existential issue of who owns and controls the physical and virtual aspects of each one of us. Finally, the need to protect a person's NIL from unauthorized use is critical as technology develops, with the expansion of virtual assets, the proliferation of social media platforms, the expansion of artificial intelligence,[18] increased use of facial recognition technology,[19] and the development of the metaverse. What is at stake is (1) whether the attributes of a person, including their name, image, and likeness, can be used by the person to increase their personal wealth and (2) whether the law will protect a person's NIL from exploitation. Seeking constitutional and fundamental bases for NIL rights, it has been suggested that NIL should be grounded on a universal, natural law concept of property law.[20] Currently, NIL law is based on the tort of a right to publicity, a legal basis that has many deficiencies.[21] Consequently, college athletes' battle for their NIL rights lays the foundation for how the law will treat the NIL rights that belong to each and every one of us.[22] Hence, whether you are a sports enthusiast or not, the nature of NIL law should be of great interest to all of us.

Endnotes

1. *See* Kenneth J. Marci, *Not Just a Game: Sport and Society in the United States*, 4 Inquiries J. No. 8, 2012, at 1 ("Sport coincides with community values and political agencies, as it attempts to define the morals and ethics attributed not only to athletes, but the totality of society as a whole").
2. Case No. 20-cv-03919 CW IN RE: COLLEGE ATHLETE NIL LITIGATION OPINION REGARDING ORDER GRANTING MOTION FOR FINAL APPROVAL OF SETTLEMENT AGREEMENT (Re: Dkt. No. 717), https://swimswam.com/wp-content/uploads/2025/06/Grant-House-vs-NCAA-Order-Granting-Final-Approval-to-Settlement.pdf.
3. *Id.*
4. Eddie Pells, A $2.8 Billion Settlement Will Change College Sports Forever. Here's How, AP News.com (updated 9:55 AM CDT, June 7, 2025), https://apnews.com/article/ncaa-house-settlement-aa3169056e8194aeebf34495641bce0b.
5. Darren Heitner, *Newsletter, Image, Likeness*, LinkedIn, https://www.chronicle.com/article/loans-fees-and-tv-money-where-colleges-are-finding-the-funds-to-pay-athletes.

6. E. Gordon Gee & Kent Syverud, *The Demise of College Sports as We Know Them*, CHRON. OF HIGHER EDUC. (Oct. 4, 2024), https://www.chronicle.com/article/the-demise-of-college-sports-as-we-know-them.
7. *Id.*
8. *Id. See also* Laine Higgins, *Is a Super League Coming for College Football?*, WSJ (Oct. 1, 2024), https://www.wsj.com/sports/football/college-football-college-student-football-league-93b7416d?mod=sports_lead_pos1 (a group of disruptive sports executives has unveiled a vision for what a break way in college football might look like).
9. Becky Sullivan, *What We Know and What We Don't about a Historic Settlement to Pay College Athletes*, NPR (May 24, 2024), https://www.npr.org/2024/05/24/nx-s1-4978680/house-ncaa-settlement-pay-college-athletes; Kristi Dosh, *10 Things To Know about The NCAA's House Settlement*, FORBES (May 24, 2024, 06:07pm EDT), https://www.forbes.com/sites/kristidosh/2024/05/24/10-things-to-know-about-the-ncaas-house-settlement/.
10. Darren Heitner, *Newsletter, Image, Likeness*, LinkedIn, https://www.linkedin.com/newsletters/newsletter-image-likeness-6995176238755545088; Pete Nakos, *NCAA to Substitute National Letter of Intent with Financial Aid, Rev Share*, On3 (Oct. 9, 2024), https://www.on3.com/news/ncaa-substitute-national-letter-of-intent-with-financial-aid:rev-share-agreements-high-school-recruiting/.
11. Email from National College Players Association to author (Oct. 8, 2024, at 11:46:02 AM CDT).
12. Kristi Dosh, *4 New Federal NIL Bills Have Been Introduced in Congress*, FORBES (updated July 31, 2023), https://www.forbes.com/sites/kristidosh/2023/07/29/4-new-federal-nil-bills-that-have-been-introduced-in-congress/.
13. *Id.*
14. *Id.*
15. *Id.*
16. *See also*, Eric Prisbell, *Examining the NCAA's Aggressive Push for Federal NIL Laws*, ON3 (Sept. 25, 2023), https://www.on3.com/nil/news/ncaa-aggressively-pushes-for-federal-nil-bill-corey-booker-lindsey-graham-tommy-tuberville-joe-manchin/.
17. *See* Darren Heitner, *Newsletter, Image, Likeness*, LinkedIn, https://www.linkedin.com/newsletters/newsletter-image-likeness-6995176238755545088; Pete Nakos, *NCAA to Substitute National Letter of Intent With Financial Aid, Rev Share*, On3 (Oct. 9, 2024), https://www.on3.com/news/ncaa-substitute-national-letter-of-intent-with-financial-aid:rev-share-agreements-high-school-recruiting/.
18. Clare Duffy, *Social Media Platforms Are Using What You Create for Artificial Intelligence. Here's How to Opt Out*, CNN (Sept. 23, 2024), https://www.cnn.com/2024/09/23/tech/social-media-ai-data-opt-out/index.html; Paul Barnwell, *What Parents Need to Teach Kids About Deepfake Videos*, WASH. POST (Sept. 11, 2019), https://www.washingtonpost.com/lifestyle/2019/09/11/common-sense-media-shares-what-parents-need-teach-kids-about-deepfake-videos/.

19. Martin Caste, *The NFL Wants to Use Facial Recognition at Games. Las Vegas Police Have Concerns*, NPR (Aug. 31, 2024), https://www.npr.org/2024/08/31/nx-s1-5094859/the-nfl-wants-to-use-facial-recognition-at-games-police-say-its-a-bad-idea.
20. Mitchell F. Crusto, *What Is Property?: A Libertarian Perspective of Name, Image, and Likeness*, 16 HARV. J. SPORTS & ENT. L. 59 (2025), https://journals.law.harvard.edu/jsel/print-edition/. *See Vidal v. Elster*, 602 U.S. 286 (2024), https://www.supremecourt.gov/opinions/23pdf/22-704_4246.pdf, where the Supreme Court supported the proposition that a person's name is that person's personal property which cannot be trademarked without their express permission. In that seminal case, the Court held that it is unlawful for a person to trademark the phrase "Trump too small" without the express consent of President Donald Trump. *Id.*
21. *Id.*
22. Mitchell F. Crusto, *Right of Self*, 79 WASH. & LEE L. REV. 533-608 (2022), https://scholarlycommons.law.wlu.edu/wlulr/vol79/iss2/3.

Further Reading

Leading Sources

NCAA, Contracts Best Practices, https://nilassist.ncaa.org/update-heading-to-contracts-best-practices/.

U.S.LegalForms,NILAgreementTemplate—FillandSignPrintableTemplateOnline, https://www.uslegalforms.com/forms/us-1341022bg/college-athlete-nil-endorsement-agreement.

Dosh, Kristi., How to Get Started with NIL: A Guide for Athletes and Parents, Business of College Sports (July 11, 2022), https://businessofcollegesports.com/name-image-likeness/how-to-get-started-with-nil-a-guide-for-athletes-and-parents/.

Darren Heitner, Newsletter, Image, Likeness, LinkedIn, https://www.linkedin.com/newsletters/newsletter-image-likeness-6995176238755545088.

NIL Guide Websites

Clapper, Leah. "How to Get Nil Deals: The Ultimate Guide." *NIL Island*, 13 Jul. 2023, nilisland.com/how-to-get-nil-deals-the-ultimate-guide/.

Day, Jeff. "A Guide to NIL: 10 Big Questions about the Revolution Sweeping College Sports." *Star Tribune*, 1 Mar. 2024, www.startribune.com/nil-guide-10-things-to-know-name-image-likeness-college-sports/600347472.

Dosh,Kristi."HowtoGetStartedwithNIL:AGuideforAthletesandParents."*BusinessofCollegeSports®*,8Aug.2024,businessofcollegesports.com/name-image-likeness/how-to-get-started-with-nil-a-guide-for-athletes-and-parents/.

Hitz, David. "Navigating Nil Deals: A Guide for Athletes—Athlete Narrative." *Athlete Narrative*, 30 May 2024, athletenarrative.com/blog/navigating-nil-deals-a-guide-for-athletes/.

Johnson, Trevor. "Playing It Smart: A Guide to Understanding NIL for Athletes and Parents." *Steeple Chase*, 8 Oct. 2024, www.steeplechasecp.com/blog/playing-it-smart-a-guide-to-understanding-nil-for-athletes-and-parents.

Petcash, Andrew. "NIL: The Ultimate Guide." *Profluence*, 14 Aug. 2024, profluence.com/nil-guide/.

Schatz, Christina. "Playbook: The Modern Athlete's Guide to Life, Money and NIL." *Morgan Stanley*, advisor.morganstanley.com/christina.schatz/documents/field/c/ch/christina-schatz/NIL_playbook.pdf. Accessed 7 May 2025.

Turner, Jacob. "The Moment Guide to NIL (Name, Image, & Likeness)." *MOMENT*, MOMENT, June 20, 2024, www.momentprivatewealth.com/post/the-moment-guide-to-nil.

Books on NIL

DeBarros, Sivonnia. *Athletes Making Moves Secure the Future by Protecting Your Name, Image, and Likeness.* Independently published, 2021.

DeBarros, Sivonnia. *What Are You Sporting About?* Independently Published, 2020.

Dosh, Kristi. *Athlete's NIL Playbook: The Complete Guide to Owning and Profiting from Your Name, Image and . . . Likeness.* John Wiley, 2025.

Grilli, Jason. *Unlocking the Power of NIL: The Keys to Monetizing Your Athletic Potential.* Keystone NIL Publishing, 2024.

Grant, Scott. *NIL Prep Kit: A Guide to Understanding Name, Image & Likeness in High School Athletics.* Triple Threat Leadership, LLC, 2023.

Haughton Esq., Elizabeth Silane. *NIL for All: A 30-Minute Guide to NIL.* Admit Hub Ref Service PR, 2023.

Kendrick, Miles. *NIL Playbook for Athletes: 7 Proven Steps to Use Your Name, Image and Likeness to Make Money.* Paperback. Independently published, 2024.

Koesterer, Mark R. & Haughton, Elizabeth Silane Haughton. *NIL For All: A 30-Minute Guide to NIL.* Independently published, 2023.

Lovell, Darrell & Mallinson, Daniel. *Name, Image, and Likeness Policies: Institutional Impact and States Responses.* Routledge, 2023.

Studstill, Johnny Jr. *The Corporation of NIL Sports: The Athlete to Entrepreneurship.* Studstill & Co, 2024.

Whitler, Kimberly A. & Hodgkins, Jay P. *Athlete Brands How to Benefit from Your Name, Image & Likeness Kimberly.* Darden Business Publishing, 2022.

Woodmore, DeCarlo. *The Basics of NIL: Name, Image, and Likeness.* Independently Published, 2024.

Sports Law Books

Berry, William W. & Daniel E. Lust. *College Sports Law in a Nutshell.* West Academic, 2024.

Davis, Timothy & N. Jeremi Duru. *Understanding Sports Law.* Carolina Academic Press, 2022.

Gray, James T. & Martin J. Greenberg. *Sports Law Practice.* LexisNexis, 2009.

Mitten, Matthew *et al. Sports Law: Governance and Regulation.* Aspen Publishing, 2024.

Ross, Stephen F. *Advanced Introduction to Global Sports Law.* Edward Elgar Publishing, 2021.

Index

A

admissions, race and, 103–105
adversity, 152–158, 177–180
affirmative action, 103–105
Alberts, Trev, 40
Alston, Shawne, 29, 30–33, 38, 43. *See also NCAA v. Alston*
Alston v. NCAA, 200
Álvarez, Canelo, 78
amateurism rule, 3, 7n17, 12, 35–41
Arnold, Jackson, 131

B

Baker, Charlie, 107
Barnes, Rick, 49n89
Beard, Chris, 49n89
Belichick, Bill, 40
Beyoncé, 122
Biden, Jill, 178
Biden, Joe, 178
Bieber, Justin, 122
Biles, Simone, 63
Bjork, Ross, 40
Black students, in college admissions, 103–105
Black women, 177, 180–182, 228
boosters, 75, 146–147
Bradley, Bill, 190
brand endorsement, 17, 122, 130, 147–149
breakout, 208–211
Brooks, Josh, 40
Brown, Mack, 76
Brown, Tommy, 15
Bueckers, Paige, 63
Burrow, Joe, 36
Bush, Reggie, 11–20
Butt, Jake, 157
Byrne, Greg, 40

C

Calipari, John, 49n89
Cavinder, Haley, 63
Cavinder, Hanna, 63
Challengers (film), 60
Chiles, Jordan, 226
Civil Rights Act of 1964, 104. *See also* Title IX
Clark, Caitlin, 2, 63, 73, 79, 205–230
coaches, compensation of, 40, 48n85
collectives, 17–18, 75–77, 146–147, 171
compensation: of athletes, 198–201; of coaches, 40, 48n85
compliance, legal, 94–95
conservatorship, 113n49
contract law, 100–101
Cuban, Mark, 216
Cunningham, T.A., 95
Curry, Steph, 122, 208, 213, 217, 224

D

D'Amelio, Charli, 126
deals, 16–18, 62–63, 72–74, 105–108, 145–149, 155–158, 175–177, 211–214
Del Conte, Chris, 40
Deutsch, Morton, 56
DeWine, Mike, 98
Dexter, Gervon, 105–106
diversity, equity, and inclusion (DEI), 104, 225
donor-driven collectives, 75

Dunne, Livvy, 16–17, 53–63, 72, 81, 86, 156, 171, 207, 211, 214, 215, 226
Durant, Kevin, 78
Duvernay-Tardif, Laurent, 192

E
eligibility rule, 3, 7n17, 35–41
Ellison, Larry, 92
Emmert, Mark, 39
End of College Football, The (Kalman-Lamn and Silva), 40
Equal Protection Clause, 8n28
estate tax, 102
Ewers, Quinn, 131
exploitation, of athletes, 8n31, 70n105, 106–109, 127, 225, 228

F
Fair Labor Standards Act (FLSA), 200
Fair Pay to Play Act (California), 8n26, 34, 39, 47n61
Federal Trade Commission, 107
Fisher, Jimbo, 49n88
Florida State University, 96–97
football conferences, 15–16
Frank, John, 192
Fritz, Robert, 170–171

G
Garnett, Kevin, 209
gender equality, 61–63
gender equity, 228–230
gender inequity, 225–228
Gerard, Harold, 56
"girl power," 221–225
Gomez, Selena, 54, 122
Gorsuch, Neil, 37
Grande, Ariana, 122

H
Harbaugh, Jim, 49n88
Hicks, Michael J., 220
high school, 124–128
Hocutt, Kirby, 40
Hoiberg, Fred, 49n89
House, Grant, 29, 33, 43
House v. NCAA, 33–34, 98, 201, 243–244
Hunter, Travis, 54, 155
Hurley, Dan, 77
Hurts, Jalen, 151

I
inclusion economics, 221–225
injuries, 60, 80–81, 152–153, 156–157, 196–198
intergenerational wealth displacement, 41–42
international athletes, 81–86
IP license, 106–107
Izzo, Tom, 49n89

J
James, LeBron, 122, 208
James, LeBron "Bronny," Jr., 16, 71–86, 126, 215
Jenner, Kendall, 122
Jenner, Kylie, 122
"jock tax," 102
Johnson, Dustin, 78
Johnson, Dwayne, 122
Johnson, Flau'jae, 181–182
Johnson v. NCAA, 200
Jones, Haley, 73
Jordan, Jasmine, 1
Jordan, Michael, 78, 212

K
Kalman-Lamb, Nathan, 40
Kardashian, Khloe, 122
Kardashian, Kim, 122
Kardashian, Kourtney, 122
Kavanaugh, Brett, 29, 36–39
Kelman, Herbert, 56
Kiffin, Lane, 122
King, Billie Jean, 212
Kohli, Virat, 122
Kromenhoek, Luke, 174

L
Lame, Khabane, 126
Lopez, Jennifer, 122

M
Mahomes, Patrick, 151
Mahomes Effect, 151
Major League Baseball (MLB), 80

Manchin, Joe, 107
Manning, Arch, 54, 119–132, 206
Manning, Eli, 120
Manning, Peyton, 120, 122
Manuel, Warde, 40
Maragos, Chris, 60
Maravich, Peter, 205, 210–211
March Madness, 77
market, rise of NIL, 74–77
Mayo, O.J., 13–14
Mbappé, Kylian, 78
McGahee, Willis, 156–157
McNair, Steve, 147
mental health, 61, 156, 178–180
mentorship, 149–150
Messi, Lionel, 54, 78, 122
Milroe, Jalen, 131
Minaj, Nicki, 122
minors, 100–101
Mok, Ken, 192
Money Game, The (docuseries), 54, 59
Mulkey, Kim, 178, 180
Mullen, Dan, 49n88
Mulvihill, Michael, 63

N

name, imagine, and likeness (NIL): collectives, 17–18, 75–77, 171; as controversial, 1; deals, 16–18, 62–63, 72–74, 105–108, 145–149, 155–158, 175–177, 211–214; defining, 2–3; importance of, 1; market, rise of, 74–77; NCAA prohibited, 3–4
National Basketball Association (NBA), 77–79
National Collegiate Athletic Association (NCAA): prohibited NIL, 3–4; Transfer Portal, 15, 170–177
National Football League (NFL), 13, 80, 120, 192–194, 196–198
National Hockey League (NHL), 80
NCAA v. Alston, 30–33, 36, 38, 41, 74–75
NCAA v. Board of Regents, 25n61, 45n19
Newson, Gavin, 39, 47n61
Nike, 2, 73, 148

O

O'Bannon, Edward, 29–30, 43
O'Bannon v. NCAA, 30, 33, 44n2
Ohio State, 12
Ohtani, Shohei, 78, 121
Orgeron, Ed, 49n88
Orji, Alex, 174

P

Payton, Walter, 147
pay to play, 94–98
Pell Grants, 39
performance-contingency, 93–94
personality rights, 8n27
Phelps, Michael, 208
popularity, 130–131
positivity, 149–152
poverty, 3, 39, 41–42
Prince, Sedona, 33
Professional and Amateur Sports Protection Act, 26n64
publicity rights, 8n267

R

race-conscious admissions, 103–105
racial diversity, 228
Raiola, Dylan, 131
Rashada, Jaden, 98–99
recruitment, 75–77
Reese, Angel, 15, 63, 169–182, 218, 221, 226–227
retirement accounts, 102
revenue sharing, 18–19
Rice, Jerry, 147
Richards, Josh, 42
Riley, Lincoln, 49n88
Roberts, John, 103–104
Robinson, Duce, 174
Rolle, Myron, 189–202
Ronaldo, Cristiano, 17, 54, 78, 122

S

Saban, Nick, 49n88
Sanders, Deion, 148, 150
Sanders, Shedeur, 54, 141–159
Sarkisian, Steve, 119
Saudi Arabia, 78
Sayin, Julian, 131

Schroeder et al. v. University of Oregon, 227
self-awareness, 170
SFFA v. Harvard, 103–104
Sharpe, Shannon, 148
Sherman Antitrust Act, 8n30, 32, 45n35, 48n68
Silva, Derekbit, 40
Singleton, Eric, Jr., 174
Skenes, Paul, 59
Sluka, Matthew, 99, 174
Smart, Kirby, 49n88
Smith, Jaylon, 157
social media, 23n34, 53–59, 63, 72–73, 107
Sörenstam, Annika, 212
Soto, Juan, 78, 121
Stricklin, Scott, 40
Swift, Taylor, 122, 157, 216, 221
Swinney, Dabo, 49n88

T

Tagovailoa, Tua, 36
tax: estate, 102; liability, 101–103
tax-exempt status, 18, 76, 114n53
Tax Reform Act of 1969, 114n53
television viewership, 63, 219–221
Thompson, Alyssa, 126
Thompson, Gisele, 126
ticket prices, 218–219
Title IX, 61–62, 199, 225, 227
Transfer Portal, 15, 170–177
Trump, Donald, 225, 247n20
Tuberville, Tommy, 107

U

Underwood, Bryce, 2, 91–109, 146, 171, 206, 211, 215
University of Alabama, 14
University of Florida, 98–99, 105–106
University of Michigan, 2, 91–92, 94, 101, 104, 109
University of Nevada, Las Vegas, 99
University of North Carolina, 40
University of Oregon, 17, 85
University of Tennessee, 97–98

W

Wagner, DJ, 73, 126
Washington Redskins, 12–13
Watkins, Juju, 73, 182
wealth inequity, 35–43
White, Byron Raymond, 192
White, Danny, 40
Whittman, Josh, 40
Williams, Jada, 126
Williams, Roy, 49n89
Wilson, Russell, 131
women, Black, 177, 180–182, 228
Women's National Basketball Association (WNBA), 59, 63, 81, 169, 170, 176, 181–182, 210, 212–215, 217–221
Woods, Charlie, 150
Woods, Tiger, 122, 150
Woodward, Scott, 40

Y

Young, Chase, 11–20
Young, Jackie, 217, 224
youth, wealth and, 41–43
Yuracheck, Hunter, 40

About the Author

Mitchell "Mitch" Crusto is the Henry F. Bonura Jr. Distinguished Professor of Law at Loyola University New Orleans. His legal scholarship focuses on the intersections between law, society, and equality, with an emphasis on property rights. He is a leading scholar on name, image, and likeness law, having published seminal law review articles with Harvard University, Stanford University, the University of Miami, Washington & Lee University, and the *Journal of Legal Aspects of Sport.* He has a J.D. from the Yale Law School, an M.A. from Oxford University, England (Marshall Scholar), and a B.A. from Yale College.